Zamumo's Gifts

Indian-European Exchange in the Colonial Southeast

JOSEPH M. HALL JR.

PENN

University of Pennsylvania Press

Philadelphia

Published by
University of Pennsylvania Press
Philadelphia, Pennsylvania 19104-4112

Printed in the United States of America on acid-free paper

10 9 8 7 6 5 4 3 2 1

Library of Congress Cataloging-in-Publication Data

Hall, Joseph M., Jr.
    Zamumo's gifts : Indian-European exchange in the colonial Southeast / Joseph M. Hall, Jr.
        p. cm. — (Early American studies)
    Includes bibliographical references and index.
    ISBN 978-0-8122-4179-2 (alk. paper)
    1. Indians of North America—Southern States—History—Colonial period, ca. 1600–1775.   2. Indians of North America—First contact with Europeans—Southern States.   3. Indians of North America—Commerce—Southern States—History—17th century.   4. Indians of North America—Commerce—Southern States—History—18th century.   5. Europeans—Commerce—Southern States—History—17th century. 6. Europeans—Commerce—Southern States—History—18th century.   7. Southern States—History—Colonial period, ca. 1600–1775.   I. Title.
E78.S65H35   2009
973.2—dc22
                                                                    2009001011

For Melissa

Contents

Abbreviations

AC Archives des Colonies, Archives Nationales, Paris, France, collected on microfilm at the Howard-Tilton Library Special Collections, Tulane University, New Orleans, La.

AGI Archivo General de Indias, Sevilla, Spain.

BPROSC *Records in the British Public Record Office Relating to South Carolina, 1663–1710*. Edited by Noel Sainsbury. 5 vols. Columbia, S.C., 1928–47.

CO 5 Colonial Office Series 5, Public Record Office, Kew, United Kingdom, reprinted in Public Record Office microfilm series, LOC.

CRSC *The Colonial Records of South Carolina: The Journal of the Commons House of Assembly 1736-*. Edited by J. H. Easterby et al. 14 vols. Columbia: Historical Commission of South Carolina, 1951–.

EC Sección de Escribanía de Cámara.

IPH *Indian-Pioneer History of Oklahoma*. Edited by Grant D. Foreman. 120 vols. OHS.

JCHA *Journal of the Commons House of Assembly, 1692–1726*. Edited by Alexander S. Salley Jr. Columbia: The State Company for the Historical Commission of South Carolina, 1907–46.

JCIT *Journals of the Commissioners of the Indian Trade, September 20, 1710-August 29, 1718*. Edited by William L. McDowell Jr. Columbia: South Carolina Department of Archives and History, 1955.

LOC Library of Congress, Washington, D.C.

México Sección de Gobierno, Audiencia de México.

MPAFD *Mississippi Provincial Archives, French Dominion*. Edited and translated by Dunbar Rowland, A. G. Sanders, and Patricia Galloway. 5 vols. Jackson: Press of the Mississippi Department of Archives and History, 1927–32; Baton Rouge: Louisiana State University Press, 1984.

OHS Oklahoma Historical Society, Oklahoma City, Okla.

SCDAH South Carolina Department of Archives and History, Columbia, S.C.

SD Sección de Gobierno, Audiencia de Santo Domingo. (Note that all correspondence is dated from St. Augustine unless otherwise indicated.)

TJCHA   *Transcripts of the Journal of the Commons House of Assembly.* Edited by John S. Green. 5 vols. SCDAH.

TJGC   *Transcripts of the Journals of the Grand Council and Proprietors' Council.* Edited by John S. Green. 3 vols. SCDAH.

TRBPROSC   *Transcripts of Records in the British Public Records Office Relating to South Carolina.* Edited by Noel Sainsbury. 36 vols. SCDAH.

Introduction

Zamumo, the chief of Altamaha, had to think carefully in the early spring of 1540. Hundreds of unknown men were apparently a two-day journey to the southwest, and they were headed toward his town in the Oconee Valley of today's central Georgia. Although the intruders did not seem violent, their strange metal weapons and the paucity of women in their party suggested a disturbing aversion to peace. Of course, Zamumo was not without power of his own. From the summit of the flat-topped pyramid of earth that his townspeople had constructed, he had close ties with the spirits who shaped the world. Its seven-meter elevation offered him a commanding view of his town and its environs. West of his mound along the banks of the Oconee River were the cane-roofed homes of his followers, who numbered perhaps as many as a thousand and occupied the largest, if not the most populous, town in the valley. Farther west, just across the river, lay extensive fields of corn, beans, and squash. Spring planting had only just begun, but the granaries still held supplies from last year's harvest, and Zamumo still enjoyed the finest deer and bear that hunters could find. A lofty position in a prosperous town reassured him, but it probably did not content him because his power depended on what he could acquire from the wide and danger-ous world beyond Altamaha. Some objects of power came from Ocute, a more prominent chief who lived a one-day journey upriver, but only in exchange for Zamumo's tribute. In this news of the visitors, then, lay a tantalizing opportunity. Perhaps, if they proved friendly, they might provide him with influence Ocute did not possess.[1]

So he sent gifts to the approaching foreigners. Women went out with food, and a messenger welcomed the intruders with an offering that their record keepers failed to name. Altamahas paddled the newcomers across the Oconee River, and there, on its banks, Zamumo met this strange party of bearded men, their immense horses, their fierce war dogs, their voracious and innumerable pigs, and their leader, Hernando de Soto. From de Soto, Zamumo received a gift of a silver-colored feather. He accepted gratefully. "You are from heaven," he replied in the words of a later chronicler, "and this your feather that you give me, I can eat with it; I will go forth to war with it; I will sleep with my wife with it."[2]

It would be easy to dismiss Zamumo's words, words recorded many years later by a chronicler who did not speak his language, as Europeans indulging their fantasies of American apotheosis, but the words tell much about a distant and forever lost world. Feathers were powerful symbols, representing lightness, purity, and power. They came from the creatures of the skies. The great bird effigy that one of Zamumo's predecessors wore as part of a headdress and took to his grave some time around 1300 C.E. remains one of the most remarkable examples of this sacred iconography.[3] Zamumo's words also fit into this larger cosmology. Three and a half centuries after the chief allegedly uttered them, one archaeologist surmised that Altamahas and many other southeastern Indians celebrated three types of rituals centered on communal cohesion and harvest, warfare, and ancestor worship. When Zamumo shared his hopes for good harvests for his followers, great success on the battlefield, and abundant offspring to support his authority and succeed him when he died, he acknowledged that his gift could serve him in all three ritual settings. He further acknowledged the power of the gift and its giver when he asked de Soto if he should offer him the tribute he usually sent to Ocute.[4] Zamumo's gifts—those he offered as well as those he received—symbolized how the power of the foreign supported the security and autonomy of the leader and his community.

With his question regarding tribute, Zamumo revealed his hopes that de Soto and Ocute might both compete for his friendship. In the Southeast, a people with multiple partners could always hope for leverage against both by pitting one against the other. Whatever his ambitions, Zamumo failed to harness these newcomers for old practices because de Soto refused to challenge Ocute during his short stay in the Oconee Valley. More ominously, he initiated a host of unforeseen changes. Within a generation of this meeting at Altamaha, the mound-building peoples of the Southeast, including the Altamahas, began to decline, and the ambitions of Europeans for the lands that some called "La Florida" began to grow. De Soto failed in his search for riches, but in the two centuries after 1540, other Europeans found wealth in trade with the Indians and in raising their own crops for sale to countrymen across the Atlantic. Exchange remained important, but by the early eighteenth century, Indians traded deerskins and captives for an ever-expanding list of European tools, weapons, and cloth. The gifts that had once tied a few leaders together with bonds of reciprocity and mutual obligation had apparently given way to commodities that bound many men and women in relations of prices and profits. As South Carolina's preeminent trader and imperialist Thomas Nairne observed of the Indians in 1708, "They Effect them most who sell best cheap."[5] Three decades later, the German traveler and artist Philip George Friedrich von Reck

Figure 1. Medlin copper plate (ca. 1300 C.E.). Measuring approximately 13.7 cm on a side, this figure of a falcon was affixed to the front of a leader's headdress at the small hole in the center. From Mark Williams, *Archaeological Excavations at Shinholser Site (9BL1): 1985 & 1987*, LAMAR Institute Publication 4 (Watkinsville, Ga., 1990), 235. Reprinted courtesy of Mark Williams.

seemed to capture British mercantile dominance over French and Spanish rivals in several watercolors of Yuchis living along the upper Savannah River. In one portrait of the chief Senkaitschi and his wife, the couple displayed the latest in English-sponsored fashion: she with a blue skirt and a white blanket trimmed with a red stripe, he with a red breechclout and blue leggings.

Such transformations had consequences far beyond material culture for Senkaitschi, his wife, and their contemporaries. Indeed, as John Stuart, the British official in charge of southeastern Indian affairs, noted in 1764, trade was the "Original great tie between Indians and Europeans."[6] His characterization includes far more than the Southeast. Exchange between Europeans and Indians had provided the foundations for all early contacts in North America, and two centuries after de

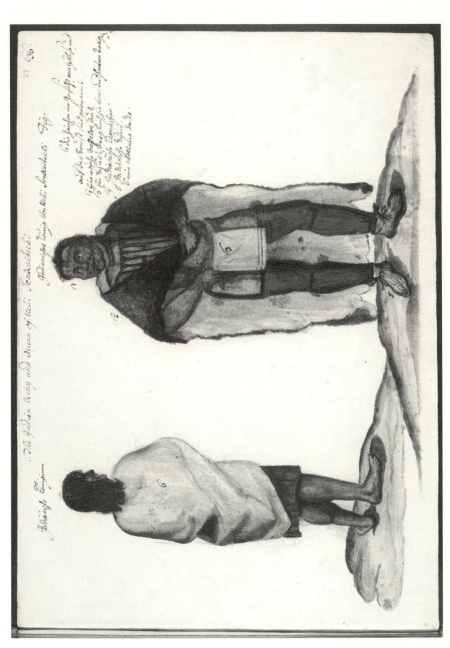

Figure 2. Philip Georg Friedrich von Reck, "The Indian King and Queen of the Uchi Senkaitschi" (1734). Senkaitschi and his wife are both wearing English woolens. A corner of her blue skirt shows just under her white blanket with red trim. His bright blue leggings contrast sharply with his red breechclout. His robe is made from buffalo skin. Courtesy of the Manuscript Department, Royal Danish Library.

Soto it remained the defining feature of Native-colonial relations west of the Appalachians. The significance of these ties has led historians to explore the variety of ways that these peoples dealt with one another through the things they traded. In most cases, historians have concluded that Indians eventually accepted European commercial norms as a first slippery step toward their economic and political subordination. In such analyses, observations like Nairne's serve as pithy epitaphs for Natives' independence.[7]

Histories of exchange deserve more sustained examination, though, and a new look at the Southeast at least makes clear that Indians continued to insist on practices that were both older than and distinct from European logics of the market even after Senkaitschi and his wife began wearing English wool. In fact, Senkaitschi probably acquired his clothes either as English gifts or at prices set by diplomats. Only a close study of the dynamics of exchange allows us to see how Indians and Europeans blended commercial and diplomatic norms. Despite their different backgrounds, both Natives and newcomers were familiar with the political and economic calculations behind exchange, whether giving generously or buying cheaply and selling dearly. Generations of negotiations meant that Zamumo, the prudent seeker of multiple patrons, became Nairne's shrewd shopper, who in turn became Senkaitschi, the material beneficiary of mid-century diplomacy. Even amid such change, though, Indians continued to seek out those who could offer power with the fewest demands, but they were doing so as peoples who had not abandoned the power of gifts. A history of Zamumo's own town of Altamaha is a testament to these resilient ideals. Although de Soto declined to challenge Ocute's claim to Zamumo's loyalty, later Altamahas managed to use other Spanish gifts to escape Ocute's orbit. In fact, Altamahas used ties with neighboring Indians, Spaniards, and eventually the English to acquire a measure of local autonomy and regional influence in 1700 that Zamumo could have never imagined in 1540. In light of such complex and shifting blends of ritual and commercial norms, it is clear that we need to look more closely at the exchanges that many historians who study the colonial period have discussed but few have placed at the centers of their histories.[8]

But first, I should introduce the setting within which these exchanges occurred. The lands that will be of greatest interest to me are those of the southeastern interior, especially those that lay between the Oconee Valley in central Georgia and the Coosa, Tallapoosa, and Alabama Valleys of central Alabama. They supported peoples who lived just beyond the limits of initial European colonization and maintained relatively regular contact with all three colonial powers, enough contact, in fact, to teach Europeans new ways to think about exchange. The rivers that fed these valleys descended, like the Oconee, from tributaries in the southern Appalachian Mountains. They reached the rolling hills of the piedmont with abundant water for crops, and the silt from their springtime floods replenished the cornfields along their banks. Their oxbow lakes and neighboring hardwood forests provided habitats for wild plants and animals that further enriched humans' diets. The rivers' relatively placid flow also made canoe travel easy among towns along the same river. Just downstream from the Georgia and Alabama piedmonts, these rivers crossed a transition zone called the fall line that separated the hardwood forests and richer ecosystems of the piedmont from the pine forests and poorer soils of the coastal plain. Besides marking a rough border between lands more and less suited to dense settlement, the fall line also served as an overland communication route. Later towns like Augusta, Georgia, or Montgomery, Alabama, grew on top of Native towns and European trading posts that took advantage of these intersections of water and land routes. Where these rivers emptied into the Atlantic or the Gulf of Mexico, they supported communities that fed themselves from riverine and also estuarine ecosystems. Poorer coastal soils limited agricultural harvests. With the exception of the fertile hill country of the Florida panhandle and the savannah country of the northern Florida peninsula, populations did not grow large along the coastal plain. In Zamumo's day, most southeastern power resided in the piedmont. It was this fact that attracted de Soto inland in search of wealth; it was also what enabled Zamumo to confront him with such confidence. After 1540, Spanish, English, and French colonists would discover in their turn why they faced little competition for the relatively poor soils of coastal Florida, South Carolina, and Alabama. In fact, only after 1700, when the English forced African slaves to turn marshes into rice plantations, would the preeminent centers of southeastern power move downstream to the coast.[9]

The book's principal protagonists inhabited these southeastern lands as the members of Indian towns or European empires. In the four or so centuries before 1540, most of the inhabitants of the lands between the South Carolina coast and the Arkansas River Valley centered their lives around towns. They supported these communities with the maize they planted and they celebrated them with the mounds they constructed. Archaeologists refer to these pre-contact peoples as "Mississippian," but even those towns that survived or were born from the changes of colonization possessed meeting places for ceremonies of war and peace, of death and fertility. Whether Mississippian or colonial, Native towns depended on networks of relationships to augment the power that they extracted from the sun, soil, and water of their river valleys. Some towns, like Ocute in 1540 or Altamaha in 1700, enjoyed influence over others, but none could dominate their neighbors because townspeople showed respect only to those leaders who provided resources to ensure local autonomy and well-being.[10] Zamumo might depend on Ocute for objects of power, but Altamahas looked to Zamumo for their strength. Their story is distinct from those of the coastal Indians who were eventually overwhelmed by colonial missionaries, traders, and settlers, but it is also intimately connected to these better-documented developments. From coastal peoples, these inhabitants of the Georgia and Alabama interior learned the value and danger of close association with Europeans.

These Europeans and their empires constitute the book's second set of protagonists. I am most interested in the colonists in La Florida, Carolina, and La Louisiane who had to consider the interests of their European and Indian neighbors in ways that superiors in Europe did not. Furthermore, these colonists enjoyed an independence from metropolitan control that routinely frustrated their European overseers. Nonetheless, monarchs and ministers, whether in Madrid, London, or Versailles, still exerted an influence disproportional to their numbers and their distance. They underwrote the grand visions of national hegemony centered on European capitals. The people of St. Augustine, Charles Town, and Mobile all possessed local interests, but they articulated them within larger imperial visions and transatlantic networks. They could not survive without the support of distant centers that gave them legitimacy and succor.[11]

The gifts and trade goods that bound European imperialists and Native townspeople also deserve brief explanation. Gifts are offered without immediate expectation of a return and are ultimately devoted to the promotion of interpersonal relationships, often one that endebts the recipient to the giver. A trade commodity, in contrast, leaves the hands of a seller only when the buyer can offer a thing or currency of equivalent value. Buyer and seller care more about the objects exchanged than their personal relationship. The contrast becomes even starker when we compare the objects that changed hands in southeastern exchanges. Most gifts that appear in the records were prestige goods, objects whose rarity symbolized the power of giver and recipient. Zamumo and de Soto both understood the silver feather as just such a conveyor of power. Most trade items were available to all who had the wherewithal to purchase them. Though the distinctions seem simple enough, the problem with them is that they exaggerate the differences between the two kinds of exchange and erroneously imply an unbridgeable divide between primitive, gift-giving Indians and manipulative, commercial Europeans, between the orderly hierarchy that preceded colonization and the egalitarian mayhem that followed it. Gifts and trade, with their attendant considerations of politics and profit, influenced nearly every colonial transaction. I am interested in the changing dynamics of giving and receiving because Indians and Europeans were constantly renegotiating their relationships through exchange. So to put it more technically, this is a study of political economies more than commercial ones, a study of power more than prices.[12]

Such a focus illuminates three topics crucial for the history of the early colonial Southeast and also, in a comparative way, colonial North America. First, because archaeologists devote much of their work to the study of objects and colonial officials wrote relatively frequently about many of these same things, a material focus provides a methodological lens for examining what several anthropologists call "the largely forgotten, but critically important, century in between" de Soto and Nairne.[13] It was a period before intensive colonization, when southeastern Indians reworked their political relationships, abandoning the singular leadership of chiefs for communal debates within large council houses, and reconfigured the intertown bonds of tribute into more broadly based alliance networks. It was also a time when Spaniards and then their English and French rivals articulated the colonial relationships that would define the eighteenth-century Southeast. A study of exchange offers important insights into both of these developments. Second, by understanding the changing nature of exchange, we can better understand these new Indian nations that populated the eighteenth-century Southeast, including the Cherokees, Creeks, Catawbas, Chickasaws, and Choctaws.[14] Among the most successful of these colonial polities were the Creeks, who played a pivotal role in the region thanks to their relative proximity to French Louisiana, Spanish Florida, and English Carolina. Despite the abundance of scholarship on the eighteenth-century Creeks, even the two most careful analyses of their history do not explain why this multilingual and multiethnic alliance worked.[15] It was through long-standing ties of trade and alliance that Creeks forged a collective identity without sacrificing local diversity. In addition to helping us appreciate the foundations of Creeks' local and national identities, a focus on exchange also reveals the foundations of Creeks' regional influence. Creeks' willingness to negotiate with all three colonial powers developed in part out of earlier efforts like Zamumo's to court multiple allies and multiple protectors.

Creeks' influence over—and close connection to—the colonial powers highlights a third benefit of a focus on gifts and trade. If John Stuart was right, then Zamumo's and de Soto's gifts were the first small knots in this "great tie" that made each a player in the other's history and bound towns and empires in a colonial Southeast. Europeans, for instance, encouraged Indians to modify their practices of diplomatic gift giving in the service of European notions of profit and debt. As the historian Alan Gallay has shown, the English of Carolina were especially effective in this endeavor between 1690 and 1715, when they promoted a brutal trade in Indian slaves that financed their expansion in the region. In fact, the success of the slave trade highlights a simple but crucial fact: Europeans' imperial expansion brought new worlds of violence into the lives of their Indian trading partners and victims.[16] And Creeks' and others' willingness to maintain relations with Europeans enabled the Spaniards to retain an underfunded military outpost for two centuries, the French to experiment with a plantation economy, and the British to construct a lucrative and brutal plantation economy on the backs of Africans. Native partnerships, in other words, helped Europeans maintain and in some instances finance the region's connection to a world of commercial and political power situated across the ocean.

But trade was a mutual relationship. Even as they helped finance imperial expansion, Indians also shaped the course of its development in the Southeast. This last point deserves particular emphasis because histories of Indians have generally fallen silently in the larger forest of colonial and imperial history. This silence should strike us as problematic because empires depended on negotiation with their constituent members, even if this negotiation sometimes occurred under the threat of imperial violence.[17] In some cases like the lands around the Great Lakes, neither Indians nor Europeans could compel the other to conform to their practices, so they developed what Richard White calls a "middle ground," a new set of norms that blended elements of the participants' cultures. Although cultural blending and adaptation were crucial to changing patterns of southeastern exchange, no middle ground formed in the Southeast because the participants were often transient or unstable. Few norms lasted more than two generations. Better instead to think of empires in the Southeast as akin to Evan Haefeli and Kevin Sweeney's "diaphanous spiderwebs connecting individual places and people."[18] *Zamumo's Gifts* explains how Europeans and Indians spun webs of exchange in the Southeast. As Indians helped construct the webs of empire, they induced Spaniards to abandon dreams of military conquest, the French to become negotiators and gift givers, and the British to build and then reform a colony dependent on trade. These developments resulted in a colonial Southeast defined by colonial ports and their military or plantation societies, but even these communities were partly constructed in reaction to the trade networks that lay largely in the hands of Indians. Indians did not seek colonization, but as they wove the violence of European expansion around older strands of local ambition, they helped fashion the fabric of empires.[19]

This history of the exchange relations that shaped the early colonial

Southeast depends primarily on documents from the three rival colonies. Spaniards were the first to struggle with colonizing the region, and the writings of political and religious officials have a surprising amount to tell about the lands that lay beyond their effective control. English traders wrote little about their extensive activities in the interior, but they and the men who governed them still said much about the larger geopolitical orientation of many groups. Although the French were later arrivals and had a less obvious impact on the history of the region east of their post of Mobile, Alabama, their colonial officials were some of the keenest observers and practitioners of southeastern diplomacy. My history of the region before 1680 draws heavily from numerous new syntheses of archaeological work, which themselves have benefited from increasingly fine-grained chronological analysis. I have read these documentary and archaeological sources in tandem with selections from Creeks' own written and oral histories, including those I learned from interviews and conversations with Muscogees (Creeks) in July 1997.[20] The stories Creeks tell are themselves legacies of this larger history of exchange. Giving and taking supported towns before and during the trials of colonization, and many stories make clear that Europeans were fundamental to a process of incorporating innovations into past practices of exchange.

Zamumo's Gifts examines this process incrementally. Before we can understand the new exchanges that de Soto and Zamumo initiated, we must first trace the rise of Mississippian towns and their networks of regional exchange. During roughly four centuries before 1540, Mississippian peoples defined the town as the center of political and cosmic life, and exchange with other communities reinforced this local autonomy. De Soto's chroniclers were among the first to record this fact, and when Spaniards sought to conquer the Southeast in the late sixteenth century and the early seventeenth, they confronted peoples who had the military capacity to defend their autonomy and demand the exchange relationships that would protect it. Although Spaniards founded St. Augustine in 1565, it was only decades later, after they accommodated these Mississippian expectations, that they secured their new outpost and its neighboring missions. Natives and Spaniards also connected Mississippian networks to a wider Atlantic world. These groups further modified their exchange relations after about 1620, when they incorporated more commercial activities within exchanges that were initially devoted to gifts and diplomacy. By 1650, these varied and sometimes competing layers of Mississippian foundations, Spanish adaptations, and Spanish-Indian innovations had broad political consequences for the region.

These consequences appeared most dramatically after 1660, when new communities of Native and English slave raiders entered the region.

As communities to the north of the Spanish missions fled these violent incursions, they drew upon and strengthened the networks of exchange that Spaniards and Indians had been developing over the previous century. By the beginning of the eighteenth century, some of these new refugees had reconfigured these ties into powerful new alliances. These alliances forced English traders from the new settlement of Charles Town and French traders from the still newer colony of Louisiana to recognize the diplomatic imperatives of exchange, even when it came at the expense of their profits. When English traders insisted on defining exchange in terms of credit, debt, and, most disturbingly, the enslavement of debtors, many of the colony's former partners decided to use war to reform the entire system. The Yamasee War of 1715–18 devastated the region. As a number of Native combatants revived older patterns of gift exchange, they also strengthened their alliance to better protect their local autonomy. Carolinians called these reorganized allies "Creeks." During the 1720s, as Creeks and their Native and colonial neighbors negotiated the norms of postwar exchange, Creeks became increasingly effective at harnessing the multilateral relations that shaped the colonial Southeast. Their success so vexed Carolinian ambitions that the colonists reorganized themselves, too, making their colony and themselves more British. In the long term, Creeks' use of exchange to support their own power, then, also made possible the survival and eventual success of the colonial peoples who most threatened the towns. This fact is more than ironic. The exchanges that lie at the heart of *Zamumo's Gifts* highlight how the history of neither Indians nor Europeans can be understood without the other.

Chapter 1

The Spirit of a Feather: The Politics of Mississippian Exchange

The Cussitas were always Bloody minded But the Pallachucola [Apalachicola] People made them Black Drink as a Token of Friendship And told them their Hearts were white And they must have White Hearts and lay down their Bodies in Token That they Should be White. . . . [The Cussitas] strove for the Tomahawk but the Apalachicola People by fair persuasion gained it from them And Buried it under their Cabin[.] The Pallachucola People told them their Captain Should all one with their People and gave them White feathers.
. . . Ever Since they have lived together And they Shall always live Together and bear it in remembrance.

—*Chekilli, 1735*[1]

In 1735, Chekilli, the principal leader of the Creek town of Coweta, told a story of his people's origins to the British of Savannah, Georgia. The British secretary's summary of the two-day account, which includes descriptions of migration, the acquisition of sacred knowledge, and encounters with friends and foes, also includes the above description of the "bloody minded" Cussitas' peace and union with the Apalachicolas. Two centuries after Zamumo had received his gift with such enthusiasm and long after mounds had ceased to serve as monuments to chiefly power and town cohesion, feathers remained symbols of power, encapsulating a spiritual iconography as old as Europe's Gothic cathedrals. But while feathers lacked the durability of stone, Zamumo's and Chekilli's small gifts sealed human relationships that were no less weighty.

What endowed insubstantial objects with such power? Marcel Mauss, one of the first anthropologists to consider the power of things in people's lives, argued that gifts were the product of an obligation to offer, to receive, and to reciprocate that he located in the "spirit" of the gift. As he explained, the object of exchange possessed its own spiritual power that compelled recipients to become givers in order to avoid suffering the ill-effects of holding on to this power too long. Exchange in turn maintained the relationships that held society together. Such gifts, as objects that had no price and offered no material gain, were different from (and, for Mauss, more important than) the commodities that promised profit through the manipulation of monetary values. Where the former promoted relations between giver and recipient, the latter promoted relations between individuals and the objects they sought. Subsequent students of giving have refined Mauss's ideas, saying that the power of any object resides not in the object itself but in the relationships that exist between giver and recipient. They have also noted how Mauss exaggerated the distinction between gifts and commodities, showing that commodities could become gifts and vice versa depending on the context of the exchange. Whatever their take, these scholars all agree that bonds within and between societies depend in some part on individuals' spirit of giving, their willingness to seal intangible relationships with material exchanges.[2]

Gifts mattered so much to Zamumo and Chekilli because reciprocity ensured the strength of the towns they led. Exchange among townspeople maintained equilibrium and hierarchy within the town while exchanges with outsiders provided leaders with rare and powerful objects. Both sets of relationships enabled townspeople to regulate their cosmos with appropriate ceremonies and to maintain friends and resist enemies with large, well-fed, and well-armed populations. Zamumo said as much when he exulted over the feather from de Soto: large harvests, powerful armies, and growing populations would all reinforce his power and perhaps his town's independence from Ocute. The calculations that informed these conclusions derived their power from centuries of practice. Zamumo was the heir to some six centuries of cultural practices that had first begun in 900 C.E., when people near today's St. Louis began constructing what would become the largest city in North America. The people of this city called Cahokia introduced a new architecture of massive earthen temple mounds, but they also introduced new relations of exchange. Other southeastern communities adopted Cahokia's new political economy, but as these successor societies grew in number and competed with one another, they expanded the networks and volume of prestige goods circulating throughout the Southeast. It was in this fluid environment of the sixteenth century that leaders like Zamumo sought new patrons like de Soto even as they acknowledged old ones like Ocute. It was also from these competitive networks of exchange that southeastern townspeople would fashion new relations with their new European neighbors, keeping the Mississippian spirit of giving alive long after mounds had become memorials to the distant (if still sacred) pasts of people like Chekilli. And stories like his testify to the capacity of ancestors to leave their descendants with gifts that could cross time as well as space. The durability of these stories that tellers adapted over generations of colonization speak as richly as any feather to the power of exchange and the resilience of local autonomy.³

The Birth and Rise of Mississippian Towns

Chekilli's story, the oldest and one of the longest written accounts of Creek origins, provides a useful point of departure for this discussion of towns, gifts, and the power of the Mississippian past. The story was written down in 1735, when Chekilli, the *mico* (or headman) of the *talwa* (or town) of Coweta, described the origins of the peoples of the Chattahoochee River and their allies to Georgian colonial dignitaries gathered in Savannah. According to a secretary's paraphrasing of the two-day talk, the people known as the Cussitas emerged from the earth somewhere to the west and migrated eastward toward the rising sun. Crossing a wide, muddy river and then a red, bloody one, they eventually came to a thundering mountain that shot fire straight upward. Taking some of this fire, they combined it with some that came to them from the north to make their sacred fire. Near this same mountain they also met three other peoples, the Chickasaws, Alabamas, and Abecas. Together the four peoples learned the attributes of the sacred plants, how some of them were necessary for purification before their annual Green Corn Ceremony, or *boosketuh*, and how menstruating women could destroy the power of the plants if they came too close. In order to determine which of the four peoples was the eldest and most powerful, they decided to erect four poles. The first to cover their pole with the scalps of their enemies would be considered the highest rank. The Cussitas finished the challenge first, followed by the Chickasaws, the Alabamas, and the Abecas, who were unable to "raise their heap of scalps higher than the knee."⁴

Also at about this time, a terrible blue bird was regularly killing these peoples. They killed their assailant with the help of a rat who was the child of the fierce bird. They then followed a path that was white, the color of peace, until they reached the Coosas. There they learned that a lion was eating one of the Coosas every seven days, and so they set a fatal trap baited with a "motherless child." After four years among the Coosas, the Cussitas relocated to a site along the river they called Calosahutchee, where they struggled to feed themselves for lack of corn. Eventually, they resumed following the white path until they came to a town that they hoped was the home of the path's makers. Unfortunately, when scouts fired white arrows into the town to indicate the Cussitas' peaceful intentions, the residents responded with red arrows of war. Displeased, the Cussitas prepared to attack the town, but when they arrived they found it abandoned, the people having apparently disappeared beneath the nearby river. When they came to another town that responded with red arrows, they attacked it and killed all but two of the inhabitants. After chasing these survivors, they came again upon the white path, which led them to the town of the Apalachicolas. The Apalachicolas welcomed the travelers, and hoping to calm their bloody-minded visitors, the hosts offered them black drink, a purificatory tea made from leaves of the cassina plant. Professing that their hearts were white, the Apalachicolas convinced the Cussitas to bury their hatchet under the meeting benches at the Apalachicolas' square ground and offered them feathers as symbols of friendship. The two peoples lived together from that point onward, with the Cussitas settling two towns, Cussita and Coweta, that became "the Head Towns of the Upper and Lower Creeks."[5]

Chekilli's story explained to his listeners the origins of his people's most important life-ways even as it also established the bonds of friendship and power that held together the Abecas, Coosas, Alabamas, Apalachicolas, and Cussitas as the people that the British colonists called "Creeks." In making their sacred fire with the fire that came to them from the north, the Cussitas first refused the fires that came to them from the west, east, and south. These four directions organized Creek space and provided Creeks with the sacred number four. Square grounds, where they met to discuss issues of general interest, always adhered to the cardinal points, with the sacred fire in the middle, and the meeting benches of the leaders facing east. One of the most important ceremonies performed at the square grounds was the Green Corn Ceremony, which the Creeks celebrated at the time of the first maize harvest, purifying themselves for the beginning of a new year. Chekilli also mentioned the importance of particular medicines and the need to protect them from the uncontrolled power of menstruating women, alluding to the division of tasks that followed lines of gender. Only women could provide children with a clan identity that would make them Creeks, which explains why the Cussitas baited their lion trap with a "motherless child." Red was the color of war and white the color of peace, and as much as war was part of Creek life, the black drink could purify and bring calm to the drinker.[6]

This account of political and cultural origins was in many respects a case for the world as Chekilli thought it should be.[7] Most basically, though, he was claiming that towns made history. Even when Creeks from other towns contested Chekilli's claim to superiority, they and many subsequent Creek historians have presented the *talwas* as the source of action and allegiance. Also like Chekilli, they have emphasized the prominence of their *talwa* in the origins of the Creeks. When two Coosas told their origin stories to the ethnologist John Swanton early in the twentieth century, they both explained that their people were the first Muskogees. Some Tukabatchees, in contrast, averred that their *talwa* came from the sky above before migrating north, south, and then finally east to settle lands among the Creeks.[8] In another version, Tukabatchees came out of the earth, later meeting the Cussitas, Cowetas, and Chickasaws. In the contest of scalps to determine seniority, the Tukabatchees and Cussitas tied, with the Cowetas following them and the Chickasaws not participating at all. For their part, Alabamas described their migration as separate from the others.[9] The Hitchitis claimed they, like the Cussitas, migrated toward the rising sun, but they did so and arrived at the sea long before the Cussitas and their companions. Thus they were revered by the later arrivals as those who went to see from where the sun came.[10] Although the differences matter a great deal, the stories agree on a number of levels, including the recurrence of sacred motifs like the sun and the cardinal directions. In every case, they also emphasize the importance of towns as the centers of historical action.

As Chekilli and others suggested in their stories, towns were old. They might move or reconfigure themselves, but their square grounds had been defining and celebrating the southeastern cosmos for centuries. But this way of life, like Chekilli's ancestors, had come from somewhere, and that somewhere lay at the American Bottom, where the Missouri and Mississippi Rivers join to create a fertile bottomland and where the city of Cahokia grew some time after 900 C.E. Still today, the city's imposing Monk's Mound rises thirty meters above the outskirts of East St. Louis, covering roughly seven hectares at its base.[11] This was among the largest of hundreds of truncated pyramids that punctuated the landscape of the American Bottom. The leaders who lived, worshiped, and were sometimes buried atop these mounds enjoyed ties of exchange with societies for hundreds of kilometers in all directions. Stored up surpluses of corn fed the people who maintained these monuments. More than large, Cahokia was unprecedented. In 1050 its population of eight thousand to fifteen thousand dwarfed any North American population center before Boston, New York, and Philadelphia reached similar sizes some seven centuries later.[12]

Unlike prior residents of eastern North America, Cahokia's builders planned their community before they built it. Some time around 1000, in one massive act of what the archaeologist Timothy Pauketat calls "urban renewal," Cahokians leveled a nineteen-hectare grand plaza and constructed the first six meters of Monk's Mound immediately to the north of the plaza. Residents even built their houses according to a prescribed layout that probably mobilized the same collective effort as the plaza and mound.[13] Equally important, this growing city promoted and depended upon an exchange network that allowed it to acquire marine shells from the Gulf Coast, copper from the Great Lakes, chert from the Ozarks, and mica from the Appalachian Mountains. From these materials Cahokian craftsmen and craftswomen made idols, tools, and ceramics that became prestigious goods exchanged throughout the Mississippi Valley. Whether peoples from the upper Great Lakes to the Mississippi Delta accepted Cahokian crafts as tributaries, allies, or outlying Cahokian trading colonies is unclear, but their participation in these exchanges enabled Cahokians to define themselves and their power in the American Bottom in terms of the peoples who lived far beyond its horizons.[14] Such contacts promoted but could not guarantee Cahokian influence, however. Between 1100 and 1300 environmental degradation, internal and external conflicts, and deepening popular dissatisfaction with the city's elite all contributed to Cahokia's collapse.[15]

The great city's legacy was far greater than even its unprecedented size would suggest. Archaeologists acknowledge its impact in their terminology. Cahokia is the standard against which they define the successor societies called chiefdoms, societies whose leaders enjoyed marked privileges compared to the commoners they ruled but who also depended on personal connections and hereditary privileges rather than bureaucracies or standing armies—institutions frequently associated with states. Mississippian chiefdoms distinguished themselves from the earlier polities most obviously in their construction of planned towns, earthen mounds, and plazas. Atop their mounds, chiefs lived, preserved their sacred fires, and celebrated communal rituals with townspeople gathered in the plaza below. When townspeople gathered to add a new layer of soil to their mounds, they affirmed their connection to one another as well as to the earth. Because most layers were added following the interment of a principal leader, mound construction also expressed a community's connection to (and elevation of) its chief. As Chekilli would have understood well, no mound and no chief existed without an associated town. However wide his ties to other farming hamlets, tributary towns, or allies, a chief resided in one particular town, where he consulted other members of the elite and conducted the ceremonies of cosmic order.[16] Not surprisingly, even after southeastern Natives ceased to define their communities through mound building, powerful chiefs, and tributary ties, they still placed their towns at the political and ceremonial heart of their world. Towns and the exchanges that supported them began with Cahokia and endured long after Zamumo and de Soto offered each other tokens of friendship and power.[17]

No southeastern community would ever reproduce Cahokia's size or success, but many would imitate it. By 1100, peoples of Georgia, Alabama, and eastern Tennessee began building new town and mound cen-

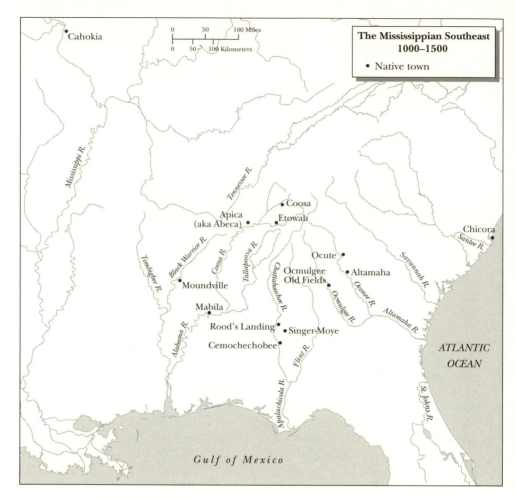

Map 1. The Mississippian Southeast, 1000–1500. Although these various chiefdoms were not contemporaneous, later communities built upon their cultural, and sometimes physical, remains.

ters of their own.[18] Archaeologists still understand relatively little about the early Mississippian societies of Georgia, Alabama, and Tennessee, and it is difficult to determine what role regional exchange played in their fortunes. By the thirteenth century, however, their successors participated in complex networks of exchange that stretched across and beyond the Southeast. Mississippian exchange provided leaders from Georgia to Oklahoma with beautifully crafted objects of copper, shell, and stone that were inscribed with a sacred iconography of bird-men, snake-birds, and other deities who blended the power of various animals and the elements of earth, air, and water.[19]

After 1200, residents of the Black Warrior River Valley in western Alabama used their place in these networks to build a Mississippian center second only to Cahokia in size. Although Moundville's population of some fifteen hundred to three thousand people was a fraction of Cahokia's, its leaders were especially effective at harnessing the dynamics of exchange and ceremony to their own quests for influence. By gaining control of the production and distribution of the finely crafted ceramics, copper ornaments, and other symbols of power, Moundville's chiefs maintained close contact with and control over neighbors who depended on these objects for their authority. By the end of the thirteenth century, peoples as far north as the Tennessee River recognized the power of Moundville and its sacred crafts, and scattered villages and hamlets began to replace more densely clustered towns in the Black Warrior Valley. Perhaps people dispersed in part because Moundville's power reduced valley residents' need for dense settlements with protective walls, but whatever the reason, this *pax Moundvilliana* incorporated the persuasive power of what its leaders gave and received.[20]

Meanwhile, between about 1250 and 1375, chiefs in western Georgia were attempting something similar. Leaders of Etowah, in northwestern Georgia, gained influence over much of the rest of the eponymous river valley, oversaw the construction of beautiful crafts, and placed these objects and themselves atop three mounds, one of which eventually grew to 21 meters in height. Etowah supported some of its influence through its access to an important route that connected chiefdoms of the Gulf Coast, Chattahoochee River, and upper Tennessee River.[21] Two hundred forty kilometers south of Etowah, elites in the Chattahoochee Valley constructed similarly large centers at Rood's Landing and Singer-Moye thanks in part to their association with prestigious goods, including the exchange of fine pottery used by elites from the Gulf Coast to the Chattahoochee fall line. Unlike the case of Moundville, it is unclear whether inhabitants of the valley produced these ceramics in their respective towns or acquired them from one town that monopolized their production. Much like their contemporaries at Moundville, though, the leaders of Singer-Moye and Rood's Landing believed that the ideas and symbols of power were best shared regionally. Leaders from the Gulf Coast to Rood's Landing 250 kilometers to the north drank from similarly decorated ceramics. Indeed, the relative similarity among commoners' pottery styles for 90 kilometers south of Rood's Landing further suggests how many people participated in the connections that bound the Mississippian world.[22]

The political and cultural integration among elites and, to a lesser extent, commoners did not last much beyond the end of the fourteenth century, when the global cooling of the "Little Ice Age" reduced the crop yields that supported these large chiefdoms. Moundville's scattered population ceased using nearly all of the mounds in the once-great town at about this time. To the northeast, external threats convinced the people of Etowah to ring their town with a trench and palisade, but new defenses could not prevent invaders from burning Etowah's palisade and desecrating its temple around 1400. Survivors abandoned the site shortly afterward. The residents of Rood's Landing also abandoned their mound center at about the same time. Only residents of Singer-Moye managed to maintain their large town for another generation or two, perhaps because they lived at some distance from the rivers that perhaps carried more war parties than prestige goods.[23]

When other chiefly polities emerged after 1400, none of these so-called Late Mississippian chiefdoms were able to replicate the success of their predecessors. The Late Mississippian Southeast—the world Zamumo inhabited and de Soto visited—was a more competitive environment than the one Moundville and Etowah had dominated. Wars flared more frequently and prestigious goods moved more abundantly, if also less widely.[24] Leaders like Ocute might enjoy the tribute of other chiefs like Zamumo, but even these lesser leaders still used their own mounds to conduct ceremonies and perhaps cast a watchful eye for enemies and a hopeful gaze for new exchange partners. In their localism, their competitiveness, and their need for allies and exchange partners, these chiefdoms were the progenitors of Chekilli's *talwas*.

The Spirit of the Late Mississippian Gift

Among these new dynamics, older patterns remained. Finely crafted objects, frequently of rare materials, still occupied the focal point of ceremonies of cosmological order, communal cohesion, and military strength. As the sites of chiefly residences and temples, the mounds continued to assert the authority of the men and (occasional) women who oversaw southeastern chiefdoms. One example of such mound-centered ceremonial power comes from a resident of South Carolina's coast, Francisco Chicorana, who spoke with the Spanish imperial historian Peter Martyr D'Anghera in the early 1500s. He explained that the Duhares, a people neighboring his own, venerated two idols "as large as a three-year old child, one male and one female," which "had their residence in the palace" atop the town's mound. Twice a year, during sowing season and harvest season, the chief of Duhare displayed these idols for the necessary ceremonies of supplication and thanksgiving. Appearing atop his mound with the idols on the appropriate days, "he and they are saluted with respect and fear by the people." During the two days of rituals, Duhare remained closely associated with these idols, which assured "rich crops, bodily health, peace, or if they are about to fight, victory."[25] Much as earlier invaders had recognized in their destruction of Etowah's temple and Zamumo later proclaimed in his speech to de Soto, sacred objects were crucial to a town's survival.

Broader access did not erase the power of these objects or the perils of acquiring them. Although most exchange probably occurred between near neighbors rather than over long distances, travel beyond the immediate protection of one's kin and community entailed significant risk. Late Mississippian ceremonies of return acknowledged both the danger that a traveler faced and the prestige that accompanied success. In 1595, the leader of the recently converted village of San Pedro, just north of St. Augustine, returned from a journey. When the man, named Juan, and his wife entered the town, the entire populace greeted them by "wailing in a high voice as if they had dropped dead before their eyes," and townspeople repeated these lamentations in Juan's presence for "many days." The Franciscan missionary who recorded this event did not allude to death accidentally. After the missionary reached St. Augustine, he learned that nearby mission Indians cried in a similar manner to honor a recently deceased leader.[26] Chekilli's own story of Cussita-Apalachicola union suggests a simple reason for this association between long-distance travel and death. It was only after many "fair persuasions" that Apalachicolas managed to calm their bellicose visitors enough to accept white feathers of peace. Beyond the norms and protections of their societies, travelers seeking peace and the goods that marked it remained vulnerable to the violence of strangers. The power of the objects that came home from these journeys, then, lay not just in their physical characteristics but also in the ways in which they were acquired.

Exchange also involved another relationship of power. Giving and receiving established relations of mutual obligation. Although a recipient acquired an obligation to reciprocate and a giver demonstrated power through generosity, a gift did not imply the unquestioned superiority of the giver. Context mattered. As Spaniards, British, and French would all learn later, when givers gave from a position of weakness rather than strength, Indians frequently accepted these offerings as tribute instead of gifts.[27] But even tributaries had claims on their supposed superiors. De Soto and his followers had good reason to believe that their weapons certainly often cowed their hosts, but when the would-be conqueror of La Florida arrived in the chiefdom of Casqui near the Mississippi River, the chief, also known as Casqui, offered "to serve" the Spaniards because, according to de Soto's chronicler Luys Hernández de Biedma, de Soto was "from heaven." In return, the chief requested help in the form of rain for his parched fields. De Soto agreed, instructed him to make a cross of two pines, and promised to return the next day with the needed heavenly sign. Casqui did not wait on his supposed superior, though; instead, as Biedma recounted, he arrived the next morning, berating de Soto for his delays despite his people's willingness "to serve us and follow us." The Spaniards were moved by the chief's devotion, but they might also have noticed that his fervor was born of a sense expectation of spiritual power the Spaniard had yet to provide. Mutual obligation confirmed the personal nature of all exchanges, but the exchange of people emphasized it more clearly still. In most instances, it is impossible to determine the motivations of the many peoples who offered men and women as burden bearers and sexual partners to the invaders, but Casqui at least acknowledged the power of human gifts when he offered captive women to the Spaniards and gave his daughter to de Soto out of his supposed "desire to unite his blood with so great a lord as he [de Soto] was."[28] Centuries later, Chekilli recounted how Cussitas had encountered a mountain where they acquired the sacred knowledge, fire, and medicines necessary to keep their world in balance. For Chekilli as well as Casqui, the capacity of a town to survive and prosper came from without. Casqui demonstrated how that survival and prosperity involved a delicate balance of generosity and obligation.

Leaders, Followers, and the Meaning of Late Mississippian Power

If it is difficult to understand this balance among towns, it is even more difficult to look within towns. To speak of the power of Mississippian towns usually implies speaking of the power of chiefs over towns. Although rare and sacred goods (and the mounds where many were buried) seem to justify this perspective, chiefs depended on the people who accorded them respect, provided them fine foods, manufactured their ornaments, and built the mounds atop which they lived and worshipped. Through the reciprocal relations of leaders and followers, of men and women, and of friends and relations, commoners negotiated the bonds that held their towns together. Such negotiations in turn influenced exchanges among towns. As much as Zamumo would have liked to convince de Soto otherwise, chiefs were not the only ones who exchanged things.

Common people, like their leaders, tended to live on their stored agricultural surpluses, especially corn, squash, and, after about 1200 C.E., beans.[29] They supplemented this diet with nuts, berries, fish, waterfowl, and deer.[30] Mississippians organized many of the tasks of subsistence along lines of gender. The men and women of pre-contact Tukabatchee, a prominent town on the Tallapoosa River, manufactured the tools necessary for their tasks in separate spaces in their homes. The stone flakes left over from men's manufacture of arrowheads litter one corner while the broken pottery from women's ceramic making lies in another. If the activities of their colonial-era descendants are any guide, Mississippian men probably cleared the agricultural fields and hunted while women cultivated the crops and gathered other seasonal foods that grew wild. Language reflected these divisions, with Muskogean grammar and vocabulary varying according to the gender of the speaker.[31] Much to their chagrin, French traders among the Natchez learned about a similar linguistic divide, for "by chiefly frequenting the women, [they] contracted their manner of speaking, which was ridiculed as effeminacy by the women, as well as the men, among the natives."[32] Men's and women's complementary roles in family and social life carried into political life as well. Among elite families, men apparently had greater access to the chieftaincy than women, and those few commoners who earned burial in or near a temple mound were usually distinguished warriors.[33] Women's importance as the principal providers of food endowed them with significant influence in the household, and senior women could help shape the ideas of their clan members who dwelled with and near them.[34] Bound together in relationships in which each provided and each received, men's and women's power depended less on control than interdependence.

Sharing also joined clans and chiefs. If the geography of the chief was the town, that of the clan was the house. Most Mississippian people inhabiting modern Georgia, Alabama, and eastern Tennessee lived in large, square homes whose floors were dug slightly below ground level and whose walls were banked with earth to provide greater insulation in the winter. Adjacent to their homes, families built raised open-air structures that could be used as summer dwellings. In the same way that chiefs buried their prominent ancestors under new layers of the mound or interred them in the nearby charnel house, many people honored their recently deceased kin by burning the homestead before burying the dead kin and rebuilding a new home over them. As further evidence of the power of kin ties, clan members within a town often built their homes near each other. Children probably grew up among their mother's family, and the most respected members of the clan were likely the occupants of the larger homes located closest to the open plaza that spread out before every temple mound.[35]

The power of clans also appeared in later stories of Creek origins, too. In some versions, clans rather than towns emerged from the earth, each clan enveloped in a fog that prevented its members from seeing the world around them. Gradually a wind began to blow, and as it did so, the clans began to recognize one another in the dissipating mist. The first to emerge from the fog became known as the Wind clan, and as others began to see the world around them, they saw different animals that became their clan's totem. As the first clan to be free of the fog, the Wind clan gained a certain prominence above all others.[36] Clans provided a fundamental bond for Creeks during the eighteenth and nineteenth centuries. "The strongest link in Creek political and social standing," noted the Creek historian George Stiggins in 1836, "is their clanship or families." According to Thomas Nairne a century earlier, even as clans grew, fragmented, and migrated to other towns, their members continued to acknowledge ties to distant kin, with "divers Tribes or nations of Different Languages . . . having constant quarrels one with the other, yet at the same time pretending kindred."[37] The connections of clans mitigated conflict by providing a network that transcended locality.

Mississippian clans were important, but their members still offered the choicest portions of the hunt and harvest to their chief, and they reaffirmed their association with the mound and its privileged occupants through their participation in the initial process of town planning and layout and the recurring rituals of mound renewal. The reciprocal relations that encouraged followers to provide labor and goods in exchange for local and cosmic security promoted the power of the few over the many. Although clan ties extended beyond the limits of the town and seemed to defy a leader's local influence, some skillful leaders could also influence neighboring chiefdoms. Mississippian titles reflected these levels of influence. Although Spanish explorers frequently referred to late Mississippian leaders by the Arawak term "caciques," Muskogean speakers like those in the Coosa paramount chiefdom differentiated their leaders with a variety of titles. An *orata*, which the chronicler Juan de la Bandera translated as *señor menor*, led small villages or groups of villages. These recognized the influence of a *mico*, or *gran señor*, who, in addition to enjoying the respect of *oratas*, also headed a town of his own. At the apex of the Coosa paramouncy was a "cacique grande" named "Cosa."[38] Apparently, the *mico* of a paramount town did not need a new title; he simply embodied the town and province over which he ruled.

Such networks enabled Coosa and other leaders with similar resources and wherewithal to integrate neighboring communities and even distant chiefs into larger regional, or paramount, chiefdoms. During his invasion of the Southeast in 1540, Hernando de Soto heard rumors of the "great lord" named "Coça" who had other towns subject to him. De Soto capitalized on Coosa's regional influence when he kept the chief as a hostage to guarantee the Spaniards safe passage through a host of towns. Only when he reached somewhere in the environs of central Alabama was this chief from northwestern Georgia no longer of any use to him. Another, more localized integration appears in the material record as well. As the town of Coosa became increasingly prominent during the fifteenth century, for example, the pottery styles of neighboring towns converged.[39] But did the bonds of hierarchy imply the bondage of commoners? Massive earthworks and the carefully crafted objects they conceal suggest that Mississippian elites claimed a monopoly on the sacred based on ancestry and knowledge of the arcane. Despite mounds' imposing stature, though, no material remains conclusively illustrate that chiefs exercised power beyond their immediate towns.[40] Sixteenth-century explorers claimed that they did, but de Soto and others spoke incessantly about chiefs and their power in part because they were hoping to find another Moctezuma or Atahualpa. Amid the ambiguity and scanty evidence, two perspectives offer some insight into the question of chiefly power.

First, the forms of warfare that secured late Mississippian power were themselves the product of a careful, if also unequal, balance between the interests of leaders and followers. Elites' inability to control sacred power as effectively as their predecessors had at Etowah, Rood's Landing, and Moundville meant that warfare served a vital role for maintaining chiefly stability after 1400, but because armies consisted of men who spent most of their time farming, hunting, and making the tools necessary for their subsistence, collective unwillingness could cripple chiefly power. Even when they did serve in massed formations at a chief's command, individuals sought to distinguish themselves through daring exploits. Individual martial skill provided families with captive slaves. Warriors often displayed the scalps of their victims from the top of a high pole, but rather than place that symbol of their prowess atop the mound of the chief, they erected it in the town's central plaza. With this act, warriors emphasized their role in a military success that belonged to their community, not their chief.[41]

But there were limits to the autonomy of warriors. However much fighting men celebrated their actions as victories for their towns and located their most basic loyalties with their homes and the clan members living in them and buried under them, chiefs organized the disciplined warriors who kept tributaries in thrall and Spanish conquistadors off balance. In 1560, Coosa convinced Spanish explorers under Tristan de Luna to join his large military conquest of wayward tributaries on the Tennessee River.[42] Twenty years earlier de Soto's forces suffered tremendous losses from a carefully orchestrated assault at the chiefdom of Mabila, somewhere in central Alabama. Although warriors were slaughtered, perhaps in the thousands, the attackers destroyed many supplies and disabused the Spaniards of their invincibility.[43] Well-organized armies enabled paramount chiefs to conduct the wars that secured their religious and tributary preeminence.

Any discussion of networks requires that we examine a second perspective, that of trade. Were chiefs the only mediators of Mississippian intertown exchange? As important as the question is for an understanding of local politics and regional exchange, it is frustratingly difficult to answer. Few non-elite goods have lasted long enough for archaeologists to find them and trace their provenance. Nonetheless, John Lawson's early eighteenth-century memoir of his visit to the North Carolina piedmont offers a tantalizing glimpse. During the annual harvest celebrations of the *boosketuh*, people gathered "from all the Towns within fifty or sixty Miles round, where they buy and sell several Commodities, as we do at Fairs and Markets." Here, then, is a possible arena in which townspeople interacted and traded with friends, kin, and strangers, a time for clan members to reaffirm their intertown relationships, perhaps an opportunity for them to share the ideas and skills that enabled people of the thirteenth-century Chattahoochee Valley or the environs of sixteenth-century Coosa to develop similar styles of pottery. But outside this ceremonial context, community leaders likely exercised more control. When the trader John Lederer traveled to the same region in 1670, his hosts shared his penchant for "higgling" over the rate of any exchange, but they also made it clear that he first had to present his goods to the town's influential elders. Part of the reason for this interposition might have been that even friends could be part-time enemies. Towns met not only to celebrate the harvest but also (and probably simultaneously) to play the ball game. This violent and grueling ancestor of lacrosse allowed peaceable neighbors to vent their hostilities without going to war against each other (hence the game's nickname: "the little brother of war"). Because spectators often wagered everything they possessed on the fortunes of their town, victors and vanquished could meet after games to exchange outside the presumed influence of their chiefs. The imbalanced nature of such interactions and the competition and violence that underwrote them probably limited the depth of such bonds, though. And perhaps this fact as much as any reminds us of the danger of trade and helps us appreciate further the ceremonial wailing that welcomed Cacique Juan back to his town, back, as it were, from the dead.[44]

All of this leaves us with a sense that chiefs enjoyed significant power if they negotiated carefully. Ocute and Coosa might personify their towns, but they could not control all of the relationships that supported their towns and their leadership. The fact that they achieved some success at controlling the people and things involved in intertown trade suggests, too, the importance of relationships to the power of the chief and the town. And when chiefs lost power at the end of the early colonial period, it should be no surprise that their followers concerned themselves more with building and maintaining networks of exchange than with restoring the power of their humbled elite. Consequently, when Chekilli told his story of his people's sacred origins in 1735, he spoke of how Cussitas, the townspeople, rather than Cussita, a chief, accepted the Apalachicolas' sacred feather.[45]

Enduring Mississippian Spirits

Despite such significant changes in the contours of Creek stories, these histories still carry the echoes and the power of the Mississippian past and demonstrate quite clearly how they shaped the colonial world. In them, Creek historians explained and today continue to explain why towns remain fundamental political units of southeastern Native life and how exchange has sustained them. Such connections can at times be quite elusive. If stories are legacies of Mississippian life-ways and indeed products of generations of exchanges of information, then how could Chekilli's story, the oldest and most detailed published account, neglect any mention of mounds? The eighteenth-century trader James Adair put the problem best during a visit to the Ocmulgee Old Fields, near today's Macon, Georgia. His Creek friends revered the site, with its remains of mounds more than six hundred years old and of a town and trading house that Indians and English had abandoned after war divided them in 1715. "They strenuously aver, that when necessity forces them to encamp there, they always hear, at the dawn of the morning, the usual noise of Indians singing their joyful religious notes, and dancing, as if going down to the river to purify themselves, and then returning to the old townhouse: with a great deal more to the same effect." So claimed his hosts, but, "Whenever I have been there," continued Adair, ". . . all hath been silent."[46]

Sometimes, though, it is a matter of listening more for stories than for specters. In 1773–74, some two decades after Adair frequented the locale, the naturalist William Bartram visited the mounds of the Old Fields as part of his itinerant study of southeastern plants and animals. There, his Creek guides taught him some of their history.

And, if we are to give credit to the account the Creeks give of themselves, this place is remarkable for being the first town or settlement, when they sat down (as they term it) or established themselves, after their emigration from the west, beyond the Mississippi, their original native country. On this long journey they suffered great and innumerable difficulties, encountering and vanquishing numerous and valiant tribes of Indians, who opposed and retarded their march. Having crossed the river, still pushing eastward, they were obliged to make a stand, and fortify themselves in this place, as their only remaining hope, being to the last degree persecuted and weakened by their surrounding foes. Having formed for themselves this retreat, and driven off the inhabitants by degrees, they recovered their spirits, and again faced their enemies, when they came off victorious in a memorable and decisive battle. They afterwards gradually subdued their surrounding enemies, strengthening themselves by taking into confederacy the vanquished tribes.[47]

As in Chekilli's story, Creeks' ancestors faced numerous military challenges on their journey east. Unlike this earlier account, mounds played prominent roles, providing strength and succor. In ways that Bartram only hinted at in his summary, Mississippians and their Creek descendants were sharing ideas that connected them to each other and to old sources of power.

In fact, Creeks frequently mentioned mounds when they explained the foundations of their *talwas'* autonomy. In 1800, Benjamin Hawkins, the United States Superintendent of the Creeks, related the account that Tussekiahmico of Cussita gave for the origin of the Creeks and their sacred fire. Much of the account paralleled Chekilli's story from six decades earlier. At one point in their migration, though, the Cussitas, Cowetas, and Chickasaws stopped at two mounds west of the Mississippi River when sacred beings from each of the four corners of the world came to them. Giving the three peoples fire, the four visitors explained that the sacred flame would preserve them and inform Esaugetuh Emissee (the Master of Breath) of their wants. Sitting around the fire on one of the mounds, the four beings also taught the traveling peoples the knowledge of the sacred plants. After the teachers departed, the Cussitas, Cowetas, and Chickasaws migrated east to the Coosa River, where they met the Abecas. In a four-year war to obtain scalps and determine seniority, Cussitas achieved the highest rank, followed by the Cowetas, Chickasaws, and Abecas. The Cussitas defeated another people inhabiting some mounds further to the east before continuing on to the Atlantic Ocean, where the recently arrived whites forced them to return inland.[48]

Another story, related by Ispahihta of Cussita to James Gregory circa 1900, described how the Cussitas, Cowetas, and Chickasaws abandoned their lands in the west because of the spread of evil. Determining that the sun was the last pure object in their tainted world, they headed east in search of its origin. After crossing the great river with the Cowetas and Cussitas, the Chickasaws abandoned the quest, preferring to live on the fertile lands along the river. Traveling far ahead of the Cowetas, Cussitas built a mound into which they dug a chamber to purify themselves.

Once purified, the warriors set out against unnamed enemies living nearby. The Cowetas, angry that the Cussita warriors had gone to war without them, threatened to kill the Cussita women and children remaining in the town. Alerted to the Cowetas' malicious intentions, the Cussita warriors returned in time to prevent the attack, punishing their partners by beating them with canes. Again the Cussitas departed, leaving the Coweta warriors to purify themselves inside the mound. When Cherokees came to attack what they thought was an undefended town, they saw, much to their astonishment and dismay, that Coweta warriors "poured up from the bowels of the earth." After routing the Cherokees, the Cowetas joined the Cussitas in a series of military victories that led them to the Atlantic Ocean. Seeing the sun rise out of the sea the following morning, they understood that the water kept the sun bright and pure. Once they had conquered neighboring peoples, the Cowetas challenged the Cussitas to the ball game to avenge their earlier caning. This contest established the distinction between the red war towns led by Coweta and the white peace towns led by Cussita.[49]

The stories that Hawkins and Gregory recorded reveal additional details about Creek culture. In the ball game, towns competed only against others that were "of the opposite fire," that is to say, red or white towns never competed against towns of the same color. Hawkins's synopsis explains the sources of this division between red towns responsible for war and white towns that took a leadership role in making peace.[50] The arrival and brief stay at the ocean shore that Hawkins described becomes more meaningful and poignant in Gregory's version. The convergence at the horizon of the Middle World where people resided with the Above World of air and order and with the Under World of water and chaos must have been a powerful sight for the migrants and for those like Ispahihta and Gregory who recounted their experience.[51] Most important, as with Bartram's account, the mounds in both stories serve as the sites of rebirth. Atop one mound, migrating peoples learned the sacred ways that would be the foundation of their common culture. Emerging from another mound, as if "from the bowels of the earth," Cowetas and Cussitas repeated their initial emergence in the west. In each case, the mounds made new people.

The people were new, but many of their basic institutions were not. Towns no longer had mounds, but by emerging from them, later Creeks acknowledged their Mississippian antecedents. Exchange also gave these towns life and strength. In the story told by Tussekiahmico and summarized by Hawkins, towns received the sacred knowledge necessary to balance the power of the cosmos; in Chekilli's account, Cussita received a feather to secure bonds of peace. Finally, the stories themselves were products of exchange. Whatever the variations among towns, the congruences also speak to centuries of people sharing information among *talwas* and across generations.

Consequently, stories that apparently deny these connections, these acts of sharing, raise interesting questions. Even with mounds figuring as prominently as they did as a rallying point in Bartram's relation and Gregory's mention that Cussitas actually built a mound as part of their migration eastward, many Creeks did not consider their ancestors responsible for them. At the end of the 1700s, Creeks claimed no knowledge of the builders of the earthworks. By 1900, some Creeks stridently asserted that neither they nor any Indian people would consent to building the mounds. As Gregory himself wrote to a Cherokee friend interested in Creek history, "None of them would entertain for one moment digging and carrying wet clay by thousands of tons by hand and building firm clay mounds a hundred feet high 400 feet long by sixty feet wide . . . No Sir! No North American Indian tribe done these things." The mounds, Gregory continued, were the product of an inferior, non-Indian people, the Mound-builders, whom the Creeks drove from the Southeast and out of North America shortly after their arrival in the Southeast.[52] Gregory made explicit what the oral histories imply: the Creeks had no ancestors other than those *talwa* or clan members who emerged from the earth.[53]

Creeks recall their origin stories to remind themselves who they are, but even in the many stories they have shared with non-Creeks, they are asserting their sense of themselves in relation to outsiders, usually their colonizers. Statements like Gregory's suggest how Europeans' involvement in southeastern exchange networks included ideas as well as objects. They also highlight the importance of the historical contexts of these stories from the last three centuries. Most briefly, Chekilli presented Georgia's leaders with his history lesson to assert his preeminence among the Creeks and also his power in relation to the new Georgia colony. Sixty years later, Tussekiahmico sought to remind Hawkins that Creeks already possessed a civilization and did not need to subscribe to the American version that Hawkins championed. When Ispahihta spoke with Gregory (and, by extension, the anthropologist John Swanton), the Creeks faced the joint political crises of allotment and Oklahoma statehood; the former threatened their land base and the latter their political independence. To assert a Creek power rooted in warfare and migration to the distant Atlantic Ocean (and to tell this to an anthropologist working for the U.S. government) offered a symbolic challenge to a nation that seemed intent on destroying them. Nearly a century later, the stories I heard during a brief visit to Oklahoma came from people who were proud of their history but who were also insistent that their history of emerging clans and migrating towns could not be entirely understood from documents in the archives or books in the library. By way of example from my own experience, when I asked Keeper Johnson about the Creeks' origins, he confidently explained his own theory, what he called a "Keeperism," that included Creek descent from the Aztecs who had fled Hernán Cortez's conquest of Mexico. His story was unique, but his attitude was not.[54]

In these stories spanning nearly three centuries lies an intellectual history of Creeks charting their future in recollections of their past. The assistance or at least the understanding of outsiders can help, but Creeks always derive their power from their traditions. As the Creek literary scholar Craig Womack contends, by presenting their own history through stories that can only be understood through Creek symbols and cosmology, Creeks "are setting themselves apart as a nation of people with distinct worldviews that deserve to be taken seriously. This is an important exercise of sovereignty."[55] In other words, the *talwa* is not just a fundamental unit of Creek identity and history, a unit important to the mound-builders as much as the mound-born; it is also the basic unit of interaction with and resistance to the last half millennium of European colonization. The Creeks rarely succeeded entirely on their terms, but when they tell stories about towns born from Mississippian mounds, they affirm centuries of exchange—of things and ideas—that created and supported their towns. This is perhaps the Mississippian period's greatest legacy, and the Creeks were among those Indians with the good fortune to keep the memory and themselves alive.

But their fortune has not always seemed so good. When the federal government forced Creeks to sell the Ocmulgee Fields in 1828, land-hungry Georgians made every effort to erase signs of the former inhabitants, who had long revered the nearby mounds. Reporting on the sale of the lands, the newspaper of the new town of Macon proclaimed, "We may expect shortly to see the springing up in these romantic retreats, handsome country seats, gardens, orchards, etc. etc. The shadows of superstition which overhung these scenes on the first settlement of the country, concealing beneath their dark mantle the spectral forms of another age, are in a manner dispersed. The goblins and spectres that were supposed to haunt the place some years back are all fled. Of late, we do not hear of unearthly phantoms, nor of unearthly voices."[56] In asserting the rights of the new occupants, it was not enough for the reporter to banish ancestral ghosts that Creeks had seen there for decades.[57] Unless any doubt remained about the Creeks' title to Georgia's lands, the reporter went on to assert that their historic roots had never been very deep to begin with. No race of "modern Indians" could have constructed earthworks reaching nearly fifty feet in height because "they exhibit in general too much labor."[58] In a short article celebrating the growth of the new town, the article affirmed the silence Adair had pondered over a half century earlier, effacing the memory of the Creeks and the work of their ancestors.

But Macon's ghosts apparently did not abandon the region. One hundred fifty kilometers northwest, Lynne and Mark Wisner bought a house near Grovetown on the banks of Euchee Creek some time in 1985, happy for the bucolic setting and even for the twenty-foot-high Indian mound located behind their house. Shortly after moving into their home, however, they were disturbed to learn that the unexcavated mound was haunted. Strange lights, drumbeats, and phantom figures dancing in the woods frequently disturbed the Wisners' sleep. "Imagine getting up in the middle of the night, looking out in the back yard and seeing this strange light going up and down just outside your window," explained Lynne Wisner. Her husband, daughter, and son-in-law had all seen similar things, and her horse, Dancer, refused to let anyone approach the mound. By 1998 they had gained local renown for the ghosts, but the Wisners had no desire to remove the mound or to leave their home.[59] Whether one believes them or not, ghost stories have an inescapable pull because they describe the past unexpectedly manifesting itself in the present. In a sense, they are like the spirit that Mauss described: they represent the remains of a past event, a relationship, that continues to live with (and perhaps haunt) giver and receiver long after an object has been exchanged. It should perhaps not surprise that Creek ghosts still haunt the lands that Indians ceded to European conquerors. It should also not surprise if those ghosts predate the nineteenth-century land cessions. They dance among towns whose roots reach back a half millennium.

Late Mississippian towns were the centers of the Mississippian world, places of sowing and harvest, tribute and bestowal, war and peace, life and death. Around each, a cosmos turned. They were the products of centuries of Mississippian development, but they were more than just smaller, distant offspring of Cahokia. They were the fractious products of the Little Ice Age and the collapse of regional centers like Moundville, Etowah, and Rood's Landing. They inhabited a more competitive world than their predecessors, one whose exchange networks provided more chiefs with more symbols of power, whose chiefs faced persistent challenges from elite rivals as well as assertive followers. When European colonizers disrupted these societies, they destroyed much of the complex ceremonies and hierarchies as well as the mounds where they were celebrated. Nonetheless, the foundations of that Late Mississippian world remained. However altered, towns survived as guarantors of cosmic balance and communal harmony. So too did the relationships, the spirit of giving, that bound them to others and ensured their survival.

Chapter 2

Floods and Feathers: From the Mississippian to the Floridian

On the fourth day the relatives and friends of the snake-man gathered at the Tcook-u'thlocco [the "Big House" or council house], as had been requested, and many others came near but remained on the outside. Presently the snake-man made his appearance, coming from the stream in which he had taken refuge, and he was followed by a stream of water. When he entered the grounds occupied by the public buildings they all sank along with the people gathered there, and this was the origin of the Coosa River. . . . The residue of the Cosa people, having thus formed a town, bitterly lamented on account of the calamity that had thus robbed them of so many of their valuable citizens. In grievous distress they cried out, "Woe is our nation!"

—Caley Proctor, ca. 1910[1]

Through the construction and maintenance of their mounds, plazas, and homes, Mississippian townspeople created monuments to their communities and their communities' relationship to the cosmos. Through the exchange of sacred objects and knowledge, they built networks that supported these towns. After 1492, they met peoples from the land called Spain who also recognized that power could come from exchange. The difference lay in the newcomers' preference for extraction over reciprocity. They hoped to incorporate Mississippian wealth and labor for the use of the distant centers across the Atlantic Ocean. As Mississippian peoples quickly realized, Spanish visions of exploitation threatened the continued existence of towns as centers of their own worlds. Although armed entrepreneurs achieved legendary success in Mesoamerica and the Andes, the peoples of the Southeast did not succumb to these so-called conquistadors so famously. Only after a half century of failed conquests did Spaniards learn to blend royal support, personal ambition, missionary zeal, and generous gifts to secure a North American beachhead at St. Augustine in 1565. As Spaniards abandoned their military conquest in favor of offering gifts, peoples who bitterly resisted them in the early sixteenth century were seeking them out in the early seventeenth. Spanish influence in the region after 1565 depended on colonists' ability to develop cooperative relations with their Native neighbors.[2]

Spaniards had to adapt, but the invasions of the sixteenth century marked the beginning of a new era in southeastern history, an era that saw the end of a Mississippian world and the beginnings of a colonial one. For some the results were catastrophic. The descendants of the once great chiefdom of Coosa recalled these years of transition as a great flood that swallowed most of their town. For others, like the residents of Zamumo's town of Altamaha, Spanish gifts provided opportunistic leaders with a new route to independence from unwanted superiors like Ocute. Throughout changes great and small, the peoples of the Southeast sought to preserve the towns that defined their worlds, and much of that stability continued to depend on exchange with outsiders. Spaniards took advantage of this fact with calculated generosity.

By the first decades of the seventeenth century, St. Augustine was the center of a new network of exchange that linked town squares throughout the region to the Atlantic outpost. Although Spanish administrative control around 1610 did not extend beyond a chain of missions near the coast, the transformative impact of Spanish Florida was regional.[3] Native networks of exchange carried Spanish gifts far inland; by the early 1600s, the peoples of the interior were gaining access to European materials. When Mississippian leaders accepted a gift such as a white feather or glass beads from St. Augustine, they probably hoped that they could incorporate these new objects into old norms regarding peace and power. Even when they succeeded in this conservative effort, Indians participated in radical change. By using European power to rebuild and maintain southeastern towns, they were connecting their lives and fortunes directly or indirectly to the people of St. Augustine. They were helping make a Mississippian region into a Floridian one.

Conquistador Invasions

This process began haltingly. Spaniards initially sought to force Indians into networks rooted in the dominance of a single center rather than the autonomy of many. They followed a well-established pattern. Ambitious men of middling means, including tailors, merchants, and lower nobility, staked their fortunes and lives on dreams of conquest, wealth, and higher social status. Although these dreams were usually tinted gold and silver, aspiring conquistadors all hoped to secure access to Native tributaries and some product of their labors. Because successful conquistadors always outnumbered the *encomiendas*, or grants of Indian tributaries, that their leaders distributed, those who lacked rank and connections were forced to seek new peoples to subdue. Consequently, Indians throughout the Americas quickly became acquainted with men seeking personal fortune in the name of a distant monarch.[4] These ad hoc designs, however grand, met universal failure in the lands called La Florida. When disease and inadequate supplies did not dash Spanish plans, Mississippian warriors did.

Shortly after Columbus's arrival in the Caribbean, Florida Natives became acquainted with a dangerous and unpredictable mix of slave raiders and shipwrecked sailors. By the time Juan Ponce de León explored the peninsula's coast in 1513, the peoples of the Atlantic and Gulf coasts were thoroughly convinced of the strangers' unfriendly intentions. Ponce's efforts to establish a colony in southwestern Florida ended in 1521 with his death from an arrow wound.[5] The aborted settlement marked an inauspicious start to four decades of unsuccessful Spanish *entradas*, or explorations, into the immense territory Ponce named La Florida. Lucas Vásquez de Ayllón brought 600 colonists to the coast of South Carolina in the summer of 1526, but disease ended his and most others' lives within months. Only 150 returned to Cuba before the end of the year. In 1528, Pánfilo de Narváez and all but 4 of his 400 soldiers died from arrows, disease, shipwreck, or enslavement, and fellow Spaniards learned of their horrible fate only when Alvar Núñez Cabeza de Vaca and three companions crossed paths with a Spanish detachment in northwestern Mexico eight years later. Hernando de Soto, flushed with the riches obtained during the conquest of the Inka, led 600 hopefuls in a fruitless search for a new empire in the southeastern interior between 1539 and 1543. When the roughly 300 survivors arrived in Veracruz, de Soto was not among them.

Of these early invasions, de Soto's probably had the greatest impact on southeastern history. At the head of 600 men, a handful of women, and thousands of horses and pigs necessary to transport and feed them, de Soto commanded a force larger than most chiefdom towns. What was significant, though, was not the *entrada*'s size—Narváez and Ayllón had pursued projects of a similar scale—but the extent of its contact with interior peoples. After landing near Tampa Bay, the expedition headed northeast in search of a kingdom reputedly rich with pearls. The army traveled through central Georgia and the chiefdom of Ocute before crossing the abandoned Savannah River Valley that separated it from its rival Cofitachequi. There the Spaniards were greeted by a "lady" carried forth on a litter who offered them lodging, visits to some of her temples, and freshwater pearls.[6] Many of de Soto's followers urged him to establish his new colony among the mounds of piedmont South Carolina. Fertile lands, abundant pearls, and supposedly easy access to Spanish shipping on the Atlantic seemed a perfect combination for future *encomiendas*. The former lieutenant of Francisco Pizarro, apparently intent on "another treasure like that of Atabalipa, the lord of Peru," disagreed, and he directed his followers west in search of the chiefdom and ruler known as Coosa. Crossing the Appalachians and entering the Tennessee River Valley, the expedition met Coosa's tributaries. When the Spaniards finally reached the paramount's central town, they took him hostage to guarantee their safe passage and their access to people as porters. As with Cofitachequi, Coosa's renown failed to translate into riches worthy of de Soto's avarice, and when the expedition reached the limits of Coosa's dominions, they released the chief, who returned, crying and humiliated, to his now distant home.[7]

Neither Cofitachequi nor Coosa resisted these brazen intruders, but as word of the Spaniards spread, so too did plans for retaliation. De Soto's next host, Chief Tascaluza, initially bided his time, offering his hospitality and accompanying the Spaniards as hostage through most of his chiefdom in central Alabama while he called on tributaries and even rivals like Coosa in a desperate bid to halt the Spanish advance. At the town of Mabila, Tascaluza sprang a massive trap. After welcoming de Soto and a small number of his party into the pallisaded town for festivities, the chief gave his order. Warriors poured from the houses, killing five almost immediately. De Soto narrowly escaped the town to rally his forces. With cavalry charges and coordinated assaults with firebrands, Spaniards breached the walls and set the town ablaze. An estimated 2,500 warriors died. Superior armor and discipline kept Spanish losses much lower, but with approximately 20 killed and 150 wounded, not to mention the loss of supplies and the freshwater pearls that constituted their meager plunder, the victors had little to celebrate.[8] And so the first year of the expedition ended. Three more remained. After wintering outside Mabila, the force headed west in the spring of 1541, crossing the Mississippi and spending much of the next year and a half living among and fighting with chiefdoms in present-day Arkansas. With de Soto's death in 1542, the survivors attempted to head overland to Mexico. When the land became inhospitable, they returned to the Mississippi River, which they followed to its mouth before 300 or so survivors sailed makeshift vessels back to Mexico in the summer of 1543.[9]

The contractual conquests that had secured Spanish control of the Greater Antilles, Mesoamerica, and the Peruvian highlands failed in the Southeast. Mississippians required new tactics, and the Spanish court's growing interest in securing the peninsula, which controlled the shipping (and silver) that flowed from the Caribbean across the Atlantic, meant that after 1550 Spain's Council of the Indies took the unusual measure of financially backing the new ventures. But unusual tactics yielded familiar results. Supply problems and poor relations with Coosa forced Tristán de Luna y Arellano to abandon his colony near modern Pensacola two years after its establishment in 1559. Frustrations abounded, but when King Felipe II learned that French Huguenots under the command of René de Laudonnière were settling Florida's Atlantic coast, he personally sponsored yet one more attempt. Under the naval commander Pedro Menéndez de Avilés, Spaniards established the fortified outpost of St. Augustine and exterminated the French colony in 1565. St. Augustine became Spain's first permanent foothold in North America in part because the region's inhabitants had forced Spaniards to adjust the principles and means of empire building. The crown helped finance a new colony and, for the first time, sent professional soldiers instead of entrepreneurial conquistadors. These would not be the first adjustments that European empires would make to the interests of southeastern towns.[10]

Of course, the residents who imparted these difficult lessons were making their own uncomfortable adjustments. The conquistadors' violence, hunger, diseases, and cultural practices destabilized many chiefdoms. De Soto frequently resorted to force when hosts did not immediately accommodate his demands, and his infrequent military engagements such as at Mabila exacted a catastrophic toll on local populations. Many communities also lost significant numbers of able-bodied men and women when Spaniards seized them as porters and sexual slaves. Feeding the visitors also took its toll. Spaniards emptied granaries and even cooked up what dogs they could find. It is little wonder that Ocute, where de Soto's chroniclers recalled a friendly reception, displayed outright hostility to missionaries entering the province fifty-seven years later. Spaniards like de Soto were dangerous and unwelcome visitors even when they were (to their minds at least) friendly.[11]

For Mississippians, such discomforts and insults initiated a series of profound social changes that convinced many to forsake their mounds and some to abandon their homes. Unfortunately, the roots of these changes continue to baffle scholars. New epidemic diseases from Europe and Africa probably had the greatest impact on the region in the two centuries after Ponce, but what exactly happened? Despite five major Spanish ventures and countless smaller raids and shipwrecks, there are no documented instances of epidemics in the interior before 1696, when a smallpox epidemic ravaged southeastern towns from the Atlantic to the Mississippi River.[12] Though the documents say nothing, archaeologists have noticed that settlements diminished in number and size after contact, but the absence of concrete evidence probably means that the horrors of the conquistadors' violence and rapine may have inflicted more damage than their diseases. Regardless of what caused some communities to struggle after 1540, the region avoided the pandemics that some have previously assumed.[13] Even when southeastern communities were spared devastating encounters with death, life also presented a host of new challenges after 1550. The dozen or so towns of Apalachees who farmed the hill country around modern Tallahassee had driven out Narváez and de Soto thanks in part to well-coordinated leadership, but political crises seem to have diminished the power of chiefs so much that by the end of the sixteenth century they had abandoned the mounds at the hearts of their communities. The people of Ocute in central Georgia also abandoned their mounds at about the same time. Altamaha, a tributary chiefdom of Ocute at the time of de Soto, moved its town away from its central mound and, by 1610, severed its tributary ties to Ocute. The peoples of the upper Coosa Valley—including the once mighty Coosa chiefdom—consolidated their shrinking populations in a series of downstream migrations. Descendants of the paramount center were now joining their former tributaries, but they came as refugees. Such movements and the shrinking populations that accompanied them also disrupted the exchange networks that had buttressed chiefly authority. As tributary populations declined and new exotic goods from Europeans became more widely available, burial goods no longer readily distinguished leaders from followers. Many southeastern peoples began to build council houses instead of maintaining chiefly mounds. In slow steps that are difficult to trace in detail, the hierarchical structures of the chiefdoms were giving way to new societies less likely to ascribe great distinction solely on the basis of birth.[14]

What this meant for the peoples of the region is nearly impossible to determine, but one tantalizing hint comes from the collective memory of the Coosas. In the 1920s, the anthropologist John Swanton published several accounts of the great town's disappearance beneath the waters of the Coosa River. In the longest version, a pair of Coosa men out hunting came across a pool of rainwater in the hollow of a tree, and in the water were fish. These were no ordinary fish. Because they were creatures of the water living on land, they transgressed a fundamental boundary of the Coosa universe. The first hunter recognized this fact, but his companion cooked and ate them. Almost immediately, the second hunter began to change into a water snake, itself one of the most dangerous creatures in Creek mythology because of its amphibian ambiguity. The first hunter then left his transformed friend in the nearby river and returned to Coosa with the sad news. Returning to the river, he signaled to his snake-friend by firing off his gun, and the two arranged a reunion with the grieving kin. When these relatives gathered in the council house and square ground to meet the snake, his visit caused the council house, the square grounds, and all of the other public buildings to sink beneath the waters of the Coosa River. Only those outside the square grounds remained to lament, "Woe is our nation! We were the greatest of all the nations; our *tus-e-ki-yås* (great warriors) were numerous, reaching out and known and dreaded the world over. . . . But it is not so now. . . . Shame and humiliation are our portion." Another version of the story recalled that some of the engulfed townspeople survived beneath the river, where "people could hear a drum beaten there when they were dancing and having their times." All of the versions agreed that the humbled and humiliated Coosa survivors decided to continue on with their town, renaming themselves Tulsa, because "*ulsee* signif[ied] in the Muscogee language 'to be ashamed.'"[15]

It is possible to read such stories as allegories for the Creeks' own humbled state in the early twentieth century, when the creation of Oklahoma in 1907 deprived them of the last vestiges of their political independence and the discovery of oil on their lands in 1913 provided their European American neighbors with new excuses to defraud them of great wealth, but the roots of this story go much deeper. After Coosa's decline sometime in the late sixteenth century, the town never returned to greatness; the trader James Adair recalled it in 1775 as "an old beloved town, now reduced to a small and ruinous village." Whatever layers of tragedy later generations placed on Coosa's demise, they lay them on top of a collapse that followed the conquistadors.[16]

But the story recalled more than tragedy; it centered that tragedy and the act of survival on the town. The people that comprised the town and the civic architecture that organized it all vanished together. That no mound existed to share this fate likely suggests some of the ways that the story had been adapted to resemble the world that tellers and listeners knew (much as the first hunter called to his snake-friend with a gun). Mounds had disappeared, but the people of the old Coosa chiefdom still spoke to their descendants, if perhaps in the muffled tones of those who are submerged. These memories of powerful warriors and great populations still had life in part because those who remained above the water did not abandon each other. Whether they in fact became Tulsas or carried on as Coosas, survivors proved the resilience of the institution of the town by establishing a new one.

Lessons in Southeastern Politics

But to say the chiefdoms were losing their luster after 1550 is not to say that their residents were losing their sense of their past or confidence in their present. However great the changes that Indians faced, Spaniards remained interlopers in a region where the world was still best understood, honored, and regulated in the town square or atop the temple mound. All of these towns needed to regulate their relations with the powerful forces that surrounded them, and all of them recognized the importance of the exchange of gifts for regulating those relations. Spaniards would have done well to take lessons from the French Huguenots they had so ruthlessly dispatched in 1565. When Laudonnière arrived off of the coast of Florida in 1564 near the "River of Dolphins" (the harbor entrance to the future St. Augustine), he paid particular attention to Native forms of generosity, which at times exceeded French notions of propriety. "Though they endeavored by every means to make us trade with them and explained by signs that they wanted to give us some presents, nevertheless for various good reasons I decided not to stay." Unwilling to accept (and potentially become beholden to) such largesse, Laudonnière continued north to the mouth of the St. Johns River, where the chief Satouriona welcomed the French commander with a deerskin painted with designs so beautiful "that no professional artist could find fault with them." The engraver Theodor de Bry depicted both of these friendly encounters, perhaps with an eye to assuring prospective colonists of the friendly receptions that awaited them. Laudonnière appreciated them with a more practical eye. For him, accepting and reciprocating this Native American brand of Southern hospitality was critical "to keep[ing] [the] friendship alive."[17]

As de Soto had shown with Zamumo, Spaniards were capable participants in such political ceremonies, but Menéndez de Avilés preferred to put more stock in his military experience and the support of Europe's most powerful monarch. He would learn soon enough that the colony would flourish or flounder less on the dreams of two great men and more on the very real and varied interests of the new colony's numerous neighbors. With a combination of violence and apathy, Native southeasterners taught Spaniards some painful lessons in Mississippian politics. Menéndez de Avilés had many tutors. In lands stretching from the Atlantic to the Gulf coasts lived perhaps fifty thousand Timucuas whose chiefs exercised significant influence over the people of their towns and who in turn acknowledged the power of one of several leaders. These paramount chiefs struggled with one another for preeminence in the lands between the Gulf and Atlantic coasts. Among these politically diverse and linguistically related peoples were the Mocamas of the coast just north of St. Augustine. Just to the north of the Mocamas lived the Guales. Unlike the more politically cohesive Timucuas, the Guale towns of the Georgia coast accorded a wavering allegiance to the paramount leaders of two or three towns and spoke a Muskogean language distinct from the Timucuas but related to the peoples of inland Georgia and Alabama. Northwest from Guale, the peoples of central Georgia's Oconee Valley, including Zamumo's town of Altamaha, inhabited dis-

Figure 3. Theodor de Bry, "The Promontory of Florida, at Which the French Touched; Named by them the French Promontory." From *La Floride Française: Scènes de la vie Indiennes, peintes en 1564* (facsimile of the 1564 original [Paris, 1928]). When de Bry showed Indians meeting Laudonnière's landing party in 1564 near the future St. Augustine (alias "F. Delfinium," or the River of Dolphins), he conveyed some sense of Europeans' and Natives' mutual interest in exchange even as he masked the disparate political interests that inspired both groups. Courtesy of the Library of Congress Rare Book and Special Collections Division. F314.L33.

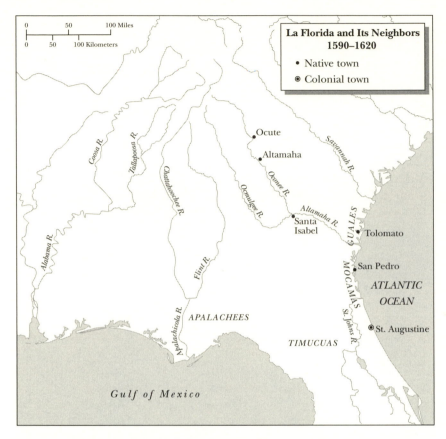

Map 2. La Florida and its neighbors, 1590–1620. St. Augustine's relationships with Natives were not extensive, but Floridanos did have contact with the Oconee Valley by 1600 and with Apalachees by 1620.

persed towns that acknowledged the primacy of Ocute. The peoples of the Deep South—even those immediately adjacent to the fledgling colony—resisted a simple template.[18]

Spaniards nonetheless sought to impose one. In the five years following the establishment of St. Augustine, Spanish soldiers, missionaries, and colonists experienced breathtakingly rapid success and failure. After founding a string of posts along the Atlantic and Gulf coasts and inland into South Carolina, Menéndez de Avilés watched helplessly as a series of Indian uprisings destroyed nearly everything. By 1570, Spaniards in St. Augustine and Santa Elena inhabited European islands in a sea of Indians who were at best mildly friendly and at worst openly hostile. Another revolt against the newly established Jesuit mission on the

Chesapeake in 1571 convinced the religious order to abandon La Florida, and many colonists followed suit after Guales and their coastal allies drove their Spanish neighbors out of Santa Elena in 1576. The Spanish colonial template had been simple, but the consequences, for Menéndez de Avilés, were simply devastating.[19]

In 1573 the increasingly frustrated governor requested permission to conduct a war that would crush the rebellious Natives and provide needed revenues from the sale of enslaved captives to Caribbean islands. The king refused, fearing that such retribution would only escalate the cycle of violence.[20] The historian Henry Kamen believes that Felipe II's distress at the violence in La Florida may have inspired his Orders for New Discoveries. Issued in 1573, the regulations required colonists throughout the Americas to incorporate "unpacified" peoples into the empire through kindness rather than conquest.[21] Menéndez de Avilés had two new resources to help him implement the new policy. Franciscans arrived in the colony in 1573 to resume the Jesuits' proselytizing mission. Equally important, beginning in 1571, a new royal subsidy, or *situado*, ensured that the colonists did not have to live on Franciscan zeal alone. These developments did not erase the human and natural obstacles to extracting wealth from the colony, though, and Pedro Menéndez de Avilés had few reasons to expect a prosperous legacy when he died in Spain in 1574.

In fact, it seemed that Spanish successes were best measured not by what Spaniards acquired but by what they gave away. De Soto was not the only Spaniard who recognized the power of gifts such as beads, feathers, metal tools, and cloth. As one missionary to La Florida explained in 1549, Indians' "friendship and affection was obviously based on what they could get from us. This world is the route to the other," he consoled himself, ". . . gifts can break rocks."[22] Not surprisingly, then, the colony's brightest developments during its first violent decade frequently followed presentations of gifts to visiting leaders. Gifts convinced a number of Mocamas in the immediate environs of St. Augustine to accept missionaries in the early 1580s, and Spanish military support against the Mocamas' inland enemies sealed these alliances by the middle of the decade. Southeastern Indians had compelled Spaniards to abandon the pike and harquebus for quieter means of conquest.[23]

Opportunity for more significant successes came in 1593, when the king provided La Florida's governor with funds to purchase gifts for visiting friendly caciques. By offering the "clothes and tools and flour" that King Felipe II stipulated, the governor would demonstrate not only his kindness but also his power. The disbursement of three years of belated *situado* payments in 1594 provided officials with the resources to meet these regulations. By 1597, they were offering hatchets and hoes; cloth of wool, linen, and a little silk; shirts, stockings, hats, glass beads, and even a pair of shoes. The Native dignitaries who received these small quantities of goods recognized them as unusual new equivalents for the copper ornaments, finely dressed skins, and shell beads that confirmed their high status and spiritual power. The new goods even began joining more familiar ones in the burials of their dead possessors.[24]

If the gifts possessed an air of familiarity that encouraged Indian leaders to accept them, they also offered possible security against the diseases that were ravaging St. Augustine's neighbors. The archaeologist Rebecca Saunders has found that by the end of the 1500s, inhabitants of one town near the Georgia coast began to decorate their pottery with an increasing number of ceremonial motifs in a much "sloppier" manner than their predecessors. Less experienced potters, apparently deprived of the benefits of their stricken elders, sought to confront these invisible scourges and sustain their societies as best as their crafts-womanship would allow.[25] While Guale potters reconceptualized their craft, chiefs had good reason to pursue remedies of a different sort. Chiefs in Guale and elsewhere sought Spanish goods with an interest that grew with Spanish generosity. They did so for reasons we can only imagine four centuries later, but two considerations likely figured prominently. Not only did Spaniards' beads, metal tools, and cloth exhibit an unusual crafting of familiar objects, but the Franciscans who frequently accompanied these gifts exhibited a remarkable power of their own. Most obviously, they walked unarmed among unfamiliar peoples and enjoyed the respect of governors and military men. They did not succumb as readily to disease as their Indian neighbors. Perhaps more relevant for peoples actually suffering disease, these spiritual men had already encountered these maladies in Europe and confidently promoted a variety of ceremonies of repentance that might end these outbreaks that they believed to be God's castigations.[26]

Spanish organization of the missions frequently confirmed Native leaders' expectation that they were adding a new and powerful people into old networks of power. Franciscans, like their new charges, preferred to organize their churches around large, settled populations. They reinforced pre-contact settlement hierarchies by establishing their missions (known as *doctrinas*) in the principal towns, making occasional visits to the outlying villages, which became *visitas*. As respectful followers were expected to do, converts had to plant a communal field, or *sabana*, for the friar's support and also gave him game from the hunt. Governors made explicit their claims to superior status by confirming the successors of deceased caciques of *doctrinas*, but they also made sure not to contravene Natives' choices. Chastened by years of failure, Spanish officials had abandoned the impositions of empire in favor of the flexibility of chiefly influence. Not surprisingly, friction remained. Indian converts did not necessarily submit fully to Roman Catholic doctrine and governors' efforts to collect tribute from townspeople directly challenged chiefly prerogatives of receiving and distributing their towns' harvests. Mission revolts during the next century exposed the limits of Indian acquiescence.[27]

But precisely because gifts could not purchase the obedience Spaniards craved, they also likely helped secure these gifts' widespread prominence. Hundreds of miles from the missions, few people had met Spaniards, but they knew of their goods and they probably heard rumors of the spiritual power that accompanied their makers. Much like the people of Coosa before them, the people of St. Augustine enjoyed regional prominence thanks to the reciprocal rather than extractive relations they had to build with their neighbors. This influence, however unintentional from the Spanish perspective, provided inland peoples with new resources to maintain their towns in a new world.

Gifts and the Reorganization of the Oconee Valley

It is not easy to determine how southeastern Indians effected these changes. The best evidence comes from the missions, but Indians there confronted other Spanish pressures and so could not always adapt as they saw fit. Nonetheless, enough fragmentary evidence exists regarding the Oconee Valley to show that Spaniards had learned well some of the norms of Mississippian gift-giving. More important, it hints at the ways that at least part of old Mississippian exchange networks were becoming part of a Floridian one. The rise of Spanish influence (or at least Spanish goods) in the Oconee Valley followed a decade of Spanish successes in St. Augustine's immediate environs. Spanish spiritual power and material generosity spurred a string of evangelical successes after 1587, including conversions among the Timucuan Mocamas and Potanos north and west of St. Augustine and even among the Guales after 1595. Hoping to build on these successes, in 1597 Governor Gonzalo Méndez de Canzo sent additional expeditions north, west, and south, beyond the limits of the mission towns. The ambitious Méndez hoped that these evangelical forays could transform the region's political and religious landscape. Although the expedition west into the peninsula would be the only one to lead to later conversions, Spaniards had a significant if subtle influence on the peoples of central Georgia. Thanks to the arrival of Spanish goods after 1597, the Indians of the Oconee Valley began to reorganize their polities. They did so within older patterns of chiefdom rivalry, but we should not overestimate the significance of such continuities. Disease may have followed these goods inland, and although chiefs and followers may have enjoyed relatively good health, the political fortunes of their societies were increasingly linked to the possession of Spanish objects.

Two Franciscans, Fr. Pedro de Chozas and Francisco de Veráscola, led the evangelical expedition north to the Oconee Valley early in the summer of 1597. Accompanying them were Gaspar de Salas, a soldier and interpreter who spoke Guale, and an escort of thirty Indians led by Don Juan, the *mico* of Guale's principal town of Tolomato. Chozas loaded them, as the Franciscan Alonso Gregorio de Escobedo put it in his epic poem, *La Florida,* "with Castillian blankets, with knives, fish hooks, and scissors, and with very fine glass beads, with sickles and cutting axes." The party set out from the Guale mission of Tolomato, expecting that the people of Altamaha and Ocute "would know the power of our people and the little which they enjoyed in their western lands." Chozas supplemented these material demonstrations with suitably dramatic preaching, and the formidable Veráscola further exhibited the power of the Spaniards and their god by successfully wrestling "chest to chest" many challengers in the towns they visited. Escobedo was writing an epic of Franciscan achievement, and we should expect some exaggeration, but even his heroic narrative described the material, physical, and cosmological power that resided in St. Augustine and east across the ocean in terms that chiefs and their followers would appreciate.[28]

One day after reaching the valley and its immense fields of ripening corn, beans, grapes, and watermelons, the travelers arrived in the town of Altamaha, where Chozas met the members of the leading family in the council house and presented to each a blanket. Impressed with the offer, the leaders permitted him to speak to the town. The following day, Chozas had "the king" place a cross in the center of the plaza, and then he and Veráscola called the community to meet inside the council house, where, after observing a grave and prolonged silence, Chozas proceeded to instruct the people about the Christian faith. A sudden rain shower convinced his listeners of his cosmological connections, and the town accepted baptism en masse and reciprocated with gifts to the Spaniards. In both acts, Altamahas expressed their own desire to build a deeper relationship.[29] Continuing inland one more day to Ocute, the visitors were again "well received." They noted with surprise and hope that the women of Ocute wore shawls similar to those of New Spain. All seemed well, but as soon as they indicated a desire to continue further on their journey, perhaps to determine the proximity of New Spain itself, the chief Ocute "obstructed them with much pleading and crying," explaining that many of those further inland still recalled de Soto's visit and hoped to kill some of those related to the ruthless invader. More troubling, the valley residents' ardor was cooling, and the missionaries failed to convert anyone in Ocute. The situation became downright perilous when, on their return through Altamaha, the formerly friendly chief sent a warrior to scalp Chozas. The Franciscan evidently possessed great power, and the chief had decided that the hair on his head—rather than the ideas in it—might improve the chief's chances of winning an imminent competition against a neighboring leader. Only a timely shot from Salas's harquebus saved the missionary. Chozas apparently could not imagine this disappointing reversal was in earnest: the next day, he still insisted on asking for porters to carry his goods. The chief's emphatic refusal made enough of an impression to send his visitors scurrying home.[30]

For the Spanish, the expedition accomplished little. Chozas, Veráscola, and Salas returned from the province they called La Tama with glorious accounts of conversions and tantalizing rumors of silver mines, but nothing ever came of either of these chimeras. Altamahas and Ocutes, and especially their leaders, had much more to appreciate from the visit. They had acquired items from the powerful new people of the coast, and perhaps the Spaniards' ally and subordinate, Juan of Tolomato, might return by way of the newly blazed trail with more such items.[31] For his part, Ocute could proudly reflect that he had maintained effective control over his subordinates and his guests. Altamaha's sudden interest in Chozas's scalp probably had something to do with Ocute's refusal to accept conversion, so the shift probably reassured the paramount leader in Ocute that the chief of Altamaha remained loyal to him. The Spaniards had heeded his injunction against venturing further inland, and they had left respectful of but not angered by Ocute's and Altamaha's displays of independence. From Ocute, prospects looked good.

Despite these positive developments, Oconee peoples' hopes of deriving new benefits from St. Augustine, whether via the hands of Franciscans, Guales, or others, took an unexpected turn shortly after Chozas's hasty departure. Late in September 1597, Guales revolted, destroying the missions, killing five Franciscans, and capturing a sixth. Despite Spaniards' two years of successes with gifts, old coercive habits died hard. Franciscans had already stacked ample tinder by attacking important Guale traditions and restricting converts' movements among the province's towns. Disputes about marriage and authority provided the incendiary spark. When Juan refused to observe monogamy as required by Christian practice, Franciscans sought to oust him in favor of his more tractable uncle Francisco. The outraged *mico* "went into the interior among the pagans, without saying anything or without obtaining permission as they were wont to do on other occasions."[32] After "a few days," Juan returned to Tolomato with some of these inland supporters (probably Guales who had fled the missions) and rallied Francisco and other followers against the missionaries.[33]

Although not directly involved in the revolt, Altamahas were never far from the minds of those who were. In the spring of 1598, Governor Méndez met with Guale leaders to ransom the captive Franciscan, offering axes, hoes, and blankets for the return of the priest. When the Guale leaders demurred, insisting on the return of some of their own sons who had been living in St. Augustine for several years, the governor became enraged and threatened to send for three hundred soldiers, "and put them to the sword, and cut down all their maize and food, and follow them as far as La Tama."[34] Guales promptly returned the missionary. Spaniards and Guales both recognized that the Oconee Valley's residents, however distant, played a pivotal role; they could be the refuge to which Guales might flee or the anvil against which Spaniards could crush them. Although they were not the only peoples that Spaniards courted, Oconee peoples' potentially pivotal role encouraged Spaniards to remain in indirect contact with them. This contact, coupled with gifts, enabled Altamahas to challenge Ocute's primacy in the valley. Indeed, Spanish gifts in the hands of Indian emissaries altered the valley far more thoroughly than de Soto or Chozas did with swords or crosses.

Altamaha's opportunity and Ocute's problems appear only fleetingly, but they were tied inextricably to Floridanos' experiments with gifts as diplomatic tools. These experiments began with Méndez's decision to pacify Guale with a new round of gift giving. The governor contented himself with this imperfect strategy because he had little choice. Despite his earlier threats of scorched-earth campaign, he acknowledged to the king that because the rebels had retreated so far inland, "there was no way that one could punish them there unless it were by the hand and order of the same Indians." Méndez's generosity, though, did enjoy some success. Raids from Spaniards and their Indian allies convinced many Guales to make peace by early 1600, and newly conciliatory Guale leaders offered to bring some of their followers to St. Augustine to work in the agricultural fields that supported the presidio and private citizens. Despite the advantages of the new labor draft—also called the *repartimiento*—for securing food supplies for St. Augustine, the new friendship had its shortcomings. Guale's nominally pacified towns continued to defy Spanish authority by welcoming French traders, and they would continue to do so for another three years. Before 1602, no Spaniard was foolish enough to think that Guales were ready to welcome new missionaries.[35] The Oconee Valley loomed increasingly large as one remedy to this persistent instability in Guale. These initial successes confirmed the value of generosity, but Floridanos were also learning that the meaning of gifts depended in part on the power of those who gave them away. If offerings were to appear as gifts rather than tribute, the colonists had to show themselves to be a formidable chiefdom in their own right. The expansion and organization of the missions served as one indicator of Spanish strength, and in 1598 one royal official believed that the governor favorably impressed "inland Indians" when he raised tribute payments among those Indians still loyal to St. Augustine.[36] And yet, two months later, as the governor sent sixteen soldiers to help defend the Mocama mission of San Pedro, the same official noted that the governor needed to send rations with these soldiers instead of expecting the Mocamas to feed them because "the inland Indians are watching to see how we aid our friends."[37] By exacting appropriate tribute from subordinate polities and providing necessary support for these same dependents, Spaniards could demonstrate their power—and the power of their goods—to observant Oconee peoples.

Although Méndez probably did not decide to provision the San Pedro garrison, he was doing his best to convince inland peoples like the Altamahas that his friendship could be of great service to them. Not surprisingly, he also had need of their friendship. As he had already acknowledged to the king, Indians would be crucial to suppressing the last of the insurgents, and Altamaha assistance would prevent the insurgents from fleeing further inland. The Spaniards knew that gifts would make this alliance possible, but to distribute these gifts Governor Méndez enlisted the help of two Christian chiefs from Mocama, Cacica María of the mission town of Nombre de Dios and Cacique Juan of San Pedro. Each cacique received gifts valued at 350 ducats—roughly equivalent to three years' pay for a common soldier—to take "into the interior land to the caciques with whom they have contact." Offering such gifts to their friends, the Christian leaders could also explain that all who joined the Spaniards could expect similar generosity from His Most Catholic Majesty.[38] Such generosity might encourage recalcitrant Guales to reciprocate with allegiance rather than continued hostility. If not, then perhaps by attracting inland peoples the governor could expand the mission system and simultaneously pressure Guales from the south and the interior.[39]

It is difficult to say with certainty what impact Governor Méndez's initiative had because he could not document it any more than he could control it. No longer orchestrating the ceremonies of "rendering obedience" in the course of presenting their gifts, Spaniards were supplying Native leaders with valuable items that they then introduced to the southeastern political economy on their terms. Cacique Juan clearly molded Spanish interests to fit his own. Two years earlier, in 1598, Governor Méndez had noted approvingly that "he spends himself into poverty giving gifts to other caciques to bring them to our obedience."[40] While Spaniards doubtless approved of such generosity in the service of their temporal and divine monarchs, Juan also had more personal interests in mind. Sometime before receiving the governor's gifts in 1600, he asked Méndez to appoint him head cacique of Guale. Perhaps the Mocama leader hoped that his growing influence among Spaniards and Indians would enable him to capitalize on the apostasy of Guale's most recent head cacique. Not surprisingly, the governor balked at the request. Juan apparently did not respond to the rejection before he died later that year, perhaps from disease.[41] Cacica María also harbored ambitions of her own: within six years of Juan's death, this cacica of Nombre de Dios included the deceased Juan's town of San Pedro in her "chiefdom" and appointed her son there as its cacique.[42] Juan's and María's fates varied, but what is significant is that Spaniards were placing gifts in the hands of Native intermediaries who were free to introduce them into older networks of exchange and influence.

Altamahas—especially their chief Altamaha—used this influx of gifts to challenge Ocute's prominence. Although there is no documentation of these gift exchanges, evidence of their consequences appears in the shifting political fortunes of Altamaha in the Oconee Valley. In 1540, when Zamumo met de Soto, Altamahas owed some allegiance to Ocute's chief. When Chozas fled the Oconee Valley in 1597, it was probably the result of Ocute's influence over the actions of its downriver tributary. Despite this long-standing relationship, Altamahas had evidently severed ties with Ocute by 1601, when they joined Guales and a number of other peoples in a final decisive attack on the remaining Guale recalcitrants. In 1602, a year after the final defeat of the Guales, another Spanish visitor noted Altamaha's independence and perhaps rising prominence when he referred to it as "the capital of the province." Such success, though, came at the expense of hostility with Ocute: when the visitor expressed interest in continuing northward toward Ocute, his hosts urged him to reconsider "so that they might not kill him."[43] With a warning that echoed the one Ocute issued to Chozas and his companions, Altamahas proclaimed a new line of independence and even hostility in the Oconee Valley. As had happened many times in previous centuries, an upstart chiefdom was moving out from the shadow of its superior. The difference was that Floridian rather than Mississippian goods had helped make this possible.

When they cautioned their Spanish visitor against traveling inland to Ocute, Altamahas made clear how much they recognized the significance of this change for their own political stability, and stability remained a precious commodity for the chiefdoms. The struggles among elites masked more fundamental shifts among the general population of the Oconee Valley. The fact that Spaniards placed these goods in the hands of leaders probably encouraged southeastern elites to draw upon these new resources in a time of political flux, but the results did not always favor chiefs' authority. One suggestive clue appears in 1604, when Governor Pedro de Ibarra met Altamahas in Guale and gave only passing mention to the "cacique of La Tama." Rather than the head of the famed inland province, he appeared in a list as one of many other dignitaries. Perhaps Spanish contact with Altamaha had become routine, or perhaps the visiting cacique was not the chief of Altamaha but one of his subordinates. Regardless, the lack of emphasis suggests that this leader was not as powerful as his Spanish title suggested. Archaeologists have uncovered additional clues regarding this power shift. For more than a century before Cacique Juan or any other emissaries ventured with gifts from St. Augustine, the Altamahas, Ocutes, and their neighbors were abandoning their towns, dispersing their homes throughout the valley. By 1580, valley residents no longer used their mounds. In other words, Altamaha leaders probably sought Spanish goods not just to escape Ocute's influence but also to maintain their own influence over an increasingly segmented population.[44]

In some respects, Altamaha's leaders were simply using new goods to confront old challenges of political instability. In other respects, these adaptations introduced far more radical consequences. Following the turn of the century, at a time when many interior populations were consolidating dwindling communities at the fall-line frontiers between piedmonts and coastal plains, Oconee peoples were also relocating. While many peoples moved in order to build new communities at locations that afforded the greatest opportunities for subsistence, some residents of the Oconee Valley were actually moving downstream of the fall line to the coastal plain. Although they now inhabited lands less ecologically diverse than their former homes, they had much easier access to the respected clothing, beads, and tools from St. Augustine. Like other inland peoples, they once again began settling in more nucleated towns rather than dispersed farmsteads, and this shift may have been a product of their leaders' rising authority.[45] Chiefs may have sought additional Spanish support for their precarious prominence by requesting Franciscans at the short-lived mission of Santa Isabel on the Altamaha River, which lasted from 1616 to about 1635. If diseases were following gifts inland, these new mission residents may have also been seeking relief from this new challenge as well. Depopulation from epidemics could have just as easily caused a dwindling population to seek the mutual protection of towns and the spiritual protection of Franciscans. Whether dealing with the old problems of inter-elite rivalry or newer ones of depopulation and community cohesion, Altamahas were looking to St. Augustine for some solutions.[46]

They did not pursue this strategy alone. In 1612, Governor Fernández de Olivera claimed that unnamed southeastern Natives' widespread interest in missionaries signified both "God's miraculous work" and the influence of the gifts and aid the governor offered to those who came. The most significant sign of this attractive power was that "[some] have arrived here from the very Cape of Apalachee and from much further away." Furthermore, explained the governor, "They assured me that they have been walking for two and a half months and that all along the way they have had safe passage and warm reception knowing that they come here."[47] Seven decades after the Apalachees of the Florida pan-handle had hounded de Soto's forces out of their province, their descendants were joining others to seek Spanish friendship and trade goods. More strikingly, other peoples were journeying eastward perhaps five hundred miles to do so.[48] St. Augustine's inhabitants, who num-bered less than one thousand in 1612, were reshaping relations among thousands and perhaps tens of thousands of Native inhabitants of the Southeast.[49] Gifts and the power that they conferred and confirmed gradually insinuated themselves into the power structures of a variety of peoples beyond the echoes of Spaniards' cannon or the peal of their mission bells.

As in the Oconee Valley, these developments probably owed much to pre-contact patterns of diplomacy and exchange, but not all of the con-sequences would prove so familiar to southeastern townspeople. Gover-nor Fernández's diplomatic triumph of 1612 also marked the eve of tragedy. Between 1613 and 1617, epidemics killed eight thousand mis-sion Indians, half of the newly converted population.[50] Whether these devastating contagions followed these new routes of travel and exchange remains an open question: continuing visits from Native dignitaries and the contemporaneous establishment of the mission of Santa Isabel may have carried the lethal microbes inland or may serve as proof of how little disease disrupted those wider contacts. Regardless, the four-year scourge stood as the most painful evidence that Spaniards were intro-ducing more than new objects for old patterns.[51]

This conjunction of gifts and diseases may help explain the sudden-ness of Spaniards' success in the region. The diseases and violence that accompanied the Spaniards disrupted chiefs' efforts to maintain the populations and cosmic harmony that would build the inspiring mounds and harvest the crucial food surpluses. As chiefs struggled, so too did skilled craftspeople lose the time and the expertise to endow their pottery, shells, deerskins, or copper with the powerful designs that leaders and followers both needed for social stability. In the midst of these crises—some grave, some merely troubling—chiefs recognized the opportunities that accompanied the people of St. Augustine. Some found answers in the new religion of the Spaniards; many saw the advantages of their gifts. Possessing a spiritual power rooted in their foreign origins and the military strength and religious zeal of their purveyors, these objects offered potential solutions for the challenges that beset southeastern elites after 1550. By 1630, Spanish beads were arriving in towns as far west as Alabama and as far north as Tennessee.[52]

Roughly one century after Ponce's *entradas*, Spaniards finally secured a stable colony, one that influenced its neighbors and altered the lives of those who never heard a mission bell. Their success, such as it was, was born of hard lessons. What began with invasions of entrepreneurial conquistadors became next a military venture and then an evangelical one. Each phase certainly involved elements of the others—missionaries accompanied Luna, Menéndez de Avilés sought personal profit, and Franciscans depended on soldiers to prevent or suppress neophyte revolts. Nonetheless, the shifts were crucial to Spanish success, and they occurred because Indians forced Spaniards to rethink their efforts. However disruptive the floods that swallowed some towns, plenty of chiefs and their townspeople had the power to enforce the norms of Mississippian intertown diplomacy. Only after 1587, when royal and religious officials regularly offered gifts to potential Native allies, effectively purchasing a friendship they could not compel, did the missions expand with any predictability. Feathers and lace accomplished much more than fire and steel. Southeastern peoples had reshaped an outpost of empire to resemble a paramount chiefdom. For the Spanish, the expansion of empire required the gifts of empire.

For many Indians, though, the gifts of empire also entailed the acceptance of empire. As the Guales knew in 1597, the missionaries who followed these gifts had more than just religious power. They also had strong ideas about how that religious power should shape Native societies. Franciscan insistence on settled communities reduced Native mobility and their access to food sources that lay outside their maize fields and the immediate environs of their missions. Chiefs might have preserved much of their authority thanks to the support of Spanish officials, but they increasingly exercised their authority in the interests of royal and religious officials, whether it was to collect tribute, enforce church attendance, or organize the labor drafts that took their townspeople to the fields of St. Augustine.[53] Along with the *situado*, the *repartimiento* labor of Indians was the only resource available for Florida elites to exploit for their personal benefit. As the archaeologist Jerald Milanich has noted and mission Indians must have increasingly realized, "Missions *were* colonization."[54] True as this was, this form of colonization was nonetheless conditioned by the demands of gift exchanges that built and maintained it. Floridians were gradually colonizing the Southeast, but they were doing so within some of the constraints of Mississippian norms. This fact would become especially apparent during the middle decades of the seventeenth century.

Profound changes were also underway in the interior: Indians were adjusting to and helping to create a new Spanish ecumene far inland from the colony's coastal foothold. Spaniards were offering items that corresponded well with the indigenous objects of copper, shell, and deerskin that traditionally marked Native leaders' ceremonial and political power. Indians of the Southeast came to recognize these new and rare objects not just as simple analogs of older symbols but also as creations from people who possessed impressive (if not overwhelming) military power and deep religious fervor. Political, economic, and perhaps epidemiological upheavals of the late 1500s and early 1600s led some Native American elites to seek these symbols of stability and strength with additional urgency. By offering gifts instead of presenting arms, Spaniards repeatedly acknowledged the failure of imperial imposition in their quest for regional influence. Accepting these items into their political and religious practices, Indians began building their eventually unbreakable ties to peoples far beyond their Atlantic shores. Subsequent observers from the eighteenth century through the twenty-first would note the transformative consequences of European goods, but most associated them with the English and French commerce that grew after 1690. Though certainly more profound after 1690, these transformations had modest but still portentious roots in the decades immediately preceding and following 1600.[55] From those roots grew a new set of relations that reworked the practices of gift exchange to fit a developing Atlantic world bound by trade and war.

Chapter 3

Seeking the Atlantic: The Growth of Trade

Way back before the Indians had any religion they were playing ball close to the ocean. They saw a ship coming on the water and ran off. The ship had come across the ocean and they discovered the Indians already here. When the Indians were all gone they brought a barrel of whisky with dippers all around it and put it at the ball pole then went back to the ship. When the Indians returned and found the barrel they all were afraid of it but one venturing closer decided to taste it. Then he drank more and the rest started to drink it. They didn't know how it would affect them so they drank too much. Some were wobbling around and others were on the ground when the strangers came back. The ones who could, ran off again but the white people captured one Indian and took him to the ship. They taught him to talk their language and brought him back to talk to the other Indians. Through him they said that they would like to be in their country and take care of them. They made an agreement—they put a cowhide in water to soak so it would be soft and would stretch. Then it was cut into a long strip. All the ground that could be encircled by this strip was to belong to the white people—about a mile square.

Later they told the Indians to go way back and one of the whites would shoot a gun. As far as the Indians could hear the gun—the whites would take the ground. They kept taking more and more ground until the Indians were in Alabama. Then they had to get up and walk clear to this country [that is, Oklahoma] as they didn't have any wagons.

—Mose Wiley, 1937[1]

In the first years of the twentieth century, long after Altamahas weighed the potential advantages of gifts and long after the Spanish missions promoted by those gifts had crumbled, the people called Creeks lived in a land called Oklahoma. Although their homes in Georgia and Alabama and later Oklahoma had never been close to the ocean, the Atlantic still played a prominent role in many stories. In those accounts, Creeks evoked the sounds of its pounding surf and the sight of the mists that rose from its waves, but more than these things, they remembered its power. The ocean had appeared in stories at least a century earlier, but it was in the time of phonographs and motorcars that some of the more subtle versions were written down. The Creek historian James Gregory recalled the Atlantic as a place of sacred power when he described the Cussitas' and Cowetas' migration to the white anthropologist John Swanton at the dawn of the twentieth century; from its waters the pure sun rose each day, and at its horizon upper, middle, and lower worlds met. Three decades later, though, when an interviewer hired by the Works Progress Administration asked Mose Wiley for stories of his past, he recounted how the ocean brought trouble rather than power to his ancestors. The newcomers initially promised friendship, but over the course of years, white demands for land pushed the Indians steadily westward, eventually to Oklahoma. Told amid the poverty of the Great Depression and in the aftermath of Creeks' economic and political dispossession, both of these stories said much about Creek lessons from the past and hopes for the future. Memories of ancient migrations and spiritual power must have reassured Creeks of their great heritage, but so, too, must references to the Atlantic have been laden with grim portents of twentieth-century troubles. Whether Gregory's or Wiley's ancestors from the seventeenth century spoke of the ocean in either set of terms is impossible to say, but they did become acutely aware that new sources of power lay in the hands of people who crossed its eastern horizons and debarked on its western shores.

Of course, leaders like Zamumo had recognized this fact decades earlier. Spaniards and their gifts provided new resources for old Mississippian networks, and by 1612, well-traveled leaders visiting St. Augustine testified to the outpost's regional status. But even as La Florida's capital gained a reputation as a new participant in southeastern networks, its inhabitants also began to change those networks. Beginning around 1620, Spaniards responded to imperial developments and Indian expectations by beginning to trade with Natives.[2] They offered their objects not as gifts in exchange for political allegiance but as trade goods in exchange for corn and deerskins. As exchanges of commodities began to accompany exchanges of gifts, Native peoples in and beyond the missions welcomed these resources for building new ties of friendship or strengthening old ones. Meanwhile, Indians' growing access to European goods allowed commoners to acquire some of the symbols of power once reserved for their leaders. These changes in intertown alliance and intratown politics appeared in striking if still fleeting fashion among the peoples of the Florida panhandle and Chattahoochee Valley. Although the new trade developed during one of the most poorly documented periods of Florida's history, it is clear that it played a vital role in the region's development. After 1620, southeastern Indians began to learn about and modify European norms of trade before it expanded rapidly and violently after 1660.[3] Gregory's and Wiley's stories do not discuss these formative adaptations, but they remind us to attend to the promise and danger of the region's growing Atlantic connections.

Setting the Foundations

As an account of the arrival of Atlantic commerce, Mose Wiley's story underscored one thing very well. Europeans initiated the first overtures for trade. Perhaps surprisingly, though, colonial commerce first arrived in Spanish ships, not those of the later arriving and more successful English, and they came in part because Spain was suffering grave financial and military troubles. By the early seventeenth century, Europe's greatest power could no longer conceal its decline, and in his novels about Don Quijote, Miguel de Cervantes made explicit what others suspected: wars for universal empire fueled by American silver had left the nation exhausted and cynical. But while peninsular Spaniards tilted at windmills in an effort to restore swiftly passing glory, their compatriots in the American colonies were exploring new routes to wealth. The shrinking size and growing unreliability of transatlantic commerce encouraged Spanish American, or Creole, elites to cultivate their American economies. Meanwhile, Floridanos hoped they might gain both riches and reliable supplies by mediating a new trade between the region's Indians and growing ports like Havana. But as much as imperial weakness and Creole activism brought trade to the Southeast, Native peoples still refused to fund Spanish wealth at their expense. In this last respect, Gregory provides an indispensable metaphor for these new encounters. Much as the Cowetas and Cussitas of his story understood the Atlantic in terms of their cosmology, so too did non-mission Indians of the mid-seventeenth century accept trade only if it came on their terms.

The foundations for change were in many respects first laid far across the ocean. Spain's economic decline only accelerated after 1618, when the nation entered a continental bloodletting later called the Thirty Years' War. Because the war proved disastrous for the peninsula's military and economic power, colonists throughout the Americas diversified their local and regional economies. Fueled largely by silver mining in New Spain, Spanish America experienced remarkable economic growth during the mid-seventeenth century. This growth reached La Florida because Havana became an important regional center. Although Havana's economy depended heavily on the Spanish treasure fleets that gathered annually at the port, local entrepreneurs also began exporting cowhides early in the century, and shipbuilding made the port a center for the Caribbean's coastal trade, licit and less so. According to route manuals from the seventeenth century, more than half of the empire's shipping routes led to the Cuban city.[4]

But trade did not arrive in La Florida simply because of New Spain's silver boom or Havana's economic expansion. Floridanos also had to want to become traders. Few people of influence saw much reason for commerce because the colony's biggest source of wealth was the royal subsidy, or *situado*. The annual appropriation provided the colony with nearly all of its necessary supplies, from communion wafers to cannonballs. It was also the colony's only access to silver coin. *Situado* funds fed and clothed the soldiers and Franciscans who justified the colony's existence, and they paid for the gifts to Indians who controlled its viability. As much as the colony depended on these subsidies, governors, treasury officials, and their close allies all sought to amass personal fortunes from the annual shipments. By controlling the sale of supplies to soldiers at a high markup, appropriating money to pay Indians for personal instead of royal service, or simply embezzling funds under the cover of obfuscatory (or nonexistent) bookkeeping, a fortunate few were able to achieve a standard of living commensurate with other parts of the empire. Elite opulence did not depend on mines of silver, plantations of sugar, or even, as Governor Gonzalo Méndez de Canzo dreamed in the 1590s, mountains of diamonds. Instead, as one soldier protested with a slightly ungrammatical pen, "the perfect diamonds is the situado!"[5]

The problem was, as the historian Amy Turner Bushnell observes, that "Spanish sovereignty, Catholic religion, and cacique authority, all three, were built on the *expectation* of royal support." Uncertain expectations, then, would have regional consequences. Unfortunately for Floridanos, the uncertainties increased during the 1620s. Spain's war with the Netherlands, one strand within the tangle of the Thirty Years' War, resumed in 1621, and the powerful Dutch navy threatened the shipping lanes vital to St. Augustine's support. Although the *situado* arrived consistently throughout most of the decade, its payment was never a foregone conclusion. European enemies regularly harassed ships sailing in and out of St. Augustine, and in 1628 the Dutch captured the entire Spanish treasure fleet outside Havana, making off with Spain's—and Florida's—entire American income for that year. In 1639, the crown seized all colonial funds, Florida's included, to pay for its military campaigns in Europe. More often, Spaniards could only blame themselves for Florida's financial troubles. If officials in New Spain regularly delayed its payment, often for years at a time, those sent from St. Augustine to collect the funds often preferred to invest them in personal ventures of varying profitability. According to the colony's royal accountant, La Florida's treasurer in one instance spent part of the *situado* while still in New

Spain "in gaming and other things that to speak with modesty and decency it is best I not refer to."[6]

Such indecencies forced Floridanos to rely increasingly on the food that they could purchase or coerce from their Indian converts. Guales and Timucuas provided corn through *repartimiento* labor in St. Augustine and through surpluses they were required to provide their missionaries. Although these two institutions existed to support the colony as a whole, royal officials regularly pocketed the proceeds of surpluses that they sold to the royal warehouse or directly to their less fortunate neighbors in St. Augustine. Franciscans were not about to be left out of such opportunities, and they usually used the proceeds of their trade to make improvements to the buildings of their *doctrinas*. Sometimes, though, the association between conversion and commerce was too close. In 1628, Fr. Gaspar de Rivota was caught privately selling food to colonists visiting his mission four leagues from the city. As he was carried under guard into the town, the wayward missionary made it clear that he did not act alone. Shouting to onlookers in a manner "disrespectful of the modesty and obligations of his order," the friar suggested that hungry colonists visit Tocoy, where "there was a store where they could buy everything that they needed." This center of illicit trade, beyond the immediate environs of St. Augustine but at the point where the east-bound trail from Timucua crossed the St. Johns River, made a logical clearinghouse for supplies coming from other missions and producers to the west. The royal prohibition that followed this scandal sought to correct an egregious breach of the Franciscans' vow of poverty, but it dealt with only one half of the problem. Franciscan transgressors might be carried off in chains, but the consumers remained. Spanish colonists were literally hungry for Indians' produce.[7]

This hunger led directly to the conversion of Apalachee, a region that had long resonated in the minds of Spaniards and other Europeans. Perhaps thirty thousand Apalachees inhabited a dozen towns in the fertile hill country around modern Tallahassee, Florida, and Spaniards had a deep, if grudging, respect for the inhabitants of this well-organized chiefdom. Apalachee warriors drove off conquistadors from Narváez's and de Soto's *entradas*. Their renown led European cartographers to name North America's easternmost mountain chain after them. By the early 1600s, governors and missionaries intent on mission expansion looked to the Apalachees as a great evangelical prize. More than a rich harvest of souls awaited, however. As the Franciscan Gerónimo de Oré reported with simultaneous emphasis and understatement in 1616, "It is a land most productive in food: maize, beans, and pumpkins. There is nothing else there." By 1625, Spaniards were purchasing Apalachee

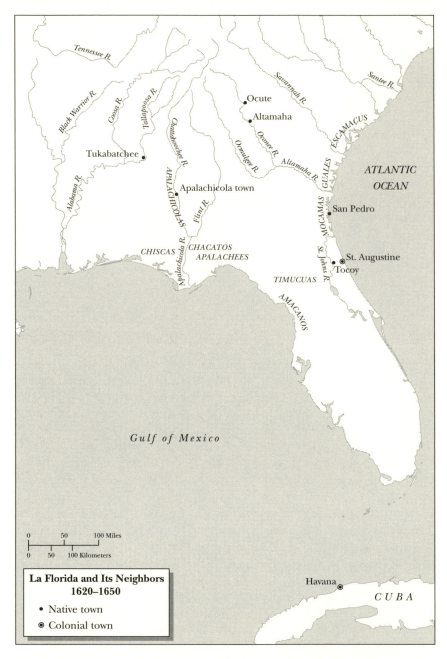

La Florida and Its Neighbors 1620–1650

• Native town

◉ Colonial town

Map 3. La Florida and its neighbors, 1620–50. Despite their limited acquaintance with the Spaniards and their missions, a number of peoples east of the Black Warrior River and south of the Tennessee River had some access to Spanish objects.

corn. By 1633, Franciscans had sufficient manpower to send two missionaries to the first *doctrina* in this long-sought breadbasket.[8]

Spaniards hungered for the harvests of Apalachee, Timucuan, and Guale fields, but these Indians set the terms for acquiring it. The simple fact remained that Indians in and beyond the missions remained in control of the region. Although missionaries introduced a host of new coercive forms into Guale and Timucuan life during the early seventeenth century, including restrictions on their movements, a greater regimentation of diet, and more frequent corporal punishment, such impositions weighed relatively lightly on most of their charges. During the rapid expansion of the missions after 1609, Franciscans were spread thinly. In 1630, for example, twenty-seven missionaries served perhaps fifty thousand Timucuas and Guales. Although each missionary resided in a convent in a town of several hundred, he also attended to an average of five other localities, to which he had to travel on foot.[9] As long as the Indian populations remained high, Franciscans and other Spaniards were an important but still relatively minor presence in the lives of most neophytes. Certainly, non-mission peoples like the Altamahas remained even further removed from Spanish influence. More important for Floridano decision making, though, was the fact that Spaniards would be foolish to antagonize peoples who could threaten the colony's dispersed and poorly defended missions. Consequently, colonists needed to build upon the norms of cooperation and exchange that colonists and Indians had devised in the colony's first decades.

No record notes the ways that Indians shaped this shift from gifts to trade, but a comparison of La Florida with other frontier mission colonies reveals the extent of Indians' influence on colonists' choices. Instead of trading with Indians, Floridanos could have followed the examples of contemporaries who also struggled to extract wealth from their marginal mission colonies. Far to the west, New Mexico's leading colonists ignored royal prohibitions against Indian enslavement and exploited the slave exchange networks between the Rio Grande and Mississippi Rivers, and when opportunity allowed, they conducted their own raids for slaves. Newly acquired prisoners augmented the wealth of the colony's elite either as servants in their homes or as commodities to be sold to the silver mines of northern New Spain. Meanwhile, the Franciscans' Jesuit brethren in Paraguay turned their new missions into plantations for the production of yerba mate, a mild stimulant that was sold to the booming silver metropolis of Potosí in the Andes. Jesuits could demand much labor from their charges in part because they provided badly needed protection from Portuguese slave raiders.[10] La Florida's peoples, especially those outside of the missions, made these New Mexican and Paraguayan options impractical. They had already demonstrated that the colony gained more from gifts than it might from slave raiding, and, at least for the time being, non-mission neighbors did not threaten Guales and Timucuas with massive enslavement. Thus, although Floridanos could imagine a number of ways to take advantage of the changing imperial economy and Havana's rise as an entrepôt, they began trading as they did—without war or massive plantation-missions—because such actions did not antagonize the peoples who remained in control of the region.

Floridanos' trade with Indians grew in importance after 1620, but the changes were subtle. While gifts remained the fundamental marker of Spanish relations with southeastern Indians for the rest of the century, by the 1620s, Spanish and mission Indian elites both sought to augment their material return from their investments in labor and leadership. Not surprisingly, much as chiefs were the principal Indian beneficiaries of Spanish gifts, they also gained the most from the new trade in corn. They received the goods that paid for the work of their townspeople who had been drafted for the *repartimiento*, and they served as agents for selling their town's surpluses to enterprising Spaniards. Despite this apparent continuity from earlier Spanish favoritism of elites, some notable shifts also appeared in the lives and attitudes of their Native followers. Some followers also enjoyed the benefits of exchanges with the Spanish. The populations of the more agriculturally productive Guale missions took to their graves a wide array of Spanish religious and decorative items.[11] The growing trade may also explain why Spanish largesse did not inspire the same kind of Indian reverence that it had a decade or two earlier. In 1627, the colony's treasurer and accountant complained that Governor Luis Rojas y Borja's spending on gifts was double the crown's annual allocation of fifteen hundred ducats. Since arriving in late 1624, the governor had distributed clothes, iron tools, and other items not just to visiting "caciques" but "generally to all of the principals and to the majority of the rest who come from inland." Worse, they complained, "today the Indians come for this clothing as if for tribute, which is what they call it."[12]

In their choice of words and attitude, Rojas y Borja's visitors hardly exhibited the deference appropriate to tributaries accepting tokens—or even diplomats accepting gifts—from a powerful host. It may be that they were articulating some of the enduring complexities of Mississippian politics. Many years before, the chief Casqui spoke to de Soto with a similar audacity when he berated his supposed superior for failing to produce the anticipated rain promptly. Perhaps, like Casqui, Native leaders and followers arrived in St. Augustine knowing that their offers of allegiance *required* Spanish largesse. Indeed, without such gifts, there was no exchange of goods or ideas, and thus no relationship. But perhaps the sense of entitlement that so rankled the royal officials grew out of new patterns rather than Mississippian ones. Indians understood any exchange of things within the context of larger relations of power. Much as they had during the Guale revolt, non-mission Indians had paid close attention to the chiefly deportment of St. Augustine's leaders, their expectations for tribute, and the extent of their generosity. As Spaniards, and especially governors, sought to profit from the colony's diplomatic relations, offering goods to followers as well as leaders, they may have evinced an inattentiveness to the rank of those with whom they traded, behavior most unbecoming a chief. By demanding tribute, Indians may have simply expressed a growing disdain for a people who no longer deserved respect.

And even as Spaniards sought to introduce trade into the delicate protocols of gift giving, they faced new competitive pressures to give more away. In 1633, six years after the royal officials complained about Governor Rojas y Borja, an Escamaçu, a Native from north of Guale near today's Port Royal, South Carolina, visited a nearby Guale mission to report that the English had established a colony in his province and "were giving away gifts of tools and other things." Furthermore, he claimed, "They gave away more [than the Spaniards]." The Escamaçu was grossly mistaken about English settlement activities, but he probably made no mistake about the English objects. The English colony of Jamestown, Virginia, had joined St. Augustine as a new source of rare objects, and peoples like the Escamaçus who were in a position to take advantage of both saw an opportunity. The value of Spain's outpost to Indians depended not only on its access to goods but on the quantities it could offer to its neighbors. If a single object symbolized a giver's power, then more probably enhanced it. In 1633, Spaniards were confronting the early stages of protracted imperial competition, and although the new commercial turn would prove decisive to the fortunes of empire, Mississippian forms of generosity remained critical to any exchange relationship.[13]

Despite the difficulties of interpretation, the incidents that inspired the royal officials' complaint and the Escamaçu's report reveal two fundamental tensions in the Spanish project, and they in turn foretell much about the colony's impact on the region after 1630. First, whatever the reasons for their expectation of "tribute" from the Spaniards, it is clear that the peoples outside the missions remained fiercely, perhaps arrogantly, independent. Far from being debilitated by contact, at least some chiefs continued to enjoy respect in their hometowns. Spaniards enjoyed some influence with them and with other inland peoples, but the gifts that made that influence possible had not compromised (and may have in fact augmented) the power of some recipients. Second,

Spaniards were starting to see these exchanges in more competitive terms. Whether they were considering their own efforts to profit from the colony or the ambitions of their imperial rival to the north, colonial leaders were beginning to think about offering more cloth and beads than they had before. Imperial developments and Floridano needs had brought Mose Wiley's shrewd traders to southeastern beaches, but, much as James Gregory's migrants had incorporated an unfathomable ocean into a familiar cosmology, so too did Indians restrain these traders within their norms of reciprocity. How this new trade affected Indians' relationships with these goods and the people who carried them appeared most clearly among Apalachees and their neighbors after 1630.

Commercial Consequences

Although missionaries arrived in Apalachee in 1633, the mercantile potential of the province and its consequences for the region were not realized for another four years. In March 1637, the first supply ship to Apalachee arrived off the coast and caused an immediate sensation. Since establishing their missions, Franciscans in Apalachee had suffered from an erratic flow of supplies. The overland route across the peninsula from St. Augustine often took weeks and depended on the backs of Timucua or Apalachee cargo bearers, who often discarded or damaged their excessive burdens. The arrival of so many goods so quickly by water reassured the province's old and new residents that royal officials were committed to keeping the province well-supplied with ecclesiastical necessities and gifts for the Apalachee elite. Within days of the ship's dropping anchor, thirty Apalachees converted. One "cacique," Anefore, joined the ship on its return to Havana, where he was baptized with Cuba's Governor Francisco de Riano y Gamboa as his godfather.[14]

Anefore and his companions must have marveled at Havana during their four-month stay. The city's population, which reached five thousand in 1620 and doubled that figure by 1650, dwarfed the one thousand or so inhabitants of St. Augustine and the fifteen hundred in the largest Apalachee towns. More than solemn ceremonies and impressive sights sealed the new link between Apalachee and Cuba. Travel between Havana and the Apalachee coast took only eight days—instead of the two months common to maritime travel from the new missions to St. Augustine. Within two years of the 1637 shipment, Cubans' ties to Apalachee were so important and so common that La Florida's Governor Damián de Vega Castro y Pardo identified the province according to its distance from the bustling port.[15]

The Apalachee trade flourished, but not with St. Augustine. By 1643,

Governor Vega was complaining that St. Augustine's new breadbasket supplied little to the famine-ridden presidio because Havana merchants were illegally shipping the produce south to Cuba. Meanwhile, in St. Augustine, a combination of irregular supplies and poor local harvests forced soldiers to forage for roots in the nearby salt marshes. In an effort to prevent Apalachee's corn from going to Havana, Governor Vega ordered soldiers overland to intercept one ship in the hopes that they could redirect its cargo to the starving garrison. The mission, which may have been successful, suggests not only the depth of the colony's troubles, but perhaps also the extent to which Havana directly challenged St. Augustine's paramountcy. Much as the Escamaçu probably appreciated English generosity and power in comparison to that of the Spanish, Anefore probably drew influence from his ties to Havana's prosperity rather than St. Augustine's privation. But there was another difference in addition to relative prosperity. Where St. Augustine's representatives secured their diplomatic and evangelical endeavors through gifts, merchants from Havana traveled to Apalachee in search of a profit. Cubans' success and Floridanos' suffering suggest just how much trade was becoming a part of Spanish relations with Apalachees. And if exchange was about relations of power, then Havana was a powerful new player in southeastern towns' development.[16]

The new trade yielded two larger changes for Apalachees and their neighbors. First, Spaniards expanded the networks of exchange and peace that bound various Native groups to each other and to St. Augustine. In 1638, a year after the first ship's arrival in Apalachee, Governor Vega sent soldiers to mediate the end of Apalachees' conflicts with the Amacanos of the Gulf Coast and two other powerful neighbors to the northwest, the Chacatos and the Apalachicolas. By using enemy captives among the Apalachees as mediators, Spanish soldiers opened the path to peace. Gifts carried inland from the Gulf helped keep that path open. The peace that the soldiers secured was, in the governor's eyes, "something extraordinary because said Chacatos have never been at peace with anyone." Another feared people, the nomadic Chiscas (whose ancestors met de Soto's forces in the Appalachian Mountains almost a century before), also joined the widening circle of peace after settling near missions in eastern Apalachee and Timucua.[17]

Second, and closely related to these economic and diplomatic successes, Spaniards expanded their exchange networks north from Apalachee. This new trade, what the Florida historian Amy Turner Bushnell believes "had the most far-reaching results" of any of Spain's mid-century colonial activities in La Florida, grew directly out of Spaniards' and Indians' efforts to craft a new relationship that balanced reciprocity and profit. Following the peace of 1638, Spaniards and Apalachees began to trade regularly with the peoples of the interior, especially the Apalachicolas, who had access to plentiful deer in the uplands and were easily accessible up the Chattahoochee River from Apalachee. Governors were delighted to promote a trade in deerskins that had a reliable, if not expansive, market in Havana, and direct trade with Havana began almost immediately after the first supply ship arrived in Apalachee in 1637. Soldiers, Franciscans, and Apalachees all joined the commerce with Apalachicola. A small number of colonists who arrived in Apalachee and western Timucua to start cattle ranches also became involved. By 1688 Governor Pedro de Aranda y Avellaneda reported that "many people regularly went to the province [of Apalachicola] to trade, with the natives there being so easy to reach that they came and went to their [the colonists'] businesses and ranches." Spanish demand for deerskins would never match later French and British markets, but the trade's impact on Apalachee and Apalachicola was undeniable. Apalachicolas and their neighbors were clearly becoming part of the world of the Atlantic.[18]

They integrated these ties to lands beyond the horizon by domesticating them. Much as Casqui had hoped to strengthen his ties with de Soto when he offered his daughter to the conquistador, Apalachicola leaders arranged marriages between prominent local women and the traders. The marriages were especially important because trade between people who were not kin always had the potential to devolve into the unregulated, and potentially violent, exchanges common to strangers. For some these ties possessed great symbolic power. In 1716, nearly seventy years after the beginning of peace and trade between Apalachee and Apalachicola, Seepeycoffee, the son of the powerful *mico* of Coweta, claimed to one Spanish official that by virtue of his wife and mother both being Christian Apalachees, "he did not consider himself an Infidel."[19] In a sense, Seepeycoffee believed (or thought it believable) that his kin connections made him a member of the nation of "Christians" to which Apalachees and Spaniards belonged. Such ties also influenced Spanish thinking about Indian exchange. Even at the beginning of the eighteenth century, Juan de Ayala y Escobar, one of St. Augustine's most prominent traders, frequently met with Indians visiting the city "and regaled them and gave them whatever he had." An expert in the colony's illicit trade, Ayala had the connections and rank to take advantage of the colony's proximity to Cuba. Much as the French and English would later do, Ayala used Indian forms of generosity to parlay Cuban goods into loyal and profitable Indian friendships. His success testified to Spaniards' and Indians' ability to blend commerce and diplomacy.[20]

However welcoming to Indians, this new trade also altered their relations with other towns and with their fellow townspeople. The trade from Apalachee did not stop along the banks of the Chattahoochee River. Apalachicolas' new ties to the south also improved their ties to the west. Many of the glass beads, bells, brass pendants, and other items of personal adornment arriving in Apalachicola eventually reached at least the Tallapoosa River. Along its banks, the buried remains of Tuka-batchee homes remain littered with these items three centuries later. Meanwhile, townspeople experienced their own political shifts. *Micos* probably still regulated relations with outsiders, but, after 1638, hunters like those from Tukabatchee could acquire the deerskins that Spaniards (or their intermediaries) sought to purchase. As this still limited but growing access to exotic goods widened, individuals eagerly pursued these symbols of the foreign. Long-standing symbols of knowledge and prestige were increasingly available to commoners. The archaeologist Vernon James Knight Jr. believes this new "economics of ostentation" spurred wider segments of the population to pursue the Spanish goods that had formerly supported the political ambitions of leaders like Juan of San Pedro, the *mico* of Altamaha, and the ambassadors who visited St. Augustine in October 1612. Although Spanish objects provided chiefs with the purported tools for building and maintaining influence in a colonial world, chiefs had reason to rue the growing availability of the European items they had once controlled. Southeastern Indians' contin-uing autonomy meant that Spaniards developed their new trade in ways that conformed to Native expectations. The consequences, however, defied even the most powerful *micos*.[21]

Two Revolts and the Widening Ripples of Contact

The regional consequences of the new trade are shadowy but sharpest in the events surrounding the Apalachee Revolt of 1647 and the Timucuan Revolt of 1655. Like a spider web visible only when struck by light at a certain angle, the strands of exchange tying the region together glinted briefly in the flash of the revolts. Some of those strands were the prod-ucts of gift exchanges; others owed their existence to a developing trade. Both types reveal the nature of Spanish influence in the region. More specifically, they suggest how peoples of the Chattahoochee and Oconee Valleys used Spanish goods to build intertown alliances even as they also refused close contact with the Spaniards who provided them.

Seeds of both revolts were planted with the arrival of the first trading vessel from Havana in 1637. As much as trade with Havana provided well-connected colonists and chiefs with new opportunities for wealth, only gifts could secure Native leaders' allegiance to St. Augustine. Unfor-tunately for colonists and their Native allies, unreliable *situados* and poor harvests in the late 1630s and 1640s constrained Spanish generosity.

Even as Spaniards' hardships reduced chiefs' access to gifts, their followers in the missions still had to fulfill their labor and grain obligations to the colonists and friars. As populations declined from disease, the burdens increased for those who remained. Growing burdens and declining compensation encouraged many to flee. As Governor Vega explained to the king in 1643, "They have very weak spirits [*tienen flacos los ánimos*], and seeing little aid, they go to the wilds with the pagans." Discontent appeared piecemeal but with increasing frequency. Unrest in Guale required military intervention in 1642. By 1645, flight from the Guale and Timucua missions was so common that towns were becoming depopulated; many Guales took advantage of old ties with Altamahas and fled to the Oconee Valley. Spaniards may have lost contact with the inland chiefdom, but, thanks to relations likely cemented with Spanish goods, Guales had not.[22]

Spaniards had problems in Guale and Timucua, but the crisis exploded in Apalachee. Writing with the benefit of hindsight, royal officials blamed the revolt on Spaniards' failure to give "as frequently (as before) what your Majesty had given them every year." Chiscas near the missions stoked the fires of rebellion by encouraging the disgruntled and threatening the uncertain with death. On February 19, 1647, Chiscas and unconverted Apalachees, who still constituted the vast majority of the population, set upon the Spanish during the celebrations for the patron saint of one of the missions. Five friars and a handful of soldiers escaped thanks to help from Christian Apalachees or because they were living close to Timucua, but three missionaries, the newly appointed lieutenant governor, his wife, and their children were all killed. After a hastily dispatched force of thirty soldiers and five hundred Timucua warriors fought to a standstill thousands of Apalachees during a daylong battle, Spaniards learned that the Apalachees, dismayed by their losses and the rapidity of the Spanish response, were again seeking peace and renewed conversions. A short and violent tour of the province ended the revolt by May, with hangings of the leaders and the institution of a labor draft as part of a general pardon. Unpacified Chiscas abandoned the missions for the relative security of a new town near the Apalachicola River.[23]

The revolt reveals much about the nature of Spanish contacts with interior towns. The unrest and its outcome were products of the influence Spanish goods had—and did not have—on the peoples north of the missions. Most obviously, the insurgents anticipated the support of other unnamed "infidels"—perhaps Apalachicolas and Chacatos northwest of Apalachee. Evidently, Apalachees and Chiscas believed that interior peoples shared their problems and would accept their violent remedy. They entertained these hopes because Spanish goods had opened and maintained peaceful lines of communication with peoples north and west of the missions. Unfortunately for the insurgents, these hopes were misplaced. Two factors relating to trade and alliance probably convinced inland peoples to remain in their towns. First, the friendship that linked the mission province to the Chacatos and Apalachicolas was barely nine years old, and lingering mistrust may have dissuaded inland peoples from joining the uprising. Second, Chacatos and Apalachicolas had different ties with the Spanish than their mission neighbors. The "infieles" of the interior suffered none of the impositions of the Spanish mission system. Furthermore, the interior peoples, linked to Spaniards more by trade than gifts and more closely to Havana than St. Augustine, shared few of the Apalachees' diplomatic ties and none of their troubles. And so they withheld their support, biding their time and providing Spaniards and Timucuas the opportunity to crush the revolt with stunning efficiency.[24]

The unrest of the late 1640s occurred within a network of relations that extended hundreds of miles north and west of St. Augustine, but it changed that network, too. Following suppression of their revolt, Apalachees were forced to contribute to the colony's labor drafts, and St. Augustine's governor reversed years of stinginess. Renewed gift giving revived or perhaps initiated St. Augustine's ties to the peoples north of Apalachee. During the years 1648–51, the Indian fund averaged four thousand pesos a year, a level of generosity that had not been seen since the spendthrift Governor Rojas y Borja two decades earlier. Apalachicolas were probably among the "caciques and principal leaders coming from many leagues inland to request missionaries" in 1650, and they met Governor Benito Ruíz de Salazar y Vallecilla during his official visit inland sometime around the same year. The revolt reminded Spaniards that however successful they were as traders, gifts remained vital to their influence in the missions and the lands beyond.[25]

The new arrangements did not eliminate old tensions. Spaniards had opened new opportunities for wealth through trade, but these opportunities weighed increasingly heavily on the backs of mission Indians who carried the gifts, trade goods, and supplies that linked the colony to the peoples outside the missions. Between 1649 and 1655, epidemics devastated the large populations that had once distributed Spanish demands broadly and lightly. Yellow fever arrived in 1649, killing Governor Ruíz and his interim replacement before it subsided in 1652. Smallpox struck St. Augustine in the winter of 1654–55, and by March "the great contagion" had reached Apalachee, where "a large number of Indians [had] died and [were] dying." While mission populations declined by a quarter or more, Spaniards provided an unwelcome measure of continuity: soldiers still came to the missions each spring to take laborers back to

St. Augustine, and if anything, Guale leaders complained, "they take by force more people than ever."[26] As if to confirm Spaniards' intent to abandon their obligations as conscientious paramounts, La Florida's new governor, Diego de Rebolledo, set out to undermine the gifts and reciprocity upon which the colony had been built. From his arrival in 1654, Governor Rebolledo refused to provide Timucuan leaders with gifts because Timucuan towns possessed nothing that could fetch a good price in Havana's markets. To those with deerskins or other vendible commodities, Rebolledo offered all the gifts the *situado* could subsidize. When these ran out, the acquisitive governor sold nearly anything else he could find, even to the point of casting new iron trading hoes from St. Augustine's cannons.[27]

But Rebolledo needed the loyalty that he was unwilling to promote. In 1655, Jamaica fell to the English, and captured English correspondence convinced Spaniards that La Florida was the invaders' next target. When he ordered caciques and head warriors from the missions to come to St. Augustine's defense, the governor unwisely stipulated that these leading men carry their own corn to the poorly provisioned outpost. For the chiefs of Timucua, the message was clear. By refusing to offer these men gifts and then commanding them to serve as cargo bearers, the governor had essentially demoted these principal men to the status of commoners. Could they be sure his sinister ambitions would stop there? Perhaps he had ordered them to St. Augustine so that he might turn *them* into commodities; perhaps he might, as some leaders later confessed, ship them to "the King so that they might be his slaves." Many in Apalachee expressed similar anxiety but only the Timucuas acted on their fears and frustrations, killing seven Spaniards in the province. Only after the summer passed without sign of English sail did Spaniards turn inland to stifle the revolt. Apalachees and Guales assisted the soldiers, and Spanish promises to pardon the leaders quickly became death sentences once the men surrendered. As further evidence of Rebolledo's commercial ambitions, the victorious governor relocated a number of Timucua missions so that they could better serve the road that linked St. Augustine with the corn, deerskins, and people of Apalachee.[28]

Revolts in Apalachee and Timucua startled Spanish leaders, but they also enabled them to refashion the missions more to their liking, drawing laborers from Apalachee and reshuffling the missions in Timucua. Both actions consolidated Spanish control in a way that neither gifts nor trade ever could. It also enabled them to expand the trade that was connecting their colony to the peoples north and west of these pacified provinces. But these successes mask another development, one remarkable for its absence, and one that tells as much about interior peoples as it does about the better-documented missions themselves. Quite simply, the trade relations that fostered the Apalachee and the Timucuan revolts also produced the colony's mid-century period of evangelical stagnation. Four decades followed the arrival of missionaries in Apalachee before the Chacatos welcomed the brown-robed Franciscans in 1674. To be sure, Floridanos do not deserve all of the blame for this sudden loss of fervor. Tens of thousands Apalachees required much of the Franciscans' resources, missionaries died faster than they were replaced, and the empire that furnished them was itself suffering tremendous setbacks at the hands of its foes in Europe.

Nonetheless, other factors tell us much about the peoples of the interior. In the half-century after 1590, Spanish gifts encouraged once hostile peoples of the coast and peninsula to accept missionaries and their attendant new demands. After about 1630, Spaniards' growing commerce had a different, if no less broad, regional impact. Because traders in Apalachee offered their cloth and hoes as trade items rather than gifts, they were effectively providing non-elite Apalachicolas and their neighbors with the objects and symbols formerly reserved for their leaders. The shift was not sudden—it may have already been underway when St. Augustine's treasury officials complained of Governor Rojas y Borja's profligacy in 1627—but it was more marked after 1650. As deerskins became the new keys to Spanish products and the power they conferred, Apalachicolas and others did not have to wait for their leaders to accept Spanish conversion to gain access to the materials they prized. As broader segments of the population acquired the material symbols of influence, non-elite Apalachicolas would have had greater resources to resist a relationship that would promote *micos'* authority at their expense. And when Spaniards expanded the labor *repartimiento* after the Apalachee revolt and relocated Indian communities after the Timucuan revolt, leaders and followers found even more reasons to refuse missionaries.[29] A 1683 map, the only surviving seventeenth-century map of La Florida done by a Floridano, offers a striking illustration of the colony's faltering mission project. The simple rendition shows strings of missions, a few "pueblos de infieles" along the Carolina coast, and a southeastern interior that is utterly empty; not even the Apalachicola River extends inland.[30] The lacunae suggest not stasis but important political change. Spaniards' ignorance was a product of southeastern societies' unwillingness to accept the burdens of evangelization.

This documentary silence regarding the interior speaks of larger changes within and beyond the Southeast itself. The order and tranquility that followed the Timucuan Revolt, however welcome to the Spaniards, was in many respects illusory. No peace could last for long in 1655 because La Florida and the lands adjacent were very much a part of a tempestuous Atlantic world, one that neither Wiley nor Gregory

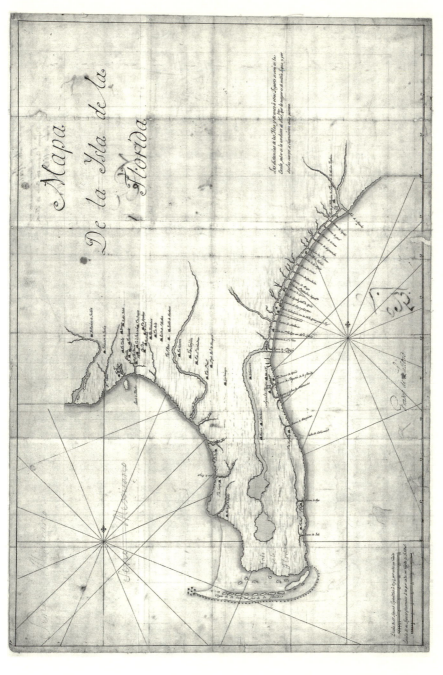

Figure 4. Alonso Solana, "Mapa de la Ysla de la Florida" (1683). This sketch map of the missions and neighboring Indian towns of La Florida illustrates Spaniards' poor understanding of the interior. Note how the source of the Apalachicola River (just west of the Apalachee missions) begins very close to the Gulf of Mexico rather than hundreds of miles inland. Courtesy of the Archivo Cartográfico y de Estudios Geográficos del Centro Geográfico del Ejército, Madrid, Spain.

recalled. On the broadest level, the ocean that had already carried so much to southeastern towns—even those that knew no Franciscans—was increasingly open to Spain's enemies. The Thirty Years' War, which ended in 1648, diminished Spain's capacity to defend its American claims, and the English seizure of Jamaica was only the most brazen challenge to Spanish power. The Spanish American colonists who had expanded their local economies during the previous three decades were in some respects exemplars of a growing European interest in America's commercial potential during the seventeenth century. Spain's European rivals were building their own mercantile empires along the northern reaches of North America and the unprotected islands of the Caribbean. As a strategic outpost on the imperial fringe, La Florida could not avoid these changes. The mid-seventeenth century, the so-called Golden Age of the missions, was at best only gilded.

Quite simply, the colony of La Florida stood upon weakening foundations. The growing trade with the interior revealed this fact as well as anything. In a sense, colonists' interest in trade was a prudent response to Indians' refusal to accept Spanish colonization on the basis of warfare, slavery, or other forms of violent or servile exploitation. By altering the contexts of exchange in their quest for profit, though, Spaniards abandoned the power that these same goods had to promote Christianity and loyalty to the governor in St. Augustine. Gifts still encouraged the allegiance of mission Indians to the Spaniards' god and king, but both the causes and consequences of the revolts in Apalachee and Timucua revealed the declining importance of gifts and the growing importance of force to securing Spanish control over the colony. Epidemics and the depopulation that followed them enabled Franciscans and soldiers to impose their cultural and economic wills on the missions after 1655, but their commands held together a colony that was increasingly brittle as the century drew to a close.

Vulnerable as the colony was, Floridanos had introduced decisive new changes to the region. Into the relatively new networks of gift exchange centered on St. Augustine, they had introduced more commercial transactions. By offering cloth, beads, tools, and other objects as trade goods as well as gifts, Spaniards promoted the influence of the many at the expense of the elite. The wider availability of these items did not erase the distinctiveness or the authority of *micos* in places like the Chattahoochee and Tallapoosa Valleys, but it did place it under growing strain. If exchanges diminished the bonds of influence that tied leaders and followers, they also strengthened some of the bonds that tied towns together. The items that Spaniards offered to their mission charges in payment for corn or labor likely joined those items that Spaniards themselves sent inland in exchange for deerskins. In the process, former belligerents like the Apalachees and Apalachicolas became better acquainted with one another, and friends like the Altamahas and Guales or Apalachicolas and Tukabatchees added new symbols to their old alliances. Given the quantities arriving in Tukabatchee, it also seems likely that more than *micos* conducted these exchanges. Leaders were perhaps maintaining old ties, but commoners were probably forging new ones with each other as well. Changing social relations in the present introduced new reflections on the past. Stories like the one Mose Wiley told about the deceptively incremental demands of these new traders and their compatriots may have begun circulating in southeastern homes and council houses, or perhaps stories that revered the Atlantic like Gregory's were adding European objects to Mississippian iconography. More likely, stories about chiefs and their sacred quests were probably already becoming stories about towns and their sacred migrations.[31] And, thanks to the same Atlantic developments that threatened La Florida and provided these towns with new and powerful bonds, the need for migration was soon to become all too apparent.

Chapter 4

Following the White Path: Migration and the Muskogees' Quest for Security

They then left that place and Travelled further till they found a White path. The Grass and all things they Saw were white that they found people had been there before that they Crossed the path and went to Sleep after which they Consulted and returned to See what path it was and what people had been there being it might be for their good to follow it.

—*Chekilli, 1735*[1]

The sea change for which Spaniards had been bracing themselves in 1655 finally washed over the Southeast four years later. Rather than English freebooters coming from the south, as Governor Rebolledo and others had feared, Indian raiders from the north initiated the new violent era. The immigrants quickly distinguished themselves with their technology and their tactics because, according to Native Americans' early reports to the Spaniards, they "use many firearms and come laying waste to the land."[2] They came for captives, whom they sold to the English of Virginia and, after 1674, the English of the newly settled Charles Town, Carolina. The Spanish called them "Chichimecos," after the nomadic peoples who had harassed the northern frontiers of New Spain in the sixteenth century. Many Muskogean speakers in the Southeast preferred their own evocative term: "Westos," meaning "enemies."[3] In the two decades following 1659, Westos seemed to range everywhere, attacking at will and destroying with impunity. This was the impression, at least, that reached the Europeans who wrote about them. According to a colonist writing in 1670 from the newly established English settlement of Charles Town, Carolina, the Westos "war against all Indians . . . and come upon these Indians here in the time of their crop and destroy all by killing Carrying away their Corn and Children and eat them."[4] About the Westos, Spaniards actually agreed with their new English neighbors and rivals. After his tour of La Florida's missions in 1674, Bishop Gabriel Díaz Vara Calderón described the Westos as "such cruel and barbarous pagans that their sole purpose is to assault the towns of Christians as well as pagans, taking their lives without regard to age, sex, or state, roasting and eating them."[5] The bishop must have appreciated the three companies of soldiers and Indians who escorted him on his visit.[6]

The Westos financed this wave of violence by selling their captives to English traders in exchange for cloth, tools, ornaments, and weapons. In doing so, they served not only their own interests but also as ruthless agents of a newly expansive English commerce in the Southeast. Natives of the Southeast, who had come to know Europeans first as conquistadors and then as paramount gift givers and then as occasional traders, learned after 1659 that this new English desire for human traffic could disrupt or even destroy their world. A river may have swallowed mighty Coosa, but now the storms of the Atlantic slave trade threatened to engulf the entire Southeast. And safe harbor would be hard to find east of the Mississippi Valley. The Westos were simply one piece of a larger cycle of trade and violence that had begun in the 1640s with Iroquois slave raids into the Great Lakes and Ohio Valley regions and expanded south and west across eastern North America, drawing towns into vortices of raiding, counterraiding, captivity, and death.

No metaphor seems adequate for the violence. The historian Richard White has described how Iroquois slave raids "shattered" the peoples of the Ohio Valley, and the anthropologist Robbie Ethridge has employed similar imagery in her reference to the Southeast as a "shatter zone."[7] While it is clear that new forms of exchange ushered in unprecedented upheavals, not all lives disintegrated. In 1675, at least one Altamaha claimed that he enjoyed his life after Westo raids forced him to abandon the Oconee Valley, sometime after 1665. After he and other Altamahas had fled their homes, they lived as nomadic raiders before settling lands near the Apalachee missions. Despite the protection that Apalachee warriors and Spanish soldiers afforded, the Altamaha missed the violent life he had left behind. As he explained to two Apalachees in 1675, and as they later explained to Spanish officials, he claimed that "in those days they had good life."[8] Because no good life could last long outside of a town—a place where people gathered to farm, protect one another, and keep the cosmos in balance—his success forces us to look for ways that even some refugees managed to preserve local coherence. Although this one Altamaha survived the slave trade by spreading its violence, he also reminds us that not even the Westos closed all paths to peace and power.[9]

Exchange provided connections and remained as important as ever to southeastern lives, but after 1659 migration enabled southeastern peoples to adapt to and eventually control this new source of upheaval.[10] As with every previous adjustment to European colonization, these movements drew upon the networks of gifts, trade, and alliance that held individual towns and the region as a whole together. When Chekilli described how Cussitas migrated in search of the makers of the white path, he described an ideal rooted in events that preceded the Westos' invasion. Cussitas' experiences would prefigure later, more desperate migrants who moved in a region revolutionized by the slave trade, and Native peoples responded to the challenges of the slave trade in a variety of ways. By 1665, the Oconee Valley towns that had so impressed Fray Chozas in 1597 were empty, their residents scattered among the Apalachicolas and various Florida missions. Several hundred miles west, the once mighty Coosas sought refuge on an island in the eponymous river. Meanwhile, a third set of migrants, the Koasatis from the Tennessee Valley, headed south to the headwaters of the Alabama River, where they joined a large resident population as well as migrants from the west called Alabamas. The responses of these migrants varied, and as the unnamed Altamaha warrior's story makes clear, they sometimes changed their minds, but all of them drew on old ties of exchange and alliance to preserve their towns. In some instances, as some Indians later explained to the Spaniards, these migrations drew explicitly on the older exchanges of Spanish goods. The violence of the era was unprecedented, and the personal tragedies staggering, but as acquaintances refashioned old ties to became new neighbors, some found opportunity amid catastrophe.

Before the Storm

The motivations and consequences of earlier migrations can tell us much about what influenced those who later fled the Westos. Many historians and archaeologists have skillfully reconstructed the routes of southeastern peoples who vanish from one site and reappear at another, but interpreting these obscure movements involves more than connecting the dots.[11] Most basically, it requires an examination of the connections that existed prior to migration and the ways that migration transformed them. Both of these elements figure prominently in Chekilli's story of Cussita migration. This story also deserves our attention both because of its relatively clear chronology and because Creeks offered and continue to offer a retrospective interpretation of this foundational event.

To summarize Chekilli's version again, during the course of their eastward journey, Cussitas visited the sacred mountain that gave them the medicines to organize their cosmos. This power likely enabled them to secure their martial preeminence over their friends and rivals, the Chickasaws, Alabamas, and Abecas. Discovering a white path, they followed it east until they arrived among the Coosas, whom they saved from the terrible blue bird. From there they continued to the town on the "Colossa River." Lack of food forced them to venture east once again until they arrived among the Apalachicolas, the makers of the white path. There, in a solemn ceremony that centered around the purificatory black drink, the two peoples pledged peace and cooperation with one another, and, Chekilli concluded, "they have lived together And they Shall always live Together and bear it in remembrance."[12]

Chekilli told this story to Georgia's officials in 1735 to emphasize the power of his people and his authority to speak for them. In asserting these points, he also described events that others have traced in the material and documentary records. At the time of de Soto's arrival in central Alabama in 1540, a town called "Casiste" occupied the middle Coosa River and apparently sent tribute to Coosa upstream. Two hundred years later, when Chekilli recalled how Cussitas protected the weaker Coosa, he may have been describing how the once mighty town had come to depend upon its former inferiors, or perhaps he was recalling how the interdependencies of exchange enabled Mississippian tributaries to simultaneously consider themselves protectors. Regardless, twenty years later, when Tristan de Luna passed through the region, he saw that Coosa retained its primacy over the town of "Caxiti." During the intervening century, the documents are silent and the material remains imprecise, but when Chekilli described how Cussitas left the Coosa Valley for the "Colossa River," he may have been referring to a site near the later town of Mucolassa, close to where the Tallapoosa River joins with the Coosa to form the Alabama River. By 1663, Cussitas had moved again and occupied the northernmost town along the Chattahoochee River. On or shortly before that year Spanish soldiers hoping to travel to the Choctaws stopped in Cussita, "the last [town] of said province of Apalachicola."[13]

In addition to key details of Cussita history, Chekilli also mentioned two closely related factors that influenced the Cussitas and probably later migrants as well. First, prior connections mattered. As Chekilli noted, Cussitas shared a powerful link to the Apalachicolas even before they met because Apalachicolas had made the white path that the migrants followed. They even knew the same ceremony of peace. Such common ceremonies and connections would have helped bridge the language barrier that separated the Muskogean-speaking Cussitas from the Hitchiti-speaking Apalachicolas. The memories of these foundational bonds remained significant for Creeks over a century and a half later, when James Gregory described how these strangers who could exchange no words somehow knew "the same secret code known to the other." Although both historians had reason to emphasize timeless Creek unity—one to warn Georgia's new colonists (and his fellow Creeks) of the Cowetas' power and the other to rally Creeks against political dissolution—both did so in terms that recalled a common Mississippian heritage.[14]

Archaeologists also see more specific political connections between the two peoples. During the late fifteenth century, the mound center at Rood's Landing on the Chattahoochee River may have exercised some influence over the towns of the lower Tallapoosa. The tributary relationship apparently declined in the mid-sixteenth century, when the Chattahoochee Valley suffered depopulation, perhaps as a result of epidemics, perhaps as declining chiefly power failed to keep older settlements together, perhaps both. Chattahoochee leaders still retained enough power to continue using and maintaining one of their old temple mounds. This ceremonial power and stability likely included ties between the two river valleys, which in turn facilitated the flow of the Spanish beads that littered the floors of seventeenth-century Tukabatchee homes. It is no coincidence that the paths that carried beads after 1639 were the same ones that carried migrants before 1663.[15]

However much these cultural, political, and material bonds encouraged prospective migrants to seek new homes on the Chattahoochee, these prior connections were only half of the equation. Friends or acquaintances were worth migrating to only if they could also provide access to peace and power. By the middle of the seventeenth century, a significant amount of both came from the Spanish trade goods and gifts that Apalachees were carrying up the Chattahoochee River. If Cussitas and their Muskogean companions moved to the Chattahoochee after 1638, they likely did so in hopes of obtaining better access to the Spanish goods that Apalachees were carrying upriver. In addition, despite depopulation in the river valley, the Apalachicolas remained powerful enough to impress Spaniards in the 1630s and archaeologists in the 1990s.[16] Cussita migrants were likely also among their admirers.

Thus, when they abandoned their homes in the Tallapoosa Valley for new ones near the Apalachicolas in the Chattahoochee Valley, older relations and admirations influenced their momentous decision. And just as those older ties promoted migration, so too did migration alter those ties. Together, Cussitas and their Apalachicola hosts had gained the respect of peoples from the Atlantic coast nearly to the Mississippi. By 1674, rumors had reached Charles Town that the Chattahoochee towns they called "Cussitaws" were a "powerful nation." One year later, Bishop Díaz referred with equal admiration to the "great population" that lived in the "province of Apalachicoli." As many as ten thousand people lived along the Chattahoochee after the migration.[17] In addition to gaining a new strength in numbers, the combined populations also enjoyed expanded ties of exchange and alliance. While the Hitchiti towns traded regularly with Apalachee traders, Cussita immigrants retained close ties to their Muskogean friends to the west. In the early 1660s, during one of the Floridanos' rare expeditions beyond the missions, soldiers met with Choctaw emissaries in Cussita. By holding the meeting at Cussita, both sets of visitors acknowledged the town's western contacts. In the sense that such ties provided them with better access to important networks of diplomacy and exotic goods, it seemed that the Cussitas and their fellow migrants had taken important steps along the white path of peace and power. Whether such successes were possible for them or their neighbors after 1659, however, remained an open question.

Southeastern Slavery Transformed

The Westos and their slave raiding inspired this new uncertainty, but their new commercial violence did not introduce slavery to the Southeast as much as transform it. Much as the European slave trade in western Africa had already begun promoting new economies and politics of violence there, so too did the new English-sponsored trade encourage Indians to refashion older forms of human capture and exchange.[18] Though the noncommercial forms of slavery that appear in de Soto's and others' records did not seem to inspire the same level of terror that the Westos cultivated, enemies who suffered capture before the arrival of the Westos still had much to dread. Lacking the protection of clan members who could provide support in times of trial and vengeance in times of injustice, a slave became a non-person. According to John Lawson, who visited the Carolina piedmont in the early 1700s, slaves were no better than domesticated animals, and the same word was used for slave as for dog, cat, or "any other thing of that Nature, which is obsequiously to depend on the Master for its Sustenance." In this dependent state, slaves suffered a social death, reduced to performing subsistence tasks like gathering wood, clearing fields, and cleaning animal skins.[19] Sometimes the pain of this status could be quite physical, as owners occasionally removed the toes and lower feet of those they feared would flee. Owners enjoyed the power that came from access to another's productive (and, potentially, reproductive) capacity. Although slaves belonged to individuals, as symbols of military victory and the subordination of outsiders, they also symbolized and augmented the power of the town to which these individuals belonged.[20]

Women's ability to bear children may help explain why many, if not

most, slaves were women. Because enslaved women lacked a clan identity, their offspring would probably have remained dependents or perhaps become family members in the household of their owner. When
the people of mission San Diego de Helaca in Timucua province fled
their mission en masse in 1648, the apostates also carried off women
from other towns to live with them.[21] Ultimately, through such raids, successful assailants asserted their power over their adversaries by gaining
the access to the productive and reproductive capacity of their women.
Spaniards' mid-century fears of outside raiders' efforts to "take control
of all of this land [of Guale]" may have accurately reflected the designs
of a people apparently intent on destroying the missions, but they may
have instead expressed the extent to which slave raiding enabled successful aggressors to augment their power at their victims' expense.[22]

To their own dismay, a few Spaniards experienced this slave system
that placed people at the center of local and regional networks of power,
warfare, and, at times, diplomacy. In 1528, Juan Ortiz was taken captive
at Tampa Bay during his fruitless search for ill-fated members of the Narváez expedition. Placed in the hands of the chief Ucita, Ortiz suffered
torture until Ucita's daughter convinced her father to spare the man as
a slave in one of the temples. Distinguished service temporarily
improved Ortiz's condition, but when Ucita again decided to kill his captive, Ortiz, with the help of Ucita's daughter, fled to a nearby rival chief,
Mocoso, who treated him much better. When de Soto brought Spaniards back to the coast in 1539, Mocoso even allowed Ortiz to return to
his countrymen.[23] Political calculations likely encouraged Mocoso's generosity. As gifts, slaves demonstrated the power of the givers and promoted peace between givers and recipients, especially when the slave
was returning to his or her people. During the early eighteenth century,
the Chickasaws of today's northern Mississippi called "killing and being
taken prisoner by the same name." To return captives was to return life
to the dead, to heal the wounds of war. Freed prisoners served as evidence of one side's good intentions and they could bridge the linguistic
divide between former belligerents. They also aimed to reduce the likelihood of future hostility, as when Mississippian leaders like Casqui
affirmed new friendships with gifts of captive women to the Spanish
invaders.[24]

Into this network of exchange of humans and power came the Westos.
Although the Westos' arrival in the Southeast appeared sudden, their
journey had been long. Before 1654, a scant five years before their
appearance south of the Savannah River, the Westos inhabited the
southeastern shores of Lake Erie, roughly between today's Buffalo, New
York, and Erie, Pennsylvania. Known as Eries or Rechahecrians, they
traded beaver pelts with the Susquehannocks of central Pennsylvania,

who themselves offered guns and other European manufactures they acquired from the English of the Chesapeake Bay. Rechahecrian rivalries with the Haudenosaunee, or Iroquois Five Nations, led to all-out war in 1653 as Iroquois warriors sought both captives to replace kin lost to disease and also beavers to trade for the commodities they obtained from the Dutch of New Netherland. In 1654, two thousand Iroquois warriors besieged a town defended by an equal number of Erie defenders. The invaders overwhelmed the town, and those who avoided death or capture fled south. By 1656, some of the survivors established a new town at the falls of the James River, just west of the Virginia colony. After a brief period of mistrust, Westos and their Virginia neighbors negotiated terms for a trade in beaver pelts and, more important, captives. By about the middle of the seventeenth century, Virginians had developed a growing tobacco export economy, but civil war in England complicated planters' efforts to maintain a reliable and affordable supply of indentured laborers. The Eries, familiar with firearms and possessing few friends in a new land, were well-positioned to answer the Virginian demand. In search of victims who did not possess their firepower, the Eries headed south to attack the peoples who came to know and fear them as Westos. Bishop Díaz was not entirely fair when he accused the Westos of wholesale cannibalism. Westos probably did consume some of their captives in ritual feasts, but they also gained much from selling them.[25]

The Westos built their power with the help of an English nation in the midst of a commercial revolution of its own. Following England's Civil War of 1642–49 and the beheading of King Charles I in 1649, the interregnum governments, first of Parliament and then of Oliver Cromwell, instituted a series of reforms designed to promote and control trade for the benefit of England. Merchants were especially well-positioned to serve their interests because, as the Venetian ambassador to London noted in 1651, "the government and commerce are in the same hands." And after King Charles II restored the monarchy in 1660, he expanded on this foundation. With the aid of strategic tariffs, a more regularized military, and an increasingly sophisticated financial network, English exports grew with new vigor in the second half of the seventeenth century. Gifts still played a role for this commercial people, but like the Spaniards and other Europeans, the English gave things away more for the purposes of negotiation, and they measured such exchanges by a larger calculus of prices to ensure equality of exchange. Traders in the Southeast learned quickly that any successful trade began with gifts, but these adventurers made their journeys in the interest of personal profit and not colonial diplomacy.[26]

Many Indians responded with enthusiasm. By the late seventeenth century, Natives in contact with the French, Dutch, and English were unanimous in their preference for firearms over bows and arrows. Although the older weapons were easier to fire and potentially more accurate, Indians recognized a number of advantages from the new technology. Besides producing terrifying sound and smoke, guns fired bullets that traveled too fast to dodge, and they usually inflicted more serious wounds than arrows. Although smoothbore muskets were renowned for their inaccuracy among Europeans, John Lawson noted in 1701 how Indians were "curious Artists, . . . sometimes shooting away over one hundred Loads of Ammunition" in the process of sighting a newly purchased musket. The results impressed Lawson. Indian men hunted birds with single balls instead of birdshot and still missed "but two shots in forty." The Westos might not have modified their muskets, but with their monopoly on firearms in the Southeast they remained fearsome enemies indeed.[27]

Between 1659 and 1674, Westos raided the peoples of today's South Carolina and Georgia, and they perhaps crossed the Appalachians. They forced Altamahas to abandon their homes along the Oconee River, harassed the Apalachicola towns along the Chattahoochee, and unsettled the missions of the Georgia coast. These last targets exposed the limits of their strength. Late in June 1661, sometime after the spring planting, a flotilla of some two hundred canoes and rafts, carrying five hundred to perhaps two thousand warriors, descended the Altamaha River and attacked the mission of Talaje located near the river's mouth. The survivors quickly fled south to a mission on neighboring Sapelo Island. The Westos' amphibious assault on the island failed when many attackers were swept out to sea and drowned. Spanish reinforcements chased the remainder inland. Spanish communications and organization (as well as the firearms that soldiers and some mission Indians possessed) thwarted all but the stealthiest of surprise attacks.[28]

Westos gained regional respect, but their preeminence was neither unlimited nor uncontested. Even without muskets, well-organized Native polities could hold their own. Apalachicolas were rumored to be "a more powerfull Nation" than the Westos in 1674, and they were not afraid to avenge their losses with raids on the Westos' own towns. Even so, plenty of easier victims remained. In 1662, Westos attacking Huyache, north of Guale, razed the settlement "and put to the knife as many people as they found in it."[29] Kiawahs and Cussoes living further up the coast fared little better. By the time of the arrival of English colonists in the new colony of Charles Town, Carolina, in 1670, the coastal Indians were "more afraid than the little children are of the Bull beggars in England." Facing the equivalents of an English childhood monster, it is little surprise that these beleaguered coastal peoples welcomed English colonists in 1670 as liberators, crying, "Hiddy doddy Comorado Angles Westoe Skorrye (which is as much as to say) English very good friends Westos are nought."[30] Through their trade pidgin, Cussoes and Kiawahs revealed their own familiarity with English traders. Perhaps the same trade that made the Westos might also defeat them.

Far across the Atlantic, the colony's seven proprietors, known collectively as the Lords Proprietor, read such reports with the hope that such friendly receptions would ensure the success of their colony and its founding ideals. Their colonial blueprint, called the Fundamental Constitutions and authored by John Locke, called for a colony based upon a landed aristocracy and guaranteed political rights, including freedom of religion, for all freeholders. This concern for social order and justice also included an interest in the rights of the "Natives of that place," over whom the colonists would have "no right to expel or use them ill."[31] Of course, the stipulations against ill treatment of Indians elegantly blended utopian and mercantile interests since the proprietors also claimed a monopoly on trade with Indians. For the proprietors, though, dreams of colonial wealth rested not on trade but on the anticipated produce of vast manorial estates. Most colonists, in contrast, modeled their aspirations on the very real example of the sugar plantations of Barbados, the prior home of most arrivals between 1670 and 1690. Sugar did not grow in Carolina's soils, but thanks to liberal land grants and astute publicity, the white population already surpassed four hundred by January 1672, and African slaves brought the total to about five hundred. As they searched for a lucrative export commodity, Carolinians learned to grow corn and began exporting beef to the Caribbean and naval stores such as wood, pitch, and tar to England. Pirates returning from tours of the Caribbean and the Florida coast refitted in the port, adding their booty to the colony's commerce. When Guales visited the port in 1678, they counted five ships riding at anchor and filled with supplies. Spanish officials, unfamiliar with more than one ship at a time in their harbor, must have learned such news with a mix of dismay and envy.[32]

Carolina's population and commerce were modest, but they grew quickly because colonists were willing to pursue the commercial endeavors available to them—even when activities like piracy directly challenged proprietary injunctions. Because the proprietors had no administrative ladder up which colonists could hope to advance, Carolinians had few incentives to please their distant overseers. This disregard for proprietors' will in pursuit of local profit had dire consequences for the region after 1674, when their agent Henry Woodward negotiated an end to the colony's desultory conflict with the Westos.[33] Colonists disregarded Woodward's new monopoly with the Westos, and they did it with impunity because the very traders who defied the proprietary monopoly were among the few who actually understood the lands west of Charles Town.[34] For their part, the Westos cared little about Carolinian squabbles and were delighted to acquire the same trade items without the arduous and dangerous journey to Virginia. The trade in captives, now tied to a Caribbean sugar economy desperate for laborers and promoted by ambitious and unscrupulous new colonists hoping to secure quick fortunes, gained new energy.

In many respects, then, Bishop Díaz's claims of Westo cannibalism may have been more perceptive than he would have liked. English traders had altered the dynamics of captivity and exchange by seeking them not for subsistence purposes but for more expansive commercial ones. Instead of eating or keeping most of their prisoners, Westos exchanged them for firearms, cloth, beads, and other trade goods from the English of Virginia and then, after 1674, with the English of Carolina. Unlike their seventeenth-century counterparts in New France, who reluctantly accepted Indian captives to reaffirm friendly relations with Native allies, or those in contemporary New Mexico, who shared with their Native neighbors certain notions of slaves as symbols of male authority, Carolinian colonists were interested almost exclusively in captives' capacity to work.[35] Living in Carolina or even in other distant colonies, Indian slaves of the English learned that shackles of iron bound them to a society that defined them not only as without kin but as property. Unlike slaves supplementing Native captors' subsistence activities, Carolinian slaves labored at the endless task of amassing wealth for their owners. Perhaps English ambitions inspired the desperation that Díaz unknowingly captured: Westos and others were not eating their captives, but their English trading partners were indeed consuming them whole.[36]

Altamaha Migration, Yamasee Emergence

The Westos visited the violence of a new commercial system on many southeastern towns. As various peoples fled the invaders, they considered factors of friendship and power, much as Cussitas and other Muskogeans had before their move to the Chattahoochee Valley. Altamahas, Coosas, Alabamas, and Koasatis all transplanted themselves, but Zamumo's people are among the best documented of these new migrants. Altamahas followed a number of different paths out of the Oconee Valley, and some joined other refugees to become a new people, the Yamasees. The results were varied, as some towns disappeared, others relocated, and still others merged to form new political entities. All drew upon older intertown connections in their searches for the

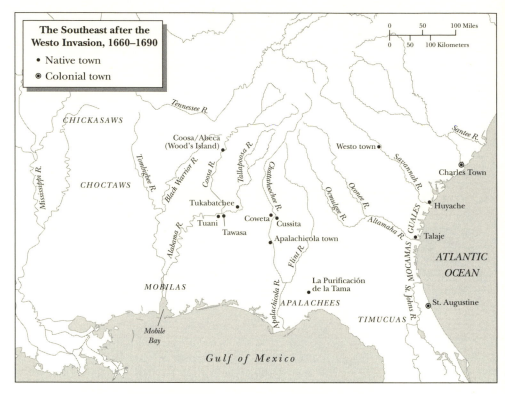

Map 4. The Southeast after the Westo invasion, 1660–90. Slave raiders from the north forced a number of peoples, including the Tuanis and Altamahas, to move south into the Alabama Valley or the Franciscan missions.

white path, a "good life," as it were. Some Altamahas were lucky enough to find it.[37]

In the middle 1600s, the Altamahas and their neighbors in the Oconee Valley probably still lived in the scattered farmsteads that they occupied when Fr. Chozas visited in 1597. Their relatively dispersed settlement pattern made them easy targets for Westo slave raids, so they fled. Many joined other coastal refugees among the missions of Guale, while others headed to Apalachee and Timucua. According to mission censuses from 1675 and 1681, nearly four hundred immigrants lived in Guale, while another three hundred lived in Apalachee and one hundred in Timucua. Although the migrants to Apalachee and Timucua accepted Franciscan evangelism, those in Guale did not. Still other migrants avoided the missions entirely and sought refuge among the

Apalachicolas. In every case, the refugees sought protectors capable of resisting the Westos.[38]

The peoples who fled the Oconee Valley, as well as others who joined them in these various refuges, cared about more than safety. Wherever they went, migrants did their best to reconstitute themselves as the towns they had left behind. That they failed to do so tells us much about new dynamics of local politics. Most obviously, the very name "Yamasee," an etymological modification of "Tama" (which was itself a synonym for "Altamaha"), first appeared in Spanish records when the refugees arrived in the 1660s.[39] The migrants had themselves adjusted to at least two developments that justified the new name. For one thing, by 1688, some of them were closely associated with mission peoples from whom they had been divided by distance and religion only thirty years before. The names of the relocated towns suggested a subtler but still significant change. The new towns in Guale included Tama and Ocotoque (which was itself probably an alias of Ocute) while those who moved to Apalachee populated the new mission of La Purificación de Tama. Other "Ocutis" and Altamahas repaired to the Apalachicolas. Town names remained, but migrants had decided not to rekindle their ceremonial fires in the same place. Such community fissures were as old as towns themselves, but the new Spanish trade probably deserved some credit for this most recent instance of fragmentation. Unlike the gift exchanges initiated by Zamumo in 1540 or Cacique Juan in 1600, followers as well as leaders were carrying Spanish goods inland after 1638. Commoners were willing to act on and strengthen these growing personal ties. Consequently, by 1686, Yamasees had "siblings and relatives" among the Apalachicolas. The fragmentation of Altamaha province suggests more than the decline of unified leadership among towns; relatively new dynamics of trade enabled lesser leaders and commoners to take questions of migration into their own hands.[40]

When one Altamaha reminisced about the "good life" that he had enjoyed with the Yamasees, he articulated a vague nostalgia for a life of security and happiness. Like the Cussitas, Altamahas and their fellow migrants recognized the importance of a white path, a path that could lead them to the friends and material resources necessary for political and spiritual balance. As with many searches for good life, though, the seekers disagreed about the best route to take. The chaos that followed Westo raids certainly encouraged uncertainty and dissension. At the same time, though, commoners or at least factions led by rival leaders were able to set out on different paths because they had established their own sets of far-flung connections in the decades prior to 1659. Building on the connections that linked them to Guales, Apalachicolas, and others, the various groups of Altamaha migrants began to develop a new collective identity called "Yamasee" that was rooted in dispersal and regional contacts. English slave hunger and Westo firearms were remaking a region at gunpoint, threatening the very existence of towns that had survived conquistadors and their pathogens. Fleeing from the depredations, some old towns were not only reevaluating old forms of leadership but were becoming new peoples.

Searching for "Light" in the Coosa and Tallapoosa Valleys

Further west, the Coosa and Tallapoosa Valleys witnessed dramatic population movements of their own in the three decades after 1659. The Coosas were among a number of peoples who continued the gradual migration down the Coosa River that they had begun in the late 1500s while Alabamas, Koasatis, and a number of other peoples settled lands near where the Coosa and Tallapoosa Rivers joined to form the Alabama. Altamahas would likely have understood the motivations behind the various moves. Security among friends in every case was key. What constituted security and who might be counted on as friends could vary, but there was no question that these two ingredients could help preserve the towns that Westos and other enemies threatened to destroy.

What we know of Coosa activities during this time of troubles is thanks to the diligent work of archaeologists. According to Marvin Smith, the principal student of the Coosas' past, the diminishing population of the former paramount chiefdom continued its movement downstream, arriving at Woods Island on the middle Coosa in about 1670. The smaller houses that they built at the new settlement may have been a sign that migration could not prevent families from shrinking. Migrants combined towns to maintain a viable population, but when Coosas built this new town with residents of the formerly tributary town of Abeca (also known as Abika), the old dynamics of power were reversed. Abeca, rather than Coosa, was the name for the new settlement, and it was this former subordinate that became the namesake for the collection of towns that English and Spaniards called Abecas after 1700. And while Coosas and Abecas negotiated their political structures of their new island community, they also welcomed refugees from the Tennessee Valley. The site offered a number of advantages to its many new inhabitants. In addition to providing an easily defensible location, the island provided important connections to the outside world. Just upstream from the town, an east-west trading path forded the Coosa River, connecting the Chickasaws of northern Mississippi with the European goods moving north and west from St. Augustine and, increasingly, Charles Town. The trading path evidently served the islanders well, too, as the vast majority of period graves contained European goods of some kind, including, for the first time in Coosa history, two guns.[41]

The desire for protection and connection motivated many others in the nearby lands, as hundreds fled downstream past Woods Island to the area where the Coosa and Tallapoosa Rivers join to form the Alabama River. Why they chose this densely populated river junction is difficult to say in part because so little is known about the region's history. According to pottery styles from the river valleys there appears to be a blurry cultural border separating the peoples living along the lower Tallapoosa from those in the immediate vicinity of the river junction and south along the Alabama. While the more westerly societies exhibited cultural ties with Moundville in central Mississippi, those to the east had more in common with the residents of eastern Tennessee and Georgia.[42] But people do not move to a place solely because they like its pottery. Besides having cultural connections to these eastern and western immigrants, residents of the three river valleys were also quite powerful. Peoples in central Alabama maintained mound centers during the late Mississippian period, and at least one town along the upper Alabama survived long enough to incorporate European goods into its rituals, what the archaeologist Craig Sheldon considers "probably the 'last gasp' of Mississippian mound ceremonialism on the upper Alabama River."[43] And however much these Mississippian leaders were struggling for breath, their successors managed to maintain relatively stable polities during the late sixteenth century and the early seventeenth. In fact, the departure of the Cussitas and other towns to the Apalachicola province some time before 1663 would have provided the remaining Tallapoosa towns with reliable access to Spanish goods. Thus, while migrants appreciated their cultural affinities with their new neighbors, they also appreciated their political stability and the access to exotic goods that seemed to ensure it.

And this appreciation appears in more than just the material record. In 1686, when Spaniards ventured to the lands where the Coosa and Tallapoosa Rivers join to form the Alabama, they heard just how much things from Havana and St. Augustine meant to people hundreds of miles from the Gulf of Mexico. The documentary details of Natives' movements and motivations come to us almost entirely from the observations of Marcos Delgado, who led a detachment in search of French interlopers under the command of René Robert Cavelier, Sieur de la Salle. He was ordered to explore Mobile Bay, where many believed the French were settling, but because the Pensacolas who controlled his route from Apalachee along the coast refused to host him, Delgado journeyed northwest to the headwaters of the Alabama River, which he could then follow downstream to Mobile Bay.[44] Although they never reached

the bay, they did at least learn it remained free of La Salle and his followers, who were already dying from starvation and fratricidal conflict on
the Texas coast. More important for our history of exchange, though,
were the remarkable changes that Delgado recorded at the forks of the
Alabama. Even as Indians confronted new forms of warfare that
uprooted entire communities, they were also facing these new challenges with time-tested institutions of leadership and power. Most striking still, they adapted to their war-torn region in part by drawing with
increasing insistence upon the power of Spanish goods. In fact, according to one heretofore mistranslated report from Delgado, some Indians
considered these objects as nothing less than "the light" that could remedy troubling new darkness of war and captivity.

Before Delgado's expedition, Spaniards had no direct contact with
the large and powerful collection of towns at the forks of the Alabama
that they called the "province of Tawasa." Delgado set out with little
more than a vague notion of the direction and Bishop Calderón's secondhand report from 1675 that listed the province's fourteen towns.
The lack of orientation became a serious liability. Delgado described an
arduous two-week journey from Apalachee "through trackless woods"
in which his company broke their largest axes and became "sick with
fevers and our legs shredded to pieces."[45] When the expeditionaries
finally arrived along the Tallapoosa River, they visited "the first town of
the province of Tabasa" and then met the next day with six chiefs sum-
moned from nearby towns, Delgado continued through two more towns
before visiting a string of six towns that had all fled from incessant
attacks. Roughly three thousand Koasati and Tuani had recently suffered raids from "the English, the Chichimeco, and another nation
called Chalaque," while another twelve hundred people in the towns of
Pacana, Culasa, and Alabama had been forced from their homes by the
populous and increasingly powerful Choctaws of central Mississippi.[46]
Towns called "Pacâna" and "Ymicolâsa" appear in Calderón's report,
so perhaps some migrants arrived over a dozen years before Delgado,
but the absence of the remainder suggests that most had arrived in the
previous decade. Even acknowledging the rough nature of Delgado's
estimates, there is no doubt that the scale of these movements was massive. Also, as the Choctaws' belligerence attests, not all of these new wars
owed their origins to English avarice, but by the 1680s not even the
Appalachian Mountains offered a barrier to English-sponsored terror.

Delgado did not indicate when these movements occurred but noted
that they were relatively recent and that the migrants had every reason
to hope for some security in their new homeland. Delgado's visit
revealed that Tawasa's influence might not have extended to all fourteen of the towns that Calderón listed, but it is clear that the leader of

"the first town of the province" enjoyed enough influence over his neighbors to convince six nearby chiefs to meet with Delgado on a day's notice. Hoping to acquire additional food supplies for his expedition, Delgado also visited the neighboring "province of Tiquipache," where he secured a little food and assurances of friendship from the town of Tukabatchee and eight others.[47] Clearly, not even the terrifying power of Westo muskets forced all southeastern peoples to abandon the hierarchies that organized their towns and wider worlds. In fact, the newly relocated towns were also organized in ways that exalted some towns over others. Those towns displaced by the Choctaws probably came together under the leadership of Pacana, which had influence over Culasa and perhaps Alabama. Tuanis, as people "of the Qusate nation," followed Koasati from the Tennessee Valley.[48] There is little doubt that old Mississippian patterns continued to decline during the late seventeenth century; what disease eroded from within, slave raiding threatened to tear apart from without. Nonetheless, migrants could still hope to preserve some older patterns among new neighbors who also remembered what it meant to have a chief.

Some refugees sought regions of political stability with a simultaneous appreciation for the Spaniards' contributions to regional exchange networks. During his visit, Delgado saw how Indians were exchanging Spanish goods throughout the Southeast and using them to promote ties of peace. Delgado's first lesson came during his efforts to reconcile the inhabitants of the forks with their downstream enemies, the Mobilas. The Mobilas controlled access to Mobile Bay, and if Delgado wanted to determine whether La Salle lurked upon its shores, he would have to end the conflict that separated him from his destination. Delgado and his gifts played a crucial role in the negotiations. When the Mobilas arrived on the upper Alabama River, the chief of Mobila and of the four towns that followed him expressed great relief. According to Delgado, "They told me that it seemed that they had emerged from a very dark night" for they had feared throughout their journey that they would suffer treachery from their upriver enemies. Not only were those fears gone, but the visiting dignitaries hoped they would never return. "Since God had brought us here," recorded Delgado, "they wanted to make friends with those of these provinces, they did not want to have wars with anyone."[49]

Delgado bolstered Mobilas' hope for peace by bringing a Mobila translator who had come to live among the Apalachees after being captured by the Chiscas. By restoring to life a man the Mobilas believed dead, the Spanish peacemaker erased one more cause for grief and rationale for conflict. The talks concluded with the former enemies embracing. However genuine the new peace, it owed much to the spiritual power of the visitors, and their gifts were the material proof of that fact. By the end of the meeting, "the gifts were all gone because the chiefs of Mobila carried off what there was."[50] The Mobilas further emphasized the capacity of Spaniards and their gifts to "bring them out of the darkness of night and showing them the light of day" when their great cacique "beg[ged]" the governor to open a trading path from Apalachee to Mobila via a more direct coastal route.[51] His supplication sought more than European things. As it was, and as the Spaniards had learned just that summer, Mobilas were already trading with "some men who are like Spaniards but who are not Spaniards." Floridanos mistook this intelligence for news of the French, but only Englishmen were capable of reaching Mobile Bay in 1686.[52] Most likely, they came among the Mobilas to buy captives, including perhaps some Tawasas among them. So when the Mobila chief requested a trade path to the Spaniards, he was not seeking trade. What he sought was a trade that did not require war.

Delgado also learned that Mobilas were not the only ones who believed Spaniards and their things could "bring them out of the darkness." Spanish gifts and the peace they promised had motivated some of the northern migrants to head to the forks of the Alabama in the first place. Shortly after arriving at their new homes, the Tuanis sent a delegation to the Apalachicolas as part of their effort to establish ties with the Spanish and Apalachees. The Apalachicolas rejected the Tuanis' overture, saying that "the friendship of the Spaniards and Christians was not good" because "their trade goods were not good, and the goods from the English and Chichimecos were better because for one thing they gave much," including "powder and shot and muskets." But according to Delgado, Tuanis rejected the Apalachicolas' breathless endorsement of English largesse because, as he recalled their explanation, "it was thanks to the English and Chichumecos that they had fled and abandoned their lands." Indeed, the Tuanis claimed that "they had not come except looking for Spanish friendship, and if they saw the light of the Spaniards they would remain [in their new homes]."[53] Delgado's arrival and his newly cleared path to Apalachee justified Tuani migration and gave them reason to stay.

The Tuanis' account of their meeting with the Apalachicolas is extraordinary on a number of levels. First, it makes clear that a century of contact with Spanish goods had made deep impressions on people as far north as the Tennessee Valley. Second, Tuanis were recognizing the significant influence that Apalachicolas had over the exchange networks that linked Europeans on the coasts with towns west of the Chattahoochee River. Third, and most important, the Tuanis' conversation with the Apalachicolas endows otherwise hypothetical networks and mute material remains with Native meanings. Much as when the Mobila chief begged for a trading path between his people and Apalachee, Tuanis rejected Apalachicolas' overtures to join their alliance with the English because they believed that the interests of traders mattered as much as the objects they traded. As important as glass beads, steel axes, or woolen blankets might have been to their possessors, these objects also symbolized human relationships that were intrinsically connected to these foreign things. And for Tuanis and Mobilas, at least, Spanish goods were particularly noteworthy as new sources of "light" in an increasingly dark and violent world

After 1660, a new nation of Europeans was looking for its fortunes in the Southeast. Instead of pikes, crosses, and gifts, they armed themselves with a newly expansionistic economy, and they ventured out from settlements where people were property, and property provided access to networks of credit for the acquisition of more property. Peoples of the southeastern interior saw little of the English of Virginia and Carolina before 1680, but they knew too much about the guns their allies carried and the prisoners they sought. Nearly every town east of the Coosa River experienced the force of English expansion. Some turned to the English, others to the Spanish; all looked to Native friends. In doing so, they sought the security that Cussitas had found along their white path to the Apalachicolas.

As a chapter in the story of colonial exchange networks in the Southeast, the events after 1659 are most obviously part of a story of migrants fleeing from a bloody new form of trade. To look at such events as a product solely of those revolutionary events, though, is to miss much (if not most) of the story. Westo violence shattered Altamaha province after 1660, but the fissures had begun forming when Spanish pathogens and gifts began moving inland a century earlier. Spanish goods helped maintain and open the paths that these and many other migrants eventually followed, but they also influenced how migrants chose their routes to safety. As an expanding trade enabled followers to acquire the exotic goods their leaders once monopolized, non-elites also deepened their acquaintance with the growing number of people who carried them. Migration demonstrated the dual influence of this new trade. Not only were townspeople willing to abandon their leaders, but they had the personal connections to follow their own paths to sanctuary, to form ties with "siblings and relatives" on their own. The networks that carried Spanish goods did not shape every migration, however. Far to the west, and in a manner that is quieter only because we possess no documents of their lives, Coosas continued to look to old tributaries for the allies who would keep their struggling town viable. In every case, though, migrants were following paths that traders and diplomats had already made white.

Besides shaping the dynamics of many migrations, Spanish trade also provided the objects and the "light" that some of the migrants desired. Zamumo had sought something similar from de Soto, but Indians a century and a quarter later needed peace (and the objects that symbolized it) with an urgency born of spreading war. According to the Tuanis, Apalachicolas championed the abundance of English power, but English commercial power did not endow English traders with a free hand in the region's networks of exchange. Spaniards' commitment to maintaining and even expanding their networks of trade and gift giving provided victims of the slave trade with new hope that they would not have to seek protection and power from their persecutors. But a dark cloud menaced this silver lining: would Floridanos' goods and their alliance be adequate protection against English colonists, whose offerings were more abundant and ambitions more violent?

Chapter 5

Creating White Hearts: Anxious Alliances amid the Slave Trade

> *Then the [Coweta] visitors addressed the [Tukabahchee] chiefs saying "We hear that you have a very powerful medicine which enables you to conquer everybody, therefore we have come to learn about it. Have you any warriors?" "Yes," said they, "we have a few." "Let us see them." "We must whoop four times in order to call them up, they said. "All right," answered the Coweta. Then they sent a messenger who returned presently with something wrapped up in a white deerskin. They unwrapped this and produced a short stick of miko hoyani-dja. Holding this they whooped once and the earth trembled and it thundered and lightened. After they had whooped the second time, the Coweta said, "That will do. You need not whoop any more." But the Tuka- bahchee answered that they must go through to the fourth now that they had begun and they did so. The Coweta said, "Let us become friends and exchange medicines." They did this and have been firm friends ever since. The Tukabahchee medicine was, as we have seen, the miko hoyani-dja; the Coweta medicine was the kapapaska.*
>
> —*Alindja, ca. 1910*[1]

Alindja said nothing to John Swanton about the wider circumstances behind the Cowetas' and Tukabatchees' alliance, but I cannot help wondering if his recollections refer to the turbulent years of the slave trade. The parallels, if not the connections, are intriguing. After 1674, as the Westos and their Carolinian trading partners destroyed and traded lives with terrifying ruthlessness, Indians in the Southeast faced two basic questions. How could one best survive? Who made the best partners for such an endeavor? Many southeastern Natives answered the first question by becoming slave raiders themselves. But if prudence seemed to encourage Carolina's new partners to join those they could not beat, slave raiding was a bloody affair for hunters as well as hunted, and the English quickly proved themselves to be dangerously unpredictable. So between 1680 and 1707, residents of Coweta, its sister town of Cussita, and other towns of the Chattahoochee Valley answered the second question in ways Alindja would have understood perfectly: They forged ties with peoples like the Tukabatchees who could reduce the risks of association with violent English partners.[2] In light of this strategy, Alindja's exchange of *miko hoyani-dja* and *kapapaska* (the former a variety of willow and the latter known in English as spicewood) is all the more evocative. Cowetas and Tukabatchees were combining medicines devoted not to war but to the purification and renewal of the Green Corn Ceremony.[3] As devoted as Carolinians were to war, profit, and empire, their Coweta, Tukabatchee, and associated Native allies remained as committed as Zamumo had been to the quest for peace, the gifts of friendship, and the power rooted in both.

However direct the lineage between these developments and Alindja's account two centuries later, his story provides not just an allegory for the years between 1680 and 1707 but a structure for exploring it. Before we can understand how and why Cowetas and Tukabatchees came to exchange powerful medicine, we must first learn how the Cowetas became such confident alliance builders in the first place. When Cowetas and the other towns of Apalachicola province finally made the difficult decision to join the English, they did so in partnership with the Yamasees. Once confederated with these eastern towns, Apalachicolas then deepened their ties with Tukabatchees and their neighbors to the west. These diplomatic successes then introduced a new question. How could these new allies keep the destructive power of war wrapped, like the Tukabatchees' medicine, in the white deerskin of peace? The allies responded by pursuing war with vigor and treating its Carolinian sponsors with circumspection, and they devoted many of the proceeds of war to the ceremonies of peace. Their answers enabled Carolinians to maintain a profitable trade, but they also gave Spaniards and the newly arrived French, who offered gifts and "light" instead of trade and war, a paradoxical security in weakness. Such balances between peace and war and among competing empires enabled these new allies to engage in a new trade while retaining old exchange patterns. And so Cowetas and their friends to the east and west were able to shape a region in a way that no European wanted.

The Apalachicolas' Quest for Balance in the East

The confidence that Alindja recalled to Swanton in 1910 and that Tuanis attributed more generally to the Apalachicolas in their conversations with Marcos Delgado in 1686 emerged out of years of tortuous debates among the Apalachicolas themselves. Carolinians promised power as well as peril. In the late seventeenth century, England's Atlantic commerce was small but growing rapidly, and the Navigation Acts of the 1660s sought to link commercial growth to imperial ambition. Even with laws that required that all colonial trade proceed on English ships and through English ports, Carolinian traders faced nothing like the Spanish regulations that funneled all transatlantic commerce through Seville and limited La Florida's commerce to infrequent shipments from Havana and Veracruz. Decentralization had its costs, however, as the absentee Lords Proprietor were largely at odds with the commercial ambitions of many colonists. For another matter, however envious Floridanos were of their neighbor's commerce, Charles Town saw only a dozen ships (not counting pirates) traveling to or from Barbados or England between 1670 and 1700.[4] Charles Town was a child of a newly mercantilist empire, but it remained for decades the immature progeny of an inexperienced parent. Worse, this child was prone to vicious tantrums. In 1680, English traders encouraged other Indian allies to destroy the Westos. Because the English colony's proprietors monopolized the trade through their exclusive access to the Westos and because trade with Native Americans constituted one of the colony's most lucrative and bitterly contested activities, traders frustrated with the monopoly decided to destroy the more vulnerable of the two partners.[5]

The Westos' destruction and dispersal placed the people of Coweta and Cussita in a particularly uncomfortable position. Beginning in 1675, they had pursued an alliance with the Westos, even to the point in 1679 of driving Franciscans away from a nascent mission in Sabacola at the southern end of Apalachicola province. But when Coweta and other Apalachicola towns offered refuge to fleeing Westos, they confronted English-sponsored raids of their own. Perhaps Spaniards offered a better option after all. They were neither so unpredictably violent nor so devoted to the mercantile logics of exchange. Between 1680 and 1685, four Apalachicola embassies visited St. Augustine requesting missionaries, the men who would ensure Native leaders' access to Spanish generosity. Despite Franciscan optimism, a second mission at Sabacola languished, and the Spanish abandoned it in 1692.[6] Missionaries failed in Apalachicola in part for the same reason that they failed to gain converts among most other people after 1650: Spaniards were offering through trade the same items that had once promoted evangelization, and newly influential commoners had no desire to accept a system that would augment their chief's power. Observant missionaries like Fray Rodrigo de Barrera, who served at Sabacola, recognized this political shift when he advised La Florida's governor in 1681 to promise Apalachicolas that he would not subject new converts to the labor drafts that Apalachees and other mission Indians had to serve. Fr. Barrera's solitary suggestion was the first official indication that Spain's evangelical project lay in the hands of thousands of circumspect commoners in and outside the missions.[7]

And so in 1685, Apalachicolas once again considered ties with the English. That summer English traders arrived among the Apalachicolas for the first of three fateful trade embassies. Perhaps this visit meant the Apalachicolas' persecutors would become their protectors. Then again, perhaps the traders sought merely to gain what fortunes they could before resuming the wars that dragged Apalachicolas into bondage. Ambivalence abounded: while Cowetas welcomed these traders to their town with signs of peace by "cleaning the paths as is usually done for the arrival of a governor," other Chattahoochee Valley residents expressed their discomfort less ceremoniously, preventing the foreigners from completing their trading houses.[8] At the least, the ceremonial display of respect was prudent. For one, the English provided the firearms that Spaniards never traded. In addition, the people of Coweta and Cussita probably also recognized that their location along the principal east-west path south of the Appalachian Mountains enabled them to control access to the large concentrations of potential captives of the Gulf plain and Mississippi Valley to the west.

But if some Apalachicolas saw white, others saw red. For months, Apalachicolas had been sending deerskins to Charles Town in the hopes of ransoming five of their people who were held captive there. Carolinians had already on two or three other occasions "failed to keep their word" and return the slaves, and this latest Carolinian embassy also arrived on the Chattahoochee River empty-handed. As Marcos Delgado learned during his meeting with the Mobilas and Tukabatchees in 1686, prisoner exchanges often formed a fundamental element of peace overtures, but the English ambassadors seemed untroubled by their diplomatic slight: in March 1686, seven months after their first embassy, English traders returned with trade goods but "without giving [the Apalachicolas] hopes of recovering the . . . slaves." As Apalachicolas examined the blankets, beads, and guns, some probably understood the traders' visit as a stark offer: trade with or be traded by the English.[9]

Apalachicolas had two good reasons for hope, though. First, the tenuous lines of commerce and credit that linked Woodward to Charles Town, Barbados, London, and elsewhere required relations of trust built upon personal—and preferably familial—ties. Thus, it was a shared hope for trust and peace that enabled Woodward to marry a niece of "Juiaui," presumably the *mico* of Coweta.[10] Second, Apalachicolas accepted the union because Woodward also brought good character references. His escort of fifty Yamasees represented a people who were both familiar to many Apalachicolas and surprising new players in southeastern power politics. Most were former residents of Altamaha and other towns in the Oconee Valley who had fled Westo raids and sought refuge among the missions and the Apalachicolas. Dispersal soon became a source of strength. When Spanish labor demands and political slights convinced Yamasees to abandon Guale in 1683, they moved north to Port Royal, the old home of some of the migrants and the new home of Scottish Presbyterians of recently established Stuart Town. Together, Scottish and Yamasee immigrants forged a friendship born of a shared hatred of the Spanish and a desire to profit from the sale of captives from the missions. These raids proved so successful that many Yamasee refugees among the Apalachicolas and the Apalachee missions also flocked to Stuart Town's environs. Between 1683 and 1703, the population mushroomed from several hundred to over four thousand. The slave trade that destroyed the Altamahas now fueled the Yamasees' remarkable rise. After 1680, proprietors and traders were all looking for a well-situated population to serve as middlemen to interior peoples, as the proprietors put it, "in the room of the Westoes." The Yamasees, with their "siblings and relatives" among the Apalachicolas, lived along the coast just north of the Savannah River, which in turn led to the upland trails heading west. These were the trails Woodward followed, and Yamasees were the ones to lead him.[11]

Yamasees did not relieve Apalachicolas of all of their concerns, though. In the summer of 1685, La Florida's Governor Juan Márquez Cabrera dispatched his lieutenant, Antonio Matheos, with 250 Apalachees and 6 soldiers into the Chattahoochee Valley in search of Woodward. Despite the imposing force and a second invasion in December and January, Matheos failed to find any English. During his second visit, he even burned the four pro-English towns of Coweta, Cussita, Colone, and Tasquique in the hopes that it would "give rise to some discord among" the Chattahoochee towns by splitting the less enthusiastic Hitchiti towns from the Muskogeans who favored the English, but here, too, he failed. A veteran of European battlefields and not woodland politics, the abrasive Matheos was clearly ill-suited for such delicate missions, but he does not deserve all of the blame for the Apalachicolas' shifting sentiments. He himself acknowledged that the Apalachicolas "are more afraid of [the English] than us." Besides neglecting to bring the five captives, the English may also have continued to sponsor slave raids on the Chattahoochee Valley.[12]

Amid such competing pressures, Yamasees proved decisive for the Apalachicolas' decision to ally with the Carolinians. As beneficiaries of the trade and with kin among the Apalachicolas, they had impeccable credentials. When a third trade embassy of five traders arrived in the Chattahoochee Valley in the spring of 1686, a lone Carolinian trader accompanied forty-five Yamasees to speak at Apalachicola town to Hit-

chitis and some immigrant Yamasees. This was the town that had probably welcomed Spanish overtures for peace in 1638 and Cussita requests
to immigrate before 1662. This town more than any other had the most
to lose from a trading path that Muskogeans controlled.[13] The solitary
Carolinian observed a prudent silence, and let those who shared ties of
language, history, and kinship make the case. The leader of the visiting
Yamasees boasted of recent military successes against the missions and
promised an imminent invasion of St. Augustine. After he finished, his
audience approved of the proposed alliance. That approval shifted
regional dynamics almost as radically as the arrival of the Westos had.
Apalachicolas were abandoning Spaniards who offered gifts for peace to
join others who promoted war through trade. Hitchitis and Muskogeans
made this new alliance for old reasons, though. Yamasees, Hitchitis, and
Muskogeans had built and renewed friendships by exchanging Spanish
goods, they had survived Westo raids by living together, and with their
agreement in Apalachicola town in 1686, they reinforced these ties. In
1688, the governor of Carolina noted to his counterpart in St. Augustine
that Yamasees were "confe[derated] with a bigger Nation than themselves, which with the Yamosyes are about 1,400 men."[14]

Spaniards sought to counteract English successes with Marcos Delgado's visit to the Alabama and Tallapoosa Valleys in 1686, three devastating raids on Stuart Town and the Yamasees in 1686 and 1687, and the
construction of a fort among the Apalachicolas in 1689.[15] This last Spanish imposition convinced even the most ambivalent Apalachicolas that
their interests were better served with the Yamasees and their English
partners. Sometime before the fall of 1691, Muskogeans and then Hitchitis abandoned the Chattahoochee in favor of what Carolinians called
"Ochese Creek" (today's Ocmulgee River in central Georgia). The Carolinians promptly constructed a trading house among what they called
the "Ochese Creek towns" to serve the migrants. While most Apalachicolas built new homes at the end of this one-hundred-mile journey, the
residents of Apalachicola town moved even farther. Wishing to remain
close to the people who drew them into the new alliance, they moved to
the lower Savannah River, thirty miles from the Yamasees of Port Royal.[16]

Through their alliance, Yamasees and the newly relocated Ocheses
blended peace and war. These ties also ensured that the newly opened
path to Charles Town did not become a path to submission. Yamasees
controlled Carolinians' access to the Savannah River, which made them,
as frustrated Carolinian traders noted in 1691, "the onely people fitt to
assist the English, in a way of trade to the Inlands."[17] Meanwhile, Ocheses had settled along the trading path that followed the fall line west
from the Savannah River and into the lands south and west of the Appalachians. The two peoples served as gatekeepers for Carolina's trade

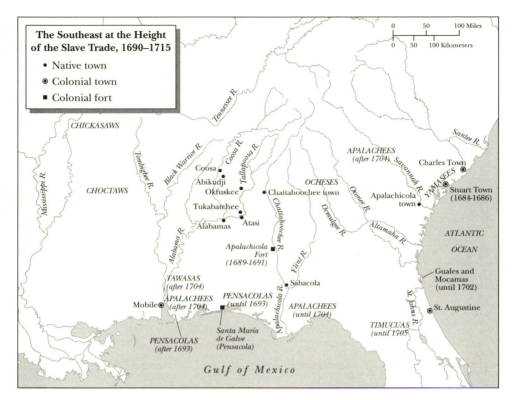

Map 5. The Southeast at the height of the slave trade, 1690–1715. New alliances before about 1695 enabled Carolinians and interior Natives to displace a number of other groups, especially after 1704.

westward even as they also stood as the colony's principal guardians against any invasion from that quarter.[18] As Zamumo knew in 1540 and Chekilli made clear in 1735, alliances secured the path to peace and power. Together Yamasees and Ocheses had found balance within the unpredictable English trading network. Together they had also become indispensable to it.

The Tukabatchees' Compelling Alliances in the West

Having achieved an influential place in Carolinians' trade network by 1690, Ocheses sought to augment that position with overtures to western friends like the powerful Tukabatchees and their neighbors on the Tallapoosa and Coosa Rivers. The second piece of this story of alliance building is harder to trace but follows a similar course as the first; old friendships became new alliances that occasioned strategic migrations. By 1690, as Tukabatchees sought to balance the imperatives of peace with the vagaries of the slave trade, they found they were best off in the company of other Native towns. The problem was that it was rarely clear whether Spaniards or English were preferable. Although Tukabatchees left no record of their debates, two sets of Spanish conversations with Natives of the Gulf Coast suggest the complexity and intensity of the discussions underway on the banks of the Tallapoosa and probably elsewhere. The first we have already heard. In the late summer of 1686, shortly after Woodward and his companions returned to Carolina from their third embassy, Mobilas affirmed to Marcos Delgado their desire for Spanish alliance founded on the "light" of peace. Unfortunately for the Spaniards, this influence depended on a new coastal trading path between their homes on Mobile Bay and the Spanish missions of Apalachee. The second conversation was a product of Spaniards' failure to open this path. In 1693, Pensacola Indians, who lived roughly halfway along the proposed path between Apalachee and Mobila, abandoned their homes on the eponymous bay. Trade and the power it provided were clearly factors in the decision. As a Tawasa man explained on their behalf five years later, the Pensacolas left because "the Spanish are not men and [the English] are."[19] In the Mobila invitation of 1686 and the Pensacola-Tawasa taunt of 1698, Gulf Coast Natives made clear how much they considered one of the colonial rivals crucial friends amid the new dynamics of war and peace, but where people like the Mobilas hoped Spanish light could spare them from English violence, Pensacolas, Tawasas, and others favored the protection of warlike masculinity.

Tukabatchees were of this latter persuasion but with an important twist. Like the Pensacolas and Tawasas, they joined the English, but they did so without sacrificing the peace that Mobilas had craved because the people of Tukabatchee province (often called "Tallapoosas" in English records), along with the Tawasas and the Alabamas of the upper Alabama Valley and the Abecas of the upper Coosa and Tallapoosa Valleys, joined Ocheses and Yamasees in the new alliance with Charles Town. We know this not because of what they said but because of what they did. Beginning in the 1690s some residents in a number of towns from the three valleys relocated eastward to help bridge the distances and differences between the Coosa River and the Atlantic Ocean. Perhaps the first to move were residents of two towns along the Tallapoosa River, Atasi and the influential town of Tukabatchee, who were eager to affirm their already close ties to the Cowetas by establishing their own satellite villages on the Ocmulgee. Cowetas reciprocated with a Tallapoosa Valley settlement some time before 1700. The Abeca town of Okfuskee settled a new satellite village on the now abandoned upper Chattahoochee to keep control of the long trading path to the Ocheses. In his map from 1711 Thomas Nairne noted the outlying settlement as "Chatahuches, 80 men," but the consequence of these and similar communities lay in their connections, not their size.[20] Reprising Apalachicola strategies with the Yamasees, these migrants from the Coosa and Tallapoosa Valleys simultaneously affirmed their alliances with the Ocheses and ensured their influence over Carolinian trade networks that stretched to the Mississippi River by 1698.[21] Much as Tukabatchee and Coweta medicines joined the powers of war and peace in Alindja's twentieth-century story, so too did their ties of trade and alliance do the same in the late seventeenth century. Tukabatchees and other Tallapoosas joined Apalachicolas and Yamasees in raids on the missions after 1690, taking captives and pillaging churches and towns. After one raid in 1694 against the Chacatos who lived northwest of Apalachee, the attackers even boasted to their prisoners that their sale would purchase the firearms necessary to "finish once and for all the Spaniards and Apalachees."[22]

The Tukabatchees, Ocheses, and their allies were formidable, but those words were probably uttered with more bravado than foresight. Administering a coup de grace to one of the region's most populous and powerful peoples required more than muskets. With a population of about 9,600 clustered into large and well-defended towns, the Apalachees were an intimidating adversary. Not surprisingly, during the 1690s, Ocheses, Tallapoosas, and their allies avoided attacking Apalachees in favor of their weaker Timucua and Chacato neighbors. If Native allies provided Apalachicolas with the best protection from meddling colonists, whose formidable power remained confined mostly to the coast, Native enemies like the Apalachees presented them with the greatest threat.[23] In such a context, all friends were indispensable. Unfortunately for the Tukabatchees, in 1694 they had reason to fear the wavering loyalty of their Tawasa and Alabama neighbors. That October, desperate emissaries from the Alabamas and Tawasas arrived in Apalachee, begging the province's Spanish lieutenant governor for sanctuary. Their fear was elegantly, if disturbingly, simple. As they explained, "The Indians of Tiquipache [Tukabatchee], Atasi, and other places threatened them each day with death because they did not want to continue in the partiality of the English." The supplicants feared so much for their lives that they requested Spanish escort to conduct them from the Alabama Valley to their new sanctuary in Apalachee.[24]

The Tukabatchees' threat probably reflected their power as much as their anxiety over losing it. Living in societies where no institution or individual possessed the power to impose their will on the reluctant, some southeastern Indians believed murder threats served as a crucial tool for forging consensus when dissent could mean disaster. In 1647, as

Apalachees were debating the merits of violently expelling the Spanish friars and soldiers among them, Spanish officials learned that neighboring Chiscas who supported the revolt "threaten[ed] the Christians to join them and leave the law of God or they will kill them all." Similar threats had enabled Coweta's *mico* to force the Sabacolas to expel their missionary in 1679. For their part, Alabamas and Tawasas were mixed in their response. While the Alabamas stayed put, some Tawasas apparently risked death and moved to Apalachee. Despite the ambiguous results of their threats, the decidedly undiplomatic Tukabatchees and Atasis made clear how much they and many other Indians had staked their security not on the English but on one another. They also intimated how much their new alliances dedicated to violence also depended on it.[25]

If the Ochese towns did not share Tukabatchee and Atasi anxiety in October 1694, they did two months later. In December, four hundred Apalachees and Chacatos and seven Spaniards retaliated for a recent Ochese attack with a raid on the Ocmulgee Valley. The Ocheses fled before their attackers reached them, and so the invaders found only empty towns. Although the defenders lost few lives, they suffered terribly from the invaders' scorched-earth tactics. Their bodies stressed by seasons of shortage in 1695, the recovering population must have been especially vulnerable to the smallpox epidemic that swept westward from Charles Town early in 1697. The epidemic, perhaps southeastern Natives' first encounter with smallpox, then followed English and Native trading paths west to the Mississippi. Successive waves of smallpox, yellow fever, and other diseases further ravaged raiders and their victims over the next fifteen years. As they watched half to two-thirds of their fellow townspeople succumb to deadly infection, Ocheses became painfully aware that not even they possessed immunity to the scourges of war, famine, and pestilence.[26]

Slave Raiding amid Imperial War

For all of their anxieties over friends and injuries from enemies, the groups who controlled these paths from Port Royal to the forks of the Alabama were among the fortunate in this increasingly violent region. Their fortune depended, much as that of Alindja's Cowetas and Tukabatchees, on their ability to balance peace and war. But how did allies maintain this balance? The question, already challenging in the 1680s and 1690s, became all the more difficult after 1699, when French colonists began building their new colony of Louisiana on the Gulf coast. Imperial rivalry became imperial war in 1702, when Europeans imported the War of the Spanish Succession to America. Between 1702 and the end of the conflict in 1713, Carolinians transformed the steel and lead of war into the silver of profit, with traders receiving commissions as militia officers and then organizing massive slave raids against the colony's enemies. They turned captives into commodities by offering competitive prices, with a captive purchasing as little as a single musket or as much, according to Nairne, as "a Gun, ammunition, horse, hatchet, and a suit of Clothes." Such rates fueled Charles Town's remarkable growth and enabled about 60 percent of Tallapoosa warriors, 33 percent of Abeca warriors, and perhaps all Alabama warriors to acquire a musket by 1710.[27] A trade from war begat the tools of more conflict, but throughout the chaos and the carnage a new collection of Native allies used their connections with one another and the English to shape a war from which they, too, hoped to benefit.

The peoples of the interior enjoyed such influence in part because there were so many European rivals to work with. French under the command of Pierre Le Moyne d'Iberville arrived on the Gulf Coast in 1699 and established their principal outpost at Mobile Bay three years later. Because of infrequent royal support, Iberville and his successor and younger brother Jean-Baptiste Le Moyne de Bienville used diplomacy to establish the regional status of their marginal colony. The French depended on gifts and exchange to find friends, but like the region itself the tokens of friendship had changed since Zamumo had received his gifts. Instead of the beads that Spaniards and English had found so useful in their early diplomacy, Mobile's colonial families quickly recognized that gunpowder had become "the most precious merchandise." The French did not hesitate to trade weapons or use force themselves, but the brothers Iberville and Bienville nonetheless set out to build Louisiana's influence on peace.[28]

Their first diplomatic mission aimed at encouraging an estimated four thousand Choctaw warriors of central Mississippi to end their long-standing conflict with the Chickasaws to their north, who, while half as large, had held their own thanks to English munitions. Hosting leaders from the two powerful nations in the spring of 1702, Iberville urged both peoples to join a French regional alliance against the English, who had no qualms about selling friends in the name of profit. As he asked the doubtful Chickasaws, "Have not the English themselves purchased some of your own brothers when your enemies have taken them prisoner? Have they not sold them into slavery to the Islands [of the West Indies] just as they have traded the Choctaw?" At the very least, Chickasaws could not deny that they had lost over a quarter of their men during the previous decade of raiding. The visitors agreed to the new alliance with the stipulation that the French provide them with their needed trade goods.[29] So impressive was Iberville's success, Alabamas visited him two months later to discuss French mediation in their war with the Mobilas. Most remarkable of all, they made their overture without any cloud of Tukabatchee and Atasi death threats. Apparently, even the Tukabatchees and Atasis were willing to see whether the French of Mobile might offer an attractive new route to power.

Unfortunately, French efforts often ran aground on the shifting shoals of poor funding and regional diplomacy. Alabamas' continuing animosities toward the Mobilas, combined with English inducements, encouraged the Alabamas to turn on their new friends a year after their 1702 visit. A decade of bitter French-Alabama conflict followed. The Chickasaw-Choctaw peace lasted until 1705, but French shortages and Carolinian generosity convinced the Chickasaws to resume raids on their old foes.[30] The English could take some credit for French troubles, but the one-dimensional nature of their power—a power rooted in war—encouraged even their closest Native friends to consider other options. As late as 1702, Ocheses still refused to abandon their ties to Apalachees and Spaniards. Although Ocheses mounted reprisals against the Apalachees' 1694 attack, significant numbers of both populations opposed this increasingly belligerent turn. When Chacatos under the command of the Lieutenant Francisco de Florencia ambushed Apalachicola hunters in 1699, the Apalachee leader Don Patricio de Hinachuba warned a trusted Spanish friend, "It is certain, sir, . . . that we will have to pay for these actions." Meanwhile, Ocheses continued to trade with Apalachees despite Spanish officials' efforts to prohibit mission Indians from trading horses, silver, or any other European imports. Although distance and conflict diminished the old trade ties, Apalachee objects still reached Ochese towns. Nonetheless, the trade remained risky. In the summer of 1702, three Apalachee traders were "cruelly killed and sacrificed" when they requested that Apalachicolas provide them with English muskets in exchange for the forbidden horses.[31]

The murders either constituted an ill-timed coincidence or reflected Ocheses' awareness of recent events in Europe. Disputes over the heir to the Spanish throne brought England into conflict with France and Spain in the spring of 1702. News of war reached Charles Town by late August and may have arrived among the Ocheses just before the unfortunate Apalachees.[32] In the late summer of 1702, Ocheses ambushed eight hundred Apalachee invaders intent on avenging the deaths of their ambassadors. The routed Apalachees left behind over three hundred casualties. Carolina's assembly affirmed the new belligerent turn with appropriations for gifts of military supplies to the Yamasees and Apalachees. Despite the expanding violence, Ocheses must have still retained some friendly sentiments. When the assembly authorized a joint English-Ochese expedition against the mission province in 1704, it expressly instructed the expedition's commander, James Moore, first "to endeavour to gain by all peaceable means possible the appalaches to our interest." Given Carolinians' obsessive fears of Apalachee invasions of the colony, who else but the Ocheses would have inspired the Carolina Assembly—an assembly closely tied to slave-trading interests—to eschew the blanket enslavement of all captives?[33]

Apalachees' and Ocheses' old ties of friendship and family yielded a confusing blend of moderation and terror. In January 1704, fifty English along with fifteen hundred Ocheses and other Indians invaded the province. In acts of violence that blended revenge, disdain for the Spanish, and calculated warnings to others who entertained resistance, the invaders burned the first town they encountered, torturing prisoners and desecrating the mission church. Other Apalachees avoided that fate with the help of timely ransoms or unbreachable fortifications, but many other towns surrendered, joining the invading force as it withdrew northward. A June invasion assisted by several dozen Apalachees convinced survivors to abandon the province before the end of August. Although many refugees fled to St. Augustine, most decided instead on a longer journey to Mobile, where they could expect to receive better supplies of food and weapons than at Spanish Pensacola. They explained to Bienville shortly after their arrival that the Spanish "did not give them any guns at all, but that the French gave them to all their allies."[34]

Like the Altamahas fleeing the Westos four decades earlier, slave raiding sent Apalachee's fortunate free in many directions. Approximately six hundred migrated north to settle lands on the Savannah River, across the river from present-day Augusta and astride the trading path between Charles Town and the Ocmulgee. Despite Carolinians' initial fears that they would turn on the colony with "barbarous cruelty," the Apalachee arrivals began new lives trading with their former partners and assailants, carrying packs for English traders heading hundreds of miles inland, and even joining them in raids on what remained of La Florida's Native and colonial population.[35] Though Apalachees had suffered defeat and many had been enslaved, the six hundred who inhabited towns on the Savannah doubtless owed some of that freedom to their Ochese captors.[36]

The removal, enslavement, and dispersal of the Apalachees erased the most immediate threat to Ocheses' well-being. The peoples of the Ocmulgee and their allies east and west had obtained a measure of security they probably had not enjoyed since the mid-seventeenth century and a position of influence that they could not have imagined a half-century earlier. The broad alliance improved its members' access to and protection from the powerful Carolinians and their violent trade. The battles for Florida's missions had ended successfully for Carolina's allies, but the war among empires continued, and Carolina's allies continued their hunts for slaves. Perhaps three thousand Chickasaws, Alabamas, and Tallapoosas, led by English colonists who came as traders and militia officers, invaded the Choctaw homeland in the fall of 1705, taking hundreds captive and burning towns and crops. Other combined forces of Ocheses, Alabamas, Chickasaws, and Tallapoosas unsettled the peoples of the lower Mississippi Valley while still others forced Chacatos and Apalachees at the six-year-old Spanish fort at Pensacola to seek new sanctuary in Mobile.[37]

Rather than slaves, though, the several hundred Indians and their English traders assaulted Pensacola in August 1707 to take the fort itself. Catching the defenders unaware, the attackers gained brief entry before being beaten back outside the walls. The ensuing month-long siege, during which the Indians employed siege trenches and grenades, failed to breach the stockade. When the invaders returned in November, twenty-one Carolinian traders and three Native war leaders, all on horseback, led a force of two hundred Alabamas and one hundred Tallapoosas, but suffering unanticipated losses, including one of the Natives' war leaders, the force abandoned the attack after a few days. Desultory raids and skirmishes continued for another three years, but the fort had survived the worst. The failure against the fort convinced many of Carolina's allies that, in the short term, they had more to gain and less to lose from slave raiding than siege warfare. The trader-lieutenants among them, more interested themselves in profits than imperialism, gladly obliged.[38]

The Indians' combined successes confirmed the wisdom of their alliances, but the continuing conflict nonetheless presented them with a serious problem, namely the Carolinians themselves. By the early 1700s, English on both sides of the Atlantic were crafting the ambitions, if not apparatus, of English imperial power.[39] In 1705, Ochese leaders, together with leaders from as far east as the Yamasees and as far west as the Alabamas, signed an accord with the Carolinians that was published in London as "The Humble Submission of the Kings, Princes, Generals, &c. to the Crown of England." The agreement, which made no mention of submission but did include an acknowledgment that "our Protection depends upon the *English*," seemed to contradict the purpose behind the alliances that Yamasees, Ocheses, Tukabatchees, and others had forged with one another. In their quest for European manufactures, perhaps they had simply avoided Spaniards' callous impositions only to become dependent mercenaries of the English.[40]

But the rhetoric, as the English well knew, hardly captured reality. Although Indian towns' continuing need to obtain power from outsiders encouraged both the slave trade and the wider process of colonization, towns retained significant influence over both. Ochese anxieties about

Apalachees provided Charles Town with an indispensable partner for the destruction of the missions in 1704, but no Carolinians could have imagined or desired that many Apalachees would be living freely on the doorstep of their colony. Even in the very act of signing the 1705 treaty, the participating leaders were collectively keeping the violent English at a distance, confining them to the red world of war that they promoted. The setting alone spoke volumes: Coweta, as Chekilli explained three decades later, was a red town. In addition, the twelve "humble" signatories were nearly all warriors. The English listed seven as a "Great Captain," "Captain," or "Head Warriour." And when the English failed to notice, the signatories did it for them. Four of the first seven men to sign the document went by some variant of the war title of "Hoboyetly." Named by their townspeople for their skill in war and their commitment to seek the power that lay beyond the town, the four men proclaimed their martial accomplishments and their qualifications for dealing with these people who sent soldiers as traders and whose favorite gift offerings were firearms, powder, and shot.[41]

Maintaining Peace amid War

The alliance seemed to keep the English at arm's length, but it is nonetheless tempting to compare Zamumo's gifts from de Soto with the Ocheses' gifts from Charles Town and see a story of declension. Even after we acknowledge the extent and power of the Ochese network of alliance and trade stretching from Chickasaw war partners to Tallapoosa and Yamasee friends and kin and then including (but not embracing) Charles Town's well-supplied and aggressive traders, it is hard not to notice a basic fact. The feather of peace in which Zamumo saw martial, procreative, and cosmological power was replaced by arms and ammunition, objects endowed with the power of death. But such an assessment would be grossly inadequate. As the conclusion of Alindja's story makes abundantly clear, war meant more than bloodshed. In fact, war, when properly conducted and contained, was a necessary foundation of peace.[42] Even when they were following the white path, the Cussitas of Chekilli's story had not shied from conflict. War could lead to peace, but, as with the older acts of turning a Gulf Coast shell, a sheet of Great Lakes copper, or even a feather into a symbol of power, the transformation required labor. In this case, however, the labor was not just of craft production but of social reorganization.

And the labor of extracting peace from the slave trade was often tremendous. Even when they did not require war, the new patterns of exchange reworked the very foundations of southeastern lives. Trade with the English and French continued to involve deerskins, and with the increase of hunting during the winter months when deerskins were thickest and most valuable, Natives abandoned their labor-intensive winter homes, with their floors slightly below ground level, in favor of unexcavated homes that could be readily abandoned as the hunt moved from one location to another. Other results appeared inside these new structures. As hunters of people and deer, men were the principal recipients of the proceeds of exchange. The weapons, tools, clothing, and ornamentation that symbolized success and made hunting and warfare possible were now of European manufacture. Women probably experienced smaller material changes. New tools such as metal hoes and pots and new cultigens such as West African watermelons and Spanish peaches supplemented but did not fundamentally alter Native diets or women's work. Even as men abandoned tools of their own making for those of European manufacture, and even though their male relatives could readily acquire copper kettles from European traders, women continued to craft their own pottery, shaping and decorating their own creations in much the same manner as their mothers. In the midst of a new colonial region, the labor of adaptation and conservation was not divided equally.[43]

Women's adjustments appeared in other parts of their lives. As the ones who, according to one trader, "[wore] the breechess" in the household, prepared deerskins for sale, and decided on the fate of captives, women played instrumental roles in the trade. They also became involved on a more intimate level. The success of Woodward's visit to the Cowetas in 1686 owed much to his marriage to one of Juiaui's nieces. Less noteworthy traders followed his lead. "The English Traders are seldom without an Indian Female for his Bed-fellow," explained the traveler John Lawson, who visited the North Carolina piedmont in 1701. In a matrilineal and matrilocal society, close ties to a woman made a trader part of a family and helped this foreigner learn local languages and customs. Ochese women gained some renown in the Southeast for their involvement in trade, whether through the "scandelous libertys" that caught the attention of English correspondents or the food and shelter that satisfied the more prosaic needs of their visitors. But Ochese women were not the only ones to take advantage of the "libertys" of English commerce. Similar activities among women along the lower Mississippi River led one old Natchez leader to lament the passing of the old times, when "our women were more laborious and less vain than they are now." Women as well as men participated in the new economy of ostentation, and when elders fretted, it may have reflected less the loss of local industry and more the end of monopolies of prestige based on age, ancestry, and gender.[44]

This shift placed unwelcome strains on the power of leaders and men in general. Instead of collecting the best of the hunt and harvest from their followers as their ancestors had done, *micos* like those among the Tallapoosas cleared the communal fields with the rest of the town and received only the first kills of each hunting season. For a champion of centralized authority like the Carolinian trader and diplomat Thomas Nairne, "Nothing is more contemptable than the authority of these Chiefs." At a time when warfare and trade provided ready access to the symbols of power, few leaders, even those responsible for peace, could ignore the opportunity for advancement that war provided. Chickasaws' respect for their leaders declined because they ceased to "be a Counterpoise to the fury of the Warriors." By failing to advocate for peace, "the chiefs' Authority is dwindled away to nothing . . . and the head Military Officers carry all the sway."[45] In a land of war, the men of war seemed to gain the most. But leaders and followers, men and women did not gain or lose power in a simple zero-sum equation. Intensified warfare did not simply alter the balance of power in Native societies; it changed the scales entirely. The anxiety that accompanied the growing likelihood of enslavement or death from wars for captives must have troubled all but the most heedless of warriors. Slave raiding was a deadly business. Thirty years of raiding and trading had transformed the Yamasees from refugees into a formidable nation of warriors and traders, but the Anglican missionary Francis Le Jau learned that between 1702 and 1713 this fearsome people lost half of their eight hundred warriors in slave raids.[46]

For some fortunate Indians, war could also be about peace. War and trade required broad adjustments, but the proceeds of conflict provided men and women alike with new tools for harmony. For one, slaves, the very proceeds of war, continued to seal the peace between those who exchanged them. And when Nairne reported that Chickasaw "ladies are so pleased to look sparkling in the dances, with the Clothes bought from the English," he cared only about whether Chickasaw women were "altogether of our party." But these were not simple baubles that symbolized Chickasaws' dependence on the English or fascination with their things. Nor did they just add new aesthetics and new sounds to old ceremonies. By making their clothes more beautiful, English beads and ornaments enabled Chickasaw women to take the proceeds and losses of men's combat and direct that work toward the critical endeavor of honoring and placating the powers of the spiritual and physical worlds. If Carolinians prized the trader-alchemists who could turn lead and steel into silver, Chickasaws and other allies celebrated communal efforts to turn red into white.[47]

Success in war also provided not just the trade goods but also the prestige necessary to preserve peace with friends. Among the Chickasaws, Tallapoosas, and probably others, when two towns or clans decided to forge a firm peace, the first appointed a man from the second who had gained "Esteem in the Wars." This *fanni mico* or squirrel king was a "protector or Friend" whose "business is to take up breaches" between two clans or two nations. Even the English, purveyors of this new war, joined such friendships. Cossitee, who was identified as "the Great Captain of the Ocphuscas" when he signed the "Humble Submission" with the English in 1705, became in 1707 the *fanni mico* joining his town of Okfuskee with the English of Charles Town. The "Great Captain" was a perfect candidate for the new relationship, and so was his partner. Thomas Nairne, Carolina's emissary to the western Indians, had also gained renown among southeastern peoples for his success in the slave trade, joining attacks on the Spanish missions and later raids far south into the Florida peninsula after the destruction of Apalachee. Also like Cossitee, Nairne hoped to harness this bloodshed and the trade it supported to ensure the greater strength and security of his people. The Scot was a tireless advocate for regulation of colonists' trade with the Indians, and when he and other Carolinian legislators finally secured passage of a regulatory law in 1707, he was appointed the first agent to oversee its enforcement. As the leader of a delegation on its way to visit the Tallapoosas, Chickasaws, and, eventually, the Choctaws, Nairne "designed to promote peace." He came with a colonial commission for Cossitee as an affirmation of Cossitee's authority and an insinuation of his dependence on Charles Town. Cossitee accepted it as the establishment of a white path between his town and Nairne's. Okfuskees and Carolinians remained allied for the purposes of war, but they now also shared people committed to a new bond of peace.[48]

But most peoples did not pursue such ties of peace with Carolina's soldier-traders, and part of the reason lay in Nairne's own motivations. Carolina's Indian agent sought to reform the trade not out of a respect for Indians' desire to affirm alliances and share power as much as in the hopes that a peaceful trade would build a stronger empire. His map of the Southeast, sketched during 1707 and printed in 1711, traced the English trading paths that justified Carolinian claims to the Mississippi Valley. Carolinian expansion was hitched to packhorses laden with trade goods, but it was also part of a much larger imperial vision forming in London. As a Scot, Nairne likely celebrated the Act of Union that joined Scotland and England in 1707 as new reason for devotion to a British, and not simply English, empire. His peace mission to the west formed part of this imperial effort. By strengthening Charles Town's ties with the Tallapoosas and Chickasaws and by making peace with the Choctaws, Nairne hoped to forge the alliance that would enable him to lead an Indian invasion force against French Mobile, destroying the key to French Louisiana and ensuring that "the English American Empire may not be unreasonably Crampt up." It was why he understood Cossitee's installation as *fanni mico* as a "coronation" that simultaneously established Cossitee's authority over the Okfuskees and his subordination to Britain. It was also why he understood the ties of friendship between Indians and English as rooted not in the ceremonial ties of peace that brought towns together but in the commercial ties of trade that bound the growing empire. As he understood Indians' love for Europeans, "They Effect them most who sell best cheap."[49]

Despite Nairne's confident claims, Bienville could still boast in 1708, "[The Chickasaws] are more attached to us than to [the English]" even though "I do not give them any presents at all." Nairne himself acknowledged that same year that the English could not shake French influence among the Chickasaws without "a much better trade and the reputation of a far greater Courage than the French." This "better trade" depended on both generous gifts and fair prices, and the French in Louisiana were especially well suited to such generosity. Because Louisiana was on the westernmost fringes of the French Atlantic economy, even Indian slaves served them primarily as symbols of their relations with Indian allies rather than as commodities to sell to the labor-hungry sugar colonies of the Caribbean. But French success depended on more than this "good faith in trading" that an older and wiser Bienville continued to champion in 1734. It also depended on the peace that the French provided and the English threatened. When Nairne noted that "2 old [Chickasaw] men of some note" continued to visit Mobile, he was witnessing how the peace that Chickasaws associated with age was something they also associated with the French. Such attitudes were not confined to Carolina's westernmost allies. "All the Indians like the French much better than they do the English," boasted Bienville to France's minister of the marine in 1706.[50]

Bienville built these alliances as he did only because he knew that Louisiana's allies and enemies determined the fate of the colony. "He gives assurance," reported his superior in France, "that when this colony is solidly established that will no longer be necessary." Nonetheless, Bienville's expedience provided Indians with important sources of peace for their towns. It enabled Alabamas to explore the possibilities of alliance with the French in 1702 without suffering the threats that they encountered for entertaining friendship with the much weaker Spanish in 1694. It encouraged Carolina's Chickasaw allies to consider peace rather than war with French and Choctaws. As later events would make even more apparent, it preserved the French outpost at Mobile from the thousands of warriors that Nairne dreamed would descend the Alabama River against it. Other scholars have noted that Nairne failed in part because Carolinians' political squabbling kept him from returning to Indian

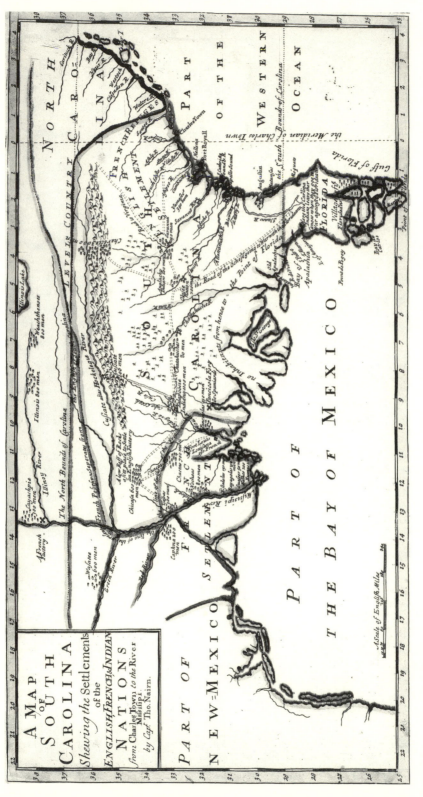

Figure 5. Thomas Nairne, "A Map of South Carolina Shewing the Settlements of the English, French, and Indian Nations from Charles Town to the River Missisipi by Capt. Tho. Nairn" (1711). The territory of "Carolina" is marked in light gray, with the borders of Louisiana and Florida outlined in dark gray. The double dashed lines are trading paths. Courtesy of the Huntington Library.

towns for the rest of the war and because slave traders could encourage more profitable and less complicated operations against France's Native allies rather than its fortified outposts. What they have heeded less was the fact that even the Chickasaws, Carolina's staunchest allies west of the Chattahoochee River, had no interest in destroying a French people willing to stake their power on the white path and powerful enough to defend it. Louisianans and their resources were invaluable to those of the region whose power depended on a careful balance between peace and war.[51]

Disease, war, migration, new materials, and trading alliances with Indians and Europeans all profoundly altered the ways Native peoples related to their fellow townspeople and their more distant friends and enemies. Peoples of the Chattahoochee had allied with Yamasees and together they had joined the Tukabatchees, Abecas, and Alabamas to the west. They sought to make the most of Carolinians' advantages without suffering the worst of their abuses. The peace they affirmed in 1705 suggests the outlines of this effort, and the trade and diplomacy they pursued confirms it. The results often took dramatic and unanticipated forms. The indecisive Carolinian and Indian siege and raids on Pensacola in 1707, for example, left a distinct impression on the Spanish. Reporting on the progress of Spanish arms early in 1708, New Spain's viceroy, the duque de Albuquerque, took particular interest in the Indian attackers. "Their form of fighting, although disorderly and undisciplined," he noted "was in the use of firearms very unlike Indians."[52]

As the most powerful figure in the American hemisphere north of Lima and resident of the continent's largest city, the viceroy was more than familiar with Indians, but the Indians he encountered on the streets of Mexico City and most of those he knew through reports from the rest of New Spain had been conquered Spanish subjects for nearly two centuries. By 1708, they occupied the lower rungs of New Spain's social, racial, and economic ladders. The putative Indians attacking Pensacola, in contrast, skillfully used weapons and military tactics that had once been the sole domain of Europeans. Had the duke been familiar with the previous four decades of correspondence between St. Augustine and Madrid, he would have recognized these tactics as one of many indigenous adaptations to the increasingly violent and commercially connected Southeast. The intrigued viceroy may have been frustrated by Indians' capacity to use shifting alliances and broad networks of exchange to maintain their stability despite marked change. He would likely have considered chiefs who could not command, women who wore English woolens, and warring towns that became newfound friends to be further proof of these Natives' lack of "Indianness." In their struggle to make sense of their new world, however, these Indians were not seeking his opinion.[53]

What mattered more were the opinions debated in each council house or each town square. As they had for generations, leaders and followers knew that outsiders were crucial to the strength and security of one's *talwa*. As Zamumo proclaimed to de Soto when he received his feather, friends brought power. From many friends came many kinds of power. Where the British brought the power of war, the French and, to a lesser extent, Spaniards brought the power of peace. More important than any of these were Native neighbors. Yamasees, Ocheses, Tallapoosas, and others sought each other out because the people of other *talwas* brought the trust and security that could only come from extended kin ties and, as Alindja recalled centuries later, the knowledge of the sacred medicines that ensured stability and strength. Exchange and alliance did more than protect *talwas* that had once fled the terror of slave raids. They enabled some to maintain balance at home at a time when violence reigned abroad. They also enabled their architects to influence the fortunes of the empires that now shared their region. And when English soldier-traders threatened this equilibrium in the years after 1707, Carolinians learned to their horror that the war cries of these allies could shake southeastern ground just as potently as Alindja's Tukabatchees had.

Chapter 6

The Yamasee War: Trade Reformed, a Region Reoriented

And they say, also, that about this period [when the Creeks were settling at the Okmulgee Old Fields] the English were establishing the colony of Carolina, and the Creeks, understanding that they were a powerful, warlike people, sent deputies to Charleston, their capital, offering them their friendship and alliance, which was accepted, and in consequence thereof, a treaty took place between them, which has remained inviolable to this day: they never ceased war against the numerous and potent bands of Indians, who then surrounded and cramped the English plantations, as the Savannas, Ogeeches, Wapoos, Santees, Yamasees, Utinas, Icosans, Paticas, and others, until they had extirpated them.

—William Bartram, 1792[1]

When the naturalist William Bartram heard the above story in 1774, Creeks had many good reasons to emphasize the strength of their relationship with the British. A year before his tour through the Southeast, Creek leaders sold a large tract of land west of the Savannah River, and a number of disgruntled warriors were attacking colonists who built farms on the newly transferred land.[2] It was with the looming threat of war that his Creek travel companions told him a story of how the Creeks had migrated from the west, settling at the Ocmulgee Old Fields (near Ochese Creek) shortly before the British founded Charles Town. They concluded the story by insisting on their "inviolable" friendship with their colonial neighbors. The Creeks' larger point was clear: the two peoples' shared origins, like their shared present, were inextricably bound. It is hard not to wonder, though, about the collective amnesia that made such clarity possible.

Not only did Bartram's teachers forget their ancestors' close friendship with the Yamasees, but they neglected to mention how they had once before abandoned their friendship with the Carolinians. Troubling questions had surfaced in the years after 1707, as Natives throughout the region reconsidered the role of Carolinian soldier-traders in their worlds. For many, the answer was war. The so-called Yamasee War of 1715–18 involved a loose and at times divergent association of peoples that destroyed the slave trade and Carolinians' pretensions of regional hegemony. Native belligerents' subsequent negotiations with the British, French, and Spaniards enabled many of them to replace the violence of the slave trade with relationships more closely related to older Mississippian norms based on gifts and diplomacy.[3]

The transformations in Indian-European exchange relations encouraged colonists and Natives to reorganize their communities as well. Two groups, Carolinians on the one hand and their former Yamasee, Ochese, Tallapoosa, Abeca, and Alabama allies on the other, were especially prominent in the regional reorganization that followed the war. Carolinians mobilized to overthrow their proprietary regime and insisted that officials in London become more involved in the colony's reconstruction. The reform of Indian relations figured prominently in Carolina's recovery, and these reforms encouraged the consolidation of a new nation that Carolinians called "Creek." The English neologism might suggest that European imaginations rather than Indian realities inspired the new name, but Creeks also played a role. Together, the Ocheses of central Georgia, the Tallapoosas and Alabamas of central Alabama, and the Abecas of northern Alabama had fought in war and, together, they crafted a new peace. Together, they also abandoned their Yamasee friends. This last act caused intense disagreement, but Creeks debated with rather than killed or ignored each other because their unity provided the best protection in a dangerous postwar landscape, where Cherokees from the north had become devoted enemies and the Carolinians remained untrustworthy friends. Alabamas, Ocheses, and their allies trusted one another because they continued to agree on the primacy of local autonomy even as they vigorously debated how to preserve it. From this blend of cooperation and debate, a new Creek nation emerged.[4] Yamasees, opposed to any peace with the Carolinians, did not participate in these foundational debates. Out of this Creek-Yamasee rupture, one of the most marked shifts caused by the war, lay an uncomfortable piece of Creek history and identity that Bartram's Creek companions preferred to forget.

Questions

"It is certain the Indians are very cruel to one another," observed the Anglican missionary Francis Le Jau in 1708, "but is it not to be feared some white men living or trading among them do foment and increase that Bloody Inclination in order to get Slaves?" Le Jau asked this question of his superiors in London in order to rebuke the traders who refused to share their trading paths with ministers hoping to spread the Good News. More than complaining about sour grapes, though, Le Jau believed that unscrupulous traders, concerned more with profit than fairness, threatened to bring the violence of the trade upon the colony itself. Despite the urgency of his question, Le Jau had no answer. "I must leave that to the Consideration of my betters," he continued, "as well as how to remedy the evil practices of the same Traders in oppressing those poor heathens; but still I must admire their sobriety [and] patience, content in their Condition and no care for time to come but to provide Corn against Winter."[5]

Le Jau's closing observation offers a salutary reminder that amid the upheavals of the slave trade, many old routines remained as they had been in Zamumo's day. Women still cultivated the corn that sustained their families. Men still hunted and made war. Towns still celebrated cosmic cycles of life, death, and renewal. Nonetheless, for all of Natives' apparent success at maintaining local balance in a region of turmoil, Le Jau could well have asked his question of his Native neighbors. Carolinian trade goods were often purchased at the high costs of slave raiders who lost their lives, and the traders who sold the tools, cloth, ornaments, and weapons that conferred power were becoming increasingly volatile in their dealings with their so-called partners, especially the colony's Yamasee neighbors. Traders killed Yamasees' horses, stole their canoes, and burned their storehouses. Others built farms and ranches on Yamasee lands. One trader forced Yamasees to build him a house while another had the gall to steal two guns from a widow. Alcohol became a more subtle challenge to the integrity of the town. Traders met returning hunters outside their towns, buying deerskins and slaves cheaply and enabling hunters to squander their proceeds unencumbered by family interest and public restraint.[6]

Yamasees and their western allies might have been even more alarmed to learn that traders were merely exhibiting the symptoms of a larger English culture, where those in authority, whether judges, husbands, or slave masters, defined their authority through violence. And traders were themselves in delicate positions of authority. Thanks to their personal connections and ample trading stocks, they possessed significant power in southeastern town squares. Nonetheless, they remained vulnerable because their power depended on a growing market economy and credit network centered on London. Reputation provided crucial collateral in such credit networks, and because of their relative poverty and their preference for life among Indians (often to flee financial or other legal troubles in Charles Town), traders were not always the most reliable debtors. Creditors rarely treat risky loans generously, so many traders faced a constant fear that debts would land them in court or even jail. Whether seizing goods from or beating ostensible Indian partners, these harried traders were often using the tools they understood to avoid the fate they feared.[7]

Of course, Yamasees could address traders' transgressions through a Native system of retributive justice, one in which injured parties could appeal to their kin to seek vengeance on the clan of a perpetrator. They did not pursue such recourses, though, preferring instead to complain to the Commission of the Indian Trade, which was created by the Carolina legislature in 1707 to regulate the trade that defined Carolinian-Native relations. Yamasees never explained why they subjected themselves to Carolinian norms of justice, but we can infer several reasons, none of which boded well for Yamasees' opinion of the colony or its traders. In the decade after 1702, Yamasees witnessed their neighbors' military successes against both imperial rivals. They saw growing numbers of colonists clearing wetlands to grow rice, a crop whose value seemed to supercede that of the lives of slaves who grew it. They saw large ships visit Charles Town with increasing frequency, especially after 1705, when the first large shipments of rice and Apalachee slaves began to leave the province. They probably had no idea that such commercial growth would make Charles Town the second busiest port in North America by 1715. They probably did not know that the Indian agent Thomas Nairne, the Indian trade commission's appointed representative, visited Chickasaw lands with the eye of one who hoped to farm them. Perhaps they did not know these things, but they realized in some way that the colony's power on the coast and its influence in the interior meant that Yamasees would subject traders to kin-based notions of justice at their peril. Unfortunately, the commissioners were often unwilling or unable to punish these traders who were both valuable emissaries and brazenly independent. And so while the commissioners could force some traders to return stolen goods or people, they failed to punish murderers and struggled to compensate for thefts. Le Jau's question about the violence of slave raiding seemed to apply to its sponsors as well.[8]

Yamasees were also uncomfortable witnesses of the ways that the same traders who undermined southeastern *talwas* as havens of peace also weakened them as makers of war. With the outbreak of the Tuscarora War in North Carolina, Altamahas and many others witnessed once again the dangerous violence of Charles Town's soldier-traders. In September 1711, bands of Tuscaroras frustrated with traders' abuses and colonial intrusion into their lands attacked their North Carolinian neighbors. Charles Town authorized two separate expeditions of colonial and Native volunteers to head north. Catawbas of the South Carolina piedmont joined Yamasees to make up the largest Native contingents, but Apalachees, Ocheses, and even some Tallapoosas and Alabamas also participated. All gained valuable opportunities to acquire slaves and sobering lessons about their colonial allies. To many Indians, Carolinian warfare was as ruthless as it was senseless, especially in the hands of John Barnwell, the leader of the first expedition in the winter and spring of 1712. When the Indians and colonists breached the walls of the Tuscarora town of Norhunta, Indians sought out captives and plunder while the colonists subdued two blockhouses inside the walls. Barnwell boasted that it was a "terror to our own heathen friends to behold us, the word was revenge." The pointless bloodletting seemed horrific enough, but Barnwell also seemed to have little regard for the blood of his own troops, who suffered twelve casualties in the unnecessary assault. War lost its luster when it drained life instead of augmenting power, but Carolinians apparently preferred such an unbalanced bargain. James Moore Jr., led a second expedition in 1713 to crush the last militants. Carolina's allies all profited from their captives, but they had also gained lessons about the dangers of opposing the British and, more disturbing, the bloodshed that accompanied helping them.[9]

Because the alliance stretched from Port Royal to the forks of the Alabama, not all members shared Yamasees' growing concerns. Though the unpredictable violence of traders encouraged many allies to turn to war in 1715, peoples at the western end of this alliance network had crucial alternatives that diminished their anxieties and would temper their involvement in the coming war. Mobile's commander, Jean-Baptiste Le Moyne de Bienville, had long recognized his colony's precarious position, so he tirelessly advocated peace with the Indians. As early as 1702 Carolinians had feared that Tallapoosas and their neighbors might "apply them Selves to the french for a Trade," so in 1712, Carolinian traders sought to end Bienville's efforts and their worries by destroying his colony with a force of Tallapoosas, Abecas, and Alabamas, but, much to the Louisianans' surprise, when canoes descended the Alabama River in March, they carried peace emissaries instead of warriors. Alabamas and their companions came not for gifts; Bienville could scarcely outfit his soldiers. Most likely they came for the peace that the British threatened and that the French, thanks to their relative weakness, promoted. British plans, despite the military alliances that backed them, were thwarted as much by Indians' need for balance as by Bienville's capacity to recognize and exploit that fact.[10]

Western Indians' quest for peace depended heavily on the young French leader, however. When Antoine de la Mothe, Sieur de Cadillac, arrived as the new governor in the colony in 1713, his obsession with serving the commercial interests of Antoine Crozat, the director of the colony's new proprietary company, meant that he obsessed more about chimerical mines than the colony's real dependence on Native allies. The new governor withheld gifts and rarely took up Bienville's mantle of peacemaker among the colony's neighbors.[11] In the middle of 1715, Bienville complained to his superiors that the new governor had "greatly alienated the minds of all the Indians": Tallapoosas, Alabamas, and others were again contemplating war with the French.[12] Crozat and Cadillac realized quickly that not even 600,000 livres (in a colony where Bienville drew a salary of 1,800 livres each year and a common soldier was allotted 108) and a heavy-handed administration could construct a colony out of lands that Indians still controlled and that French ships could rarely supply.[13]

French troubles confounded Bienville's peace initiatives, but, paradoxically, a declining slave trade only increased Indians' anxieties. The very diseases and warfare that halved the Yamasees' population had also reduced the populations of potential captives between La Florida and the Mississippi Valley. Worse, the British were less interested in purchasing those that their allies did offer for sale. In 1713, the Treaty of Utrecht ended the War of the Spanish Succession. At about this same time, Britain's northern colonies began prohibiting the importation of Indian slaves, largely out of fear that these products of war and revolt were themselves, in the words of a 1712 Massachusetts law, dangerously "malicious, surly, and revengeful."[14] Carolinians had lost the diplomatic sanction and commercial incentive for sponsoring raids against La Florida's and Louisiana's Natives, but the slave traders' declining interest in promoting war may have convinced Indians less of Britons' newfound pacifism and more of their continuing desire to destroy Indians' power. Even as Carolinians' most lucrative export declined in value and volume, Indians' debts did not. The Yamasees, probably the most heavily indebted of the colony's trading partners, owed the astronomical equivalent of about one hundred thousand deerskins, or roughly what the colony exported on a very good year.[15]

Yamasees experienced violence and debt as a local crisis, but through conversation they recognized it as a regional one. As Yamasee and Ochese ambassadors explained to the governor in St. Augustine after the war broke out, they all suffered trader abuses, but "they did not completely understand until learning that in all of their towns [*lugares*] they were experiencing the same thing."[16] And understanding brought alarm as well as commiseration because the allies realized that "the English traders, whom the Governor of San Jorge [Charles Town] placed there as lieutenants, . . . took some children, and hiding them from their parents, they boarded them on ships and sent them to be sold in other lands as slaves."[17] Among those raising such alarms was a powerful

Coweta war leader that Carolinians called "the Emperor Brims."[18] Thanks to the influence of men like him, such news reached far beyond the paths connecting Ocheses and Yamasees. In 1715, when Alexander Longe, himself a fugitive from Carolina justice, warned the Cherokees "that the Einglish was going to make wars with them and that they did design to kill all their head warriors," Cherokees had already heard the news "from their friendly Indians."[19] And so the chilling news spread.[20]

But was it true? Unfortunately, there was no way to be certain. By the end of June, the people best qualified to answer this question, the Commissioners of the Indian Trade and their agent, Thomas Nairne, were too embroiled in internecine conflicts with political rivals to bother with Indians. Meanwhile, traders passed through the towns as part of a region-wide census. Were colonists enumerating their future slaves?[21] And then traders killed Brims's "heir" during a dispute over debts. While the Carolinians remained inscrutable, if not belligerent, Ocheses and Yamasees met at the Yamasee town of Pocotaligo to discuss their debts early in the winter of 1714–15. There, Brims made a radical proposal. As his emissaries explained to St. Augustine's governor, Francisco Córcoles y Martínez in July 1715, Brims thought that the best way to avoid future violence from traders and the continued enslavement of children would be "to offer to the English payment for the muskets, arms, munitions, and other things that they had given in the form of pigs, rice, maize, chickens, lard, and other fruits of the land and [also] skins of deer, otter, and beavers because they saw the impossibility of repaying them [*darles sattisfación*] in the form of Indian slaves brought from lands of Spanish dominions."[22] More than an effort to change the objects of exchange, Brims's idea would change the very foundations of Carolina's relations with its Native allies. No longer would Carolinian traders have reason to lead their Native partners to war; no longer would warriors risk their lives in pursuit of the blankets, bells, and weapons that conferred power and prestige. Brims was in effect seeking to replace a Carolinian trade based on war with an older set of relations that Apalachicolas had enjoyed with Spaniards before 1685, when deerskins and corn acquired many of these objects.[23]

Carolina's governor, Charles Craven, apparently responded favorably to the proposal and even promised to restrain the traders who threatened Carolina's relations of trade and friendship. Unfortunately, as Brims's emissaries later explained to Córcoles, some Indians also believed that "he commanded the fortification of plantations and the construction of stockades in Carolina, by which they realized it was true that they [the Carolinians] planned to enslave them by force."[24] Contrary to what Brims told Córcoles, Carolinians were making no preparations for war before April 1715. Whether Brims was lying or mis-

informed is less important than the fact that many Indians now associated the uncertainty of their old trade relationship with the violence of
their imminent enslavement. As more people questioned the Carolinians' ambitions, the intertown alliances begun in 1685 appeared as prudent as their devotion to war seemed inadequate. In early April 1715,
the wife of the trader William Bray (herself probably a Yamasee) learned
from a dissident Yamasee that "the Creek Indians had a Design to cut
of the Traders first and then to fall on the Settlement, and that it was
very near."[25] Meanwhile, runners from the Ochese towns discussed the
possibility of war with all who would listen. In each town square, they
added another knot to the deerskin strands that symbolized this new alliance of the anxious. And in this detail, too, lay persistent patterns. The
attendants in every town square shared bonds of exchange, alliance, and
influence that made them Yamasee as well as Altamaha, Ochese as well
as Coweta, Tallapoosa as well as Tukabatchee. Many knew each other as
allies, but as they sought to thwart Charles Town's perceived ambitions,
the supporters of war in each town square still tied their own new knot.
Indians' anxieties bound them regionally, but they still acted locally.[26]

Answers

The alarming news from Bray and others spurred the Commissioners of
the Indian Trade to dispatch their agent, Thomas Nairne, as well as his
rival and predecessor, John Wright. Several other traders accompanied
the ill-matched pair to the Yamasees' principal town of Pocotaligo. On
April 14, 1715, they explained to the Yamasees that Governor Craven
would meet with them, the Ocheses, Apalachees, and Yuchis and offer
"them all sort of satisfaction for the wrongs [that] had been done to
them." The reassurances pleased the Yamasees. If they could gain reassurances for their questions, if they could reform the old relationship
through negotiation, so much the better. If only. After the Carolinians
had retired for the night, Wright returned to threaten the Yamasee warriors that the British actually intended to enslave them all, even the men,
"for he said that the men of the Yamasses were like women." The threats
revived dark fears, and dawn brought no comfort. Before sunrise on
Good Friday, April 15, Wright, Nairne, and their companions were
roused by terrifying war cries and the sight of Yamasee warriors painted
red and black, the colors of war and death. One trader escaped to
spread the alarm, and another was forced to hide temporarily near the
town. He reached safety with grim testimony of Carolinian captives tortured and killed. The unfortunate Nairne, deeply respected even in captivity, suffered for three days before he was allowed to die.[27]

Once begun, the war quickly consumed the colony and the region.

The Yamasees struck out immediately against Port Royal, a town whose traders most immediately threatened their lives and whose farmers and ranchers had long coveted their lands. Residents of the town, alerted by one of the escaped traders, quickly took shelter aboard a ship at anchor in the harbor. Yamasees destroyed the town, livestock, and plantations, taking all they could carry. Meanwhile, other townspeople throughout the Southeast debated whether to join the Yamasees. Ocheses were likely the first to enter the fray. As Abecas recalled a decade later, "We were Brought into it By the Tallapoops Coweetawes and other of the Lower People [that is, Ocheses]."[28] Ocheses killed the traders among their towns and then hunted others who were receiving sanctuary elsewhere. Coweta warriors visiting the Chickasaws managed to kill four Carolinians, while two traders under Cherokee protection died at the hands of stealthy Abecas.[29] Within two months of the Good Friday killings, ninety of Carolina's one hundred or so traders died at the hands of their embittered partners.[30]

The spreading violence revealed common ties and common uncertainties. Cherokees in one town gathered six Carolinians together for protection. After celebrating and feasting with the traders, they shot them. One escaped with the horrible tale.[31] Hundreds of miles west, Chickasaws gathered a number of English traders into a cabin where they, and a misidentified Frenchman, were also shot.[32] Another house provided fleeting sanctuary for traders in Apalachicola town. According to Creek conversations with William Bartram in 1773, many traders fled at the first news of war to Apalachicola town, a "white" town whose ceremonial role was to end, not begin, war. Unfortunately, according to Bartram, "whilst the chiefs were assembled in council, deliberating on ways and means to protect them, the Indians in multitudes surrounded the house and set fire to it." No trader survived. Forty years after the killings, Apalachicolas, believing that the blood of eighteen or more traders still haunted their town, abandoned their homes. Some sought relatives in Florida while most migrated up the Chattahoochee River.[33] The same trading paths that enabled Indians to share their anxiety before the war remained busy after its outbreak. Chickasaws, Cherokees, and Apalachicolas shared stories, confirmed fears, and ensured that many of their victims, burned or shot in supposed sanctuaries, met similar fates.

Carolinians also communicated with one another, but they did so primarily on the increasingly crowded streets of Charles Town or in plaintive letters to those beyond the sea. By early May, news had reached Charles Town that nearly all traders among the Indians were dead. "Enemies surround us . . . from the borders of St. Augustin to Cape Fear," lamented Le Jau. "We have not one nation for us."[34] By the end of May, colonists had abandoned all but the most well-defended plantations for the safety and squalor of Charles Town, where starvation and disease became imminent threats.[35] One resident, George Rodd, begged his unnamed patron in London, "If you judge that nothing will be done for us, I pray you will arrange for the governor and council to permit me to return to England."[36] Those who could fled on any ship willing to take them.

The Indians had humbled the region's most powerful people, but they killed, tortured, and burned in their disparate efforts to resolve particular problems. Although they seemed to strike their common enemy in unison, Yamasees and their allies eventually recognized that each had their own answers to the questions of the previous decade. It is in these disparate answers that various peoples laid foundations for the postwar region. Despite their early involvement in the war, for instance, most Cherokees and Chickasaws decided that Carolinians were vital to their future security. In contrast, most Yamasee towns thought exactly the opposite. Ocheses and their Tallapoosa, Abeca, and Alabama allies to the west agreed with both of these apparently irreconcilable answers. They did not trust the Carolinians and rejected the violence that underpinned Carolinian trade, but they still valued the colonists' power and the things they offered. So they reconfigured their alliance with one another to protect themselves from the traders they desired. Carolinians, for their part, still wanted to recover their old alliances, and so they, too, adjusted their commerce and colony. All of these stories are related, but they must be told separately.

The first reforms came from those who most wanted peace. Cherokees and Chickasaws both opted to negotiate with the Carolinians by the end of 1715. Because the inhabitants of the mountains had only recently become close trading partners with the colony and because the Chickasaws had received reassurances of Carolinian friendship in the fall of 1714, neither collection of towns felt particularly threatened by the threat of Carolinian abuses or enslavement. In late November, a number of Cherokee leaders visited Charles Town to offer peace, exchanging clothes with Carolinian leaders, according to Francis Le Jau, as symbols of "reconciliation and friendship." For their part, Chickasaw leaders informed the Carolinians in December that they opposed the killings and wished to meet with Governor Charles Craven and keep "their friendship which they had before."[37] But the old friendship had died with the traders. While southeastern Natives reconsidered their relations with Charles Town, Carolinians were making adjustments of their own. In mid-1716 the Commons House of Assembly enacted new trade regulations that limited most colonial contact with Indians to several trading houses, or "factories," situated at various forts that also protected strategic points of entry to the colony. Savannah Town, near modern Augusta,

Georgia, was the most distant of these and the one most important for the Cherokees and all peoples living west of the Savannah River. The "factors" who ran these posts served as traders and diplomats, but they performed both duties as public servants more than as private entrepreneurs. Even after the monopoly collapsed in 1718 under Indian and Carolinian complaints, it left behind a fundamentally altered commercial and political landscape: however important to the colony, private traders never returned inland as powerful colonial emissaries.[38]

For their part, Cherokees and Chickasaws had reforms of their own to suggest. The legislature's most striking and longest lasting reform was also the product of Cherokee expectations. When Cherokee and Carolinian leaders exchanged clothes in November 1715, they laid the groundwork for negotiations the following spring that fixed new trading prices for all goods "as they are always to be sold." Despite Carolinian reticence, Cherokees also insisted on gifts. A year later, the colony's agent complained to the Board of Trade that "the last time the Charachees were here, they Insulted us to the last degree. And Indeed by their demands (with which we were forced to comply) made us their Tributaries." Exchange linked people at peace, but like La Florida's Indians in the 1620s who accepted Spanish gifts as "tribute," Cherokees used the new friendship to assert a new dominance over their beleaguered partners. Equally important, the new price agreements, which would last largely unchanged for five decades, enabled Indians to purchase more with a deerskin after the war than they could before it. By the end of 1717 Chickasaws had negotiated prices equal to those the Cherokees paid. Although traders to the Chickasaws traveled further than to the Cherokees, prices would mark equivalence of friendship rather than costs of transport. Thanks to the Yamasee War, Carolina's trading partners made a crucial modification to Carolinian trade practices, one that hearkened back to the Mississippian protocols that Zamumo had introduced to the Spaniards.[39]

While Chickasaws and Cherokees looked for reform in Charles Town, Yamasees sought redress in St. Augustine. Carolinians' summertime counterattacks convinced Yamasees to retreat to St. Augustine in the fall of 1715, doubling the town's nearby Indian population to nearly one thousand.[40] There they found new protectors, new suppliers of firearms, new markets for their Carolinian plunder, and new homes and freedom for their captured African slaves. The Yamasees' fears about Carolinians' encroachment before the war and of Carolinian reprisals after it convinced them that their old friends were best left as new enemies. They came to St. Augustine without all of their fellows, however. At least one Yamasee town joined the Ocheses, and by 1718, three towns of Apalachees and Yamasees inhabited lands in Apalachee.[41] As it had in the 1660s, war had splintered the Yamasees.

As the war was born of many local anxieties, it is not surprising that Yamasees and Cherokees could pursue such divergent courses. What is remarkable is how Ocheses and a number of their western allies charted a course somewhere between these two poles of friendship and hostility with Carolina. Ocheses began their more complicated journey in the company of Yamasees. Within weeks of the murders at Pocotaligo, four emissaries, two Ocheses and two Yamasees, met Governor Francisco Córcoles y Martínez to make peace in the "voice and name of the Great Cacique of Coweta" and also in the name of Cherokeeleechee, an Ochese *mico* who fervently supported Spanish alliance. They had come to see if the governor would offer them "shelter and assistance." The Spaniards accepted the request with as much incredulity as anticipation, and Brims, "the Great Cacique of Caveta" himself, arrived two months later to ratify the new accord.[42]

But in their efforts to revive an older set of relations, Ocheses declined to join the Yamasees' war alliance with St. Augustine and instead worked with their western allies, the Tallapoosas, Alabamas, and Abecas, to build ties of trade with Pensacola and Mobile that were also rooted in peace. While Brims was beginning his journey to St. Augustine and colonists like George Rodd cowered in Charles Town, the "principal Indian" of the Tallapoosa town of Tallassee arrived in Pensacola with forty other Tallapoosas and three Spanish prisoners sent by Brims. The well-traveled Coweta leader could not visit Pensacola, but by offering the prisoners he made clear "the good union and harmony which he desired to observe with the Spaniards." Later in that busy and fateful summer of 1715, "the Emperor of the Caoüitas" (that is, Brims) joined chiefs from the Alabamas, Choctaws, and "other nations" to discuss a new relationship. Bienville agreed to a request by the Alabamas for a fort near their towns and also promised to all to "trade with them for their produce and peltries." The latter offer echoed provisions that Brims and other leaders had sought from Charles Town and secured from St. Augustine. Though the Ocheses and their allies were hardly pacifists, by dismantling the slave trade through war with the British on the one hand and diplomacy with the Spanish and French on the other, they could now hope that the trade that supported violence beyond their towns would not also depend on it.[43]

These answers raised new questions and new problems. Was this war with the British necessary now that the Ocheses, the war's very instigators, had achieved much of what they sought? Perhaps not. In late 1715, Cherokees used their position as Carolina's new friends to interpose in negotiations. When Carolinian militia arrived in late December to mobilize a Cherokee war party against the Ocheses, some of the cooler Cherokees restrained their belligerent brethren and convinced the militia officers to talk peace instead. So the militia halted its march and waited for an Ochese embassy. And waited. Were the Ocheses having second thoughts about peace with their former tormentors and instead plotting to "kill the white men," as some Cherokees claimed? Or did they distrust Cherokees, some of whom remained eager for war and many of whom still considered slave trading the best way "to buy ammunition and Clothing"? Unfortunately, although ambassadors arrived in the Cherokee town of Tugaloo in late January, they never had a chance to explain themselves to the Carolinians. By the time Carolinians finally heard the Ocheses had arrived, they were already dead.[44]

Cherokees had slain the Ochese dignitaries, and generations would pass before the victims' countrymen forgave what they considered an act of treachery, but in the face of Cherokee hostility, Ocheses and their Yamasee, Yuchi, and Apalachee neighbors worried less about revenge than retreating to the safety of the Chattahoochee Valley.[45] In a series of subsequent discussions that foreshadowed the carefully revised history that Bartram heard in 1773, these allies debated their uncertain future with selective retellings of the past. From these debates emerged the first outlines of new postwar order, one in which no European colony enjoyed a distinct advantage and in which many Indian towns reaffirmed a once vulnerable autonomy. From this new position of security, Ocheses, Tallapoosa, Abecas, and Alabamas would craft new trade relations that placed a greater emphasis on what Bienville would call "good faith" over "good prices."

Many Ocheses, especially Cherokeeleechee, found greatest hope in a Spanish alliance. He and other Ocheses welcomed Lieutenant Diego de Peña and four soldiers to Apalachicola town in August 1716. With echoes of the reception Delgado had received among the Alabamas in 1686, Peña's hosts thanked the men for releasing them from a dark "cell or dungeon" into the brightness of Spanish peace. During the following spring, Cherokeeleechee reminded Governor Juan de Ayala y Escobar in St. Augustine of the "ancient tradition" regarding the Ocheses' "stable and permanent" obedience to the Spaniards. He wanted a new fort at the port of San Marcos in Apalachee, but his selective history lesson made clear that he hoped to revive the gifts and trade that had sustained Apalachicolas' and Spaniards' friendship before 1704. Ayala was the perfect man for such a message. Before becoming interim governor in 1715, he served as an officer in the garrison and used his contacts in Havana and his less-legitimate ones in Charles Town to supply colonists and friendly Indians. Cherokeeleechee and others still remembered how Ayala welcomed visiting Indians into his house "and regaled them and gave them whatever he had." In Ayala, Ocheses had a man who knew how to combine the commercial considerations of trade with the generous gifting of diplomacy. Unfortunately, Ayala's stature was a product of the colony's financial straits. He made his money on the black market, supplying colonists at exorbitant prices because the *situado* remained erratic. Even as governor, his commercial connections could not support the expectations of all Ocheses, much less their western friends.[46]

This obvious fact inspired a number of other Ocheses to pursue the British friendship they had shunned. In the spring of 1716, a few months before Cherokeeleechee invited Peña to the Chattahoochee Valley, two Ochese leaders opened peace overtures to Charles Town by returning a captive trader and declaring Brims's and the Ocheses' desire "to fall upon the Yamsees and endeavour to extirpate them." When Peña arrived on the Chattahoochee, about 130 Coweta women and a few Coweta men abandoned the town to protest the Spanish military gifts that omitted the cloth and tools that made women's lives easier.[47] And while Cherokeeleechee taught his version of Ochese history to Ayala in the spring of 1717, Brims and other Ocheses welcomed the Carolinian trader John Jones to their towns with the old promise that they would have no peace with the Yamasees, "whom they are resolved to destroy though under the walls of St. Augustine for having drawn them into a war with [the Carolinians]." The Ocheses' revisionist history needed further revising, though, because Brims in fact had no desire for peace with the colony. And then only one headman, Boocatee, appeared at the Savannah garrison to meet with the colony's officials in June. He requested more time, saying that the Ocheses wanted to wait until after the harvest; the busk or Green Corn Ceremony that marked the new year would likely enable them to ritually abandon old animosities. Ocheses contradicted themselves and refashioned their pasts because there were many stories by which to chart the future. Neither Spanish light nor British cloth alone could keep Ocheses secure and together.[48]

Brims's own apparent about-face regarding peace with the British revealed how these contradictions could divide an individual, even a man whom the Lords Proprietor in London considered "as great a Politician as any Governor in America."[49] His "son" (who, because of matrilineal kinship norms, was probably his sister's son) and presumed successor, Seepeycoffee, strongly favored the Spanish. One of his sisters, Qua, supported the British with equal fervor. And one of his "daughters," Coosaponakeesa, served as an intermediary with British negotiators, eventually marrying one. Troubling questions and close kin ties pulled in many directions the man the Europeans called "Emperor," but his influence over the newly resettled Chattahoochee towns and

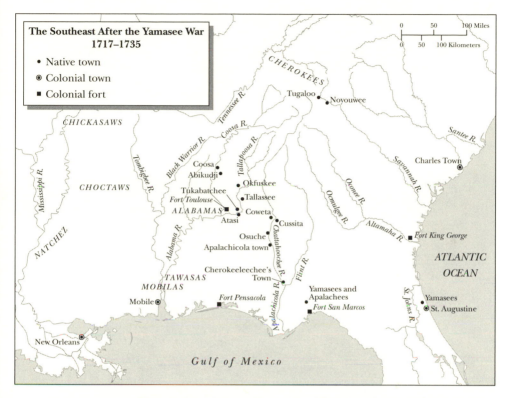

Map 6. The Southeast after the Yamasee War, 1717–35. As all three colonies revived their exchange networks after the Yamasee War, Creek towns were well positioned to trade with French, Spaniards, and British.

even over some Tallapoosa towns gave him a better chance than most to resolve this ambivalence on his terms.[50] European observations reveal several patterns to his efforts. First, Brims recognized that he needed the help of his Tallapoosa, Abeca, and Alabama allies. Second, they cooperated because, regardless of their differences, they agreed that the slave trade was no longer a tenable cornerstone of commerce or diplomacy. Third, Brims and other leaders came to believe that the best way to balance his and others' ambivalence toward the British required alliances or, at the very least, cautious neutrality, with all three imperial powers. Not surprisingly, then, even as Cherokeeleechee visited St. Augustine and Brims welcomed Jones, some Tallapoosas set out from Pensacola to visit the viceroy of New Spain in Veracruz, and Alabamas welcomed the construction of a new French Fort Toulouse at the strategic junction of the Coosa and Tallapoosa Rivers.[51]

These multiple overtures produced a series of intensifying confronta-
tions beginning in the summer of 1717. While the French laid out the
lines of their Alabama stockade, Qua and other Ochese women welcomed the cloth, ribbons, and beads that accompanied Carolinian
trader-ambassadors who spoke more of diplomacy than of war. Coosaponakeesa and other Ocheses ratified this new relationship when she
agreed to marry the trader John Musgrove. When Peña inadvertently
crashed the party in August, Brims's cold reception all but sent the Spaniards scurrying south in the company of Cherokeeleechee and Seepeycoffee. Meanwhile, ten of the Carolinian traders visited the Tallapoosas.
French and Alabamas drove them back to the Ocheses, but Fort Toulouse's commander, Le Blond de la Tour, could offer only a "handful of
powder" to the Alabamas to answer for the four hundred livres worth of
British gifts that the Tallapoosas accepted.[52] But the British successes
were deceptive. Even after Ocheses met with Governor Nathaniel Johnson in Charles Town in November to end hostilities and resume trade at
appointed trading houses, mistrust lingered. As Francisco Domínguez,
one of Peña's translators, learned during the Spaniards' unsuccessful
trip up the Chattahoochee, many Ocheses still believed that the British
"have two words or intention[s]: to come and seek peace and if unsuccessful, to enter by force of arms" and take all of them prisoners.[53] However much Carolinian traders offered after 1717, it was hard for Ocheses
to forget what those men had almost taken before 1715. La Tour noted
this ambivalence in early 1718: "The Emperor is a great politician and
great traitor. He has his heart entirely for the Spanish and loves or fears
the English because he wants to have them absolutely."[54]

When La Tour offered this assessment, Brims and his Native allies
were headed toward a fateful reckoning. In February, Tallapoosas
returned home from Veracruz, but their welcoming celebrations with
Tallapoosas, Ocheses, and soldiers from the Pensacola garrison were
interrupted by the disturbing news that thirty Carolinian traders were at
Cussita. These had been sent under the command of John Musgrove
with the Carolina trade commissioners' urgent charge to show the Indians "of our real Intention and Ability to supply them, before any Others
that shall attempt the like." In the meeting with Brims, Cowetas and Carolinians confirmed the new peace by breaking a knife and a bow and
arrow. Seepeycoffee, Brims's son, then followed the Cherokees' and
Chickasaws' lead and laid out the exchange rates for the new trade with
the Carolinians. Meanwhile, La Tour, who had already invited Brims and
other Tallapoosa and Abeca leaders to meet with him at Fort Toulouse,
sweetened his offer with news from Bienville that three ships laden with
trade goods had arrived in Mobile.[55] To further complicate matters, runners from Cherokeeleechee's town asked Joseph Primo de Rivera, the

commander of the still incomplete Fort San Marcos, to hurry to Coweta in an effort to rally those who favored St. Augustine. With representatives from Mobile, Pensacola, Charles Town, and St. Augustine either in or headed toward their towns, Ocheses and Tallapoosas gained an unusual opportunity to address the larger questions regarding colonial relations and regional trade that had driven their fighting and negotiations since April 1715. On March 23 Primo de Rivera reported that the joint council resolved "to live in friendship with us [the Spanish of St. Augustine], Pensacola, Mobile, and the said English."[56]

If the Yamasee War was the product of disturbing questions, this agreement, what the historian Steven Hahn has called the "Coweta Resolution," seemed the war's most definitive answer.[57] Although Ocheses and Tallapoosas were the principal (if not the only) Indian participants, the resolution affirmed a new set of relations they had been building in partnership with Abecas and Alabamas. Trade with the British remained important, but it had become one devoid of slaves and defined by predictable prices that would hopefully diminish the power of traders and affirm the power of the leaders who regulated the relationship. Gifts and limited trade with the French and Spaniards would serve as additional insurance of British goodwill. A half century after Westos had introduced English trade at the point of a gun, Ocheses and their allies had begun to pacify it.

Consequences

Much as Spanish gifts, the deerskin trade, and the slave trade had before, the new exchange norms created new power dynamics in the region. The multilateralism of Ocheses and their allies provided French Louisiana with space for a period of unprecedented (if evanescent) growth, renewed Spanish dreams of control of the Atlantic coast north of St. Augustine and influence in the Chattahoochee Valley far to the northwest, and forced the British to reorganize their colony in their efforts to salvage dreams of regional hegemony. As the architects of this new colonial order debated the best way to adjust to the postwar region, many decided they had much to gain from a closer association with one another. These partners, whom the British called "Creeks," were devoted to exchange relations that would protect their towns from colonial encroachment, especially from the people from Charles Town, who remained the region's preeminent traders. Creeks' uncertain blend of desire for and fear of the British forced them to make some uncomfortable decisions, including lying to some friends and leaving others. As Bartram's companions later implied, the fates of the people called Creeks and the reformed colony of Carolina were inseparable. As their omissions suggested, the Yamasees in particular would present troubling obstacles to this new union.

Plenty of people were facing new choices after 1717 in part because Carolina's misfortune revived the fortunes of La Florida and Louisiana. Less concerned with a British invasion, French investors led by John Law invested heavily in the Gulf colony. They financed the construction of a new colonial port and capital at New Orleans in 1717, and Louisiana's population ballooned from fewer than four hundred Europeans in 1718 to fifty-four hundred Europeans and six hundred Africans three years later. The population explosion alarmed Governor Nathaniel Johnson of Carolina, who fretted to the Board of Trade in 1720, "If there should ever be a war between the Crowns of France and England, this province would fall easy prey to them." He had less cause for fear than he imagined. Although Fort Toulouse reasserted French influence in the Alabama Valley, the small post had to compete with settlers' dreams of tobacco plantations along the Mississippi and officials' interest in westward routes to the silver of New Spain. Extravagant French ambitions only made Louisiana's reality more painful. Inadequate food and abundant disease caused half of the newcomers to die or leave by 1726.[58] Meanwhile, Governor Ayala of La Florida staked a new Spanish claim to the abandoned lands of Apalachee with the completion of Fort San Marcos in 1718, and Yamasees continued to harass Carolina with regular raids on the plantations near Port Royal. So generous was Ayala's successor, Antonio Benavides, with the Yamasees living near St. Augustine and Fort San Marcos that in 1722 they and their Ochese friends appealed to King Felipe V himself to extend the appointment of a man they considered nothing less than the "son of the sun."[59] Although the hopes that inspired this acclamation would fade in subsequent years, Benavides went on to serve another decade.

While their imperial rivals dreamed of expansion, Carolinians fretted over internal political and economic concerns. The winter of 1719–20 was beset with fears of Spanish invasion, which among other things convinced the newly elected Commons House of Assembly to overthrow the proprietary governor and request royal control. With spring came the discovery of a planned slave uprising. Not until the arrival of the new royal governor, Francis Nicholson, in May 1721 did someone again take charge of Indian affairs.[60] Commercial developments also diverted attention away from the once lucrative trade with Indians. Although deerskin exports returned to prewar averages of just over fifty thousand skins per year after 1720, even doubling by 1735, their commercial significance declined relative to other commodities. By 1720, the exports of choice were rice and naval stores like tar and pitch. Where officials had once covered public debts with deerskins and slaves, in 1720 they backed

£25,000 in bills of credit with a tax on rice. Unfortunately, this effort to pay war debts with paper money only sank the colony's devastated economy under rampant inflation. With seven pounds of this new Carolina currency worth one pound sterling by 1722, merchants struggled to pay their overseas creditors. And then Britain ended its subsidies for naval stores in 1724. "By 1725," according to the economic historian Converse Clowse, "South Carolina was in the midst of a serious depression."[61] Internal instability only seemed to encourage external threats. Nicholson's fears of the French and the Spanish invasion scare of 1719 suggested just how much Carolinians had lost their confidence. And then there were the very real Yamasee raiders who harassed new rice plantations near Port Royal and carried off the African slaves who represented much of the planters' available wealth and labor.[62]

Desperate for answers, Carolinians looked to London to help them deal with the Natives they still needed as allies. At about the same time that Charles Town was bracing for a nonexistent Spanish invasion and Governor Johnson was noting French power in Louisiana, the veteran Indian fighter John Barnwell was traveling to London to convince the Board of Trade, which oversaw colonial policy, to fortify the frontier. After 1717 trade no longer sufficed as a bond for empire in the Southeast. In fact, some time after 1717, Barnwell or someone who thought much like him indicated as much when he edited a copy of Nairne's 1711 map. At the junction of the Coosa and Tallapoosa Rivers he noted a "french fort" that now intruded into Nairne's old empire of trade. This author evidently believed the British should respond in kind, so he also added symbols for proposed forts that would protect the paths for traders (or, perhaps from raiders) to the west and south of Charles Town.[63]

Whether these additions reflected Barnwell's thinking is unclear, but he did insist strongly on a fort near the mouth of the Altamaha River that might thwart overland invasions from the south or west. In addition, he suggested that the Board of Trade authorize the distribution of medals to the leaders of Carolina's Native allies as emblems of their ties to Britain (and not just Carolina). Upon the old decentralized system of trade and Native military alliance that Thomas Nairne and others had championed before the war, Barnwell hoped to use imperial backing to protect the colony. As his request for medals made clear, he and other Carolinians were looking west as well as east for their security. A newly regulated relationship with western Natives, especially the newly named "Creeks," would make possible this new empire anchored in London. By introducing medals into old exchange relations, Carolinians hoped they might foster the hierarchies that would bind Creek followers to their leaders and Creek leaders to Carolinian interests. To further

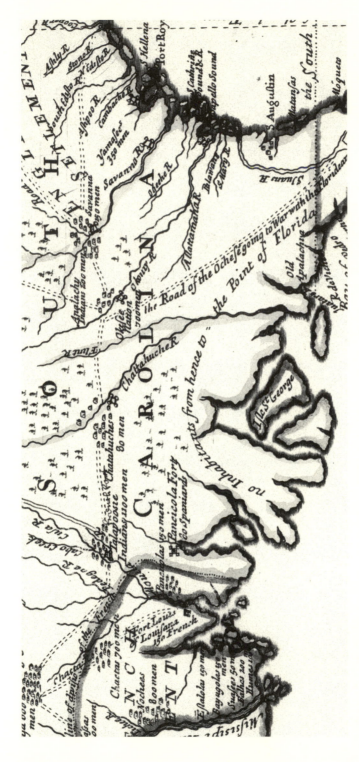

Figure 6. Thomas Nairne, "A Map of South Carolina Shewing the Settlements of the English, French, and Indian Nations from Charles Town to the River Missisipi by Capt. Tho. Nairn." (1711), detail. The handwritten label "french fort" begins above the "p" in "Talapoosie," and its corresponding symbol is just to the left of the "T" in the same word. Other unlabeled symbols for forts appear near "Chatahuches," "Okese Nation," "Savanna," "Savanna R.," and at the mouth of the "Allattamaha R." Courtesy of the Huntington Library.

manipulate relations rooted in exchange, in 1718 Carolinian officials appointed Theophilus Hastings to serve as a resident trade factor at Cussita. Although his principal tasks included regulating traders, he often used gifts and trade to promote the Creek unity that Carolinians craved.[64]

Of course, the name itself was an effort to create a united Native people and a more rationalized British empire in a place where neither yet existed. Carolinians first referred to these new allies as "Creeks" in December 1717 when they agreed "to sell Arms and Ammunition (without Restraint) to any of the Indian Nation, called Creeks, in Amity with this Government."[65] Colonial officials recognized the awkwardness and imprecision of the term when they employed circumlocutions like "Indian Nation, called Creeks" or "Indians (commonly called Creeks)."[66] Since about the beginning of the century, "Creek" had been synonymous with "Ochese," but after the war, the Commissioners of the Indian Trade and traders themselves began applying it to Tallapoosas, Alabamas, and Abecas.[67] Whether reflecting their understanding of a new unity or their interest in regulatory uniformity, the commissioners appointed a single representative to oversee the trade among these peoples in 1718.[68] By 1723, the broader definition of Creek had become common enough that Brims's son Ouletta (or at least his translator, Jehu Barton) referred to all peoples between the Chattahoochee and Alabama Rivers as "Creeks."[69] With this new name, Carolinians distinguished between Lower and Upper Creeks, with the former referring to the Ocheses of the Chattahoochee Valley, who were best reached along the lower, or more southerly, trading path from Savannah Town, and the Tallapoosas, Abecas, and Alabamas constituting the Upper Creeks who lived at the end of the upper path.[70] Such cohesion mattered not just for the purposes of crafting the well-regulated empire that Carolinians hoped would protect them from another Yamasee War. If Carolinians could unite the Creeks against the Yamasees they could weaken the colony's last Indian enemies just as they would also, as Spaniards later acknowledged, "Separate [the Creeks] from our friendship and have them more firmly in theirs."[71]

Creeks accepted these developments in part because they posed no immediate threat to their well-being. The Board of Trade was itself only in the earliest stages of drafting centralized strategy regarding the interior of North America, and Barnwell's fort provided a sorry illustration of British hegemony. A triangle of earthen walls and a rotting blockhouse twenty-six feet square held a garrison of one hundred soldiers who were more familiar with scurvy and malaria than the rising tide of British imperialism.[72] In addition, some of these developments overlapped with their own interests. The unity that Carolinians sought among Alabamas, Tallapoosas, Abecas, Ocheses, Yuchis, Apalachees, and even some Yamasees owed more to decades of their own cooperation than it did to the grand imaginations of Carolinian imperialists. Such close cooperation in turn provided protection from the colony that many wanted but few trusted. Thus, while Carolinians hoped that the new trade regulations might unite Creeks in the colony's interest, Creeks demonstrated over the coming years how their intertown alliance enabled them to accept Carolinian objects more as new sources of personal and local power. If the British were to colonize the region, they would also have to conform. Forts and medals would only work in tandem with older norms of exchange that affirmed influence.

Creeks and Carolinians worked out the contours of their new relationship primarily in the context of their relations with the Yamasees. Where Carolinians believed that the destruction of the Yamasees would ensure the friendship of the Creeks and the viability of a new economy based on rice cultivated by African slaves, Creeks debated whether friendship with Charles Town required war with kin and friends. During one Ochese raid against Yamasees in the fall of 1719, one of the Ochese scouts raced ahead to advise members of his own family to flee. Once warned, these few, "having Friends being Creeks living among the Yamasees," further spread the alarm, and most of the intended victims escaped.[73] After the Carolina's new royal governor, Francis Nicholson, arrived in 1721, he presented the Coweta leader Ouletta with medals to take to his father Brims, who was in turn empowered to keep one and bestow the other on anyone else he wished to carry Nicholson's "talk" calling for war on their Yamasee kin.[74] With these carrots also came a stick. The trade factor Theophilus Hastings was to embargo all trade with those Ocheses who refused to war on the Yamasees. Such conditions convinced one aspiring Cussita warrior, Cussabo, to lead a party against the Yamasees in Apalachee in the spring of 1723. Although Ochese warnings enabled all but three to escape capture or death, Hastings still rewarded Cussabo with "clothes of all kinds until they piled up to his shoulders, and after that they gave him a barrel of liquor, a musket, all of the ammunition he wanted, and to those who accompanied him they also gave good gifts."[75] Carolinian generosity quite literally suited Cussabo and his friends.

It also inspired the Tallapoosas, who had fewer ties to the Yamasees than the Ocheses. Shortly after Cussabo's raid, the Tallapoosa leader known as Oulatchee, or the Tukabatchee Captain, used his own gifts from Governor Nicholson to raise a large body of Tallapoosa and Abeca warriors against the Yamasees. On their way south, he and six head warriors stopped in the Ochese towns to deliver the governor's "talk" of war and make sure they would not be molested on their journey. So hostile were most Ocheses to his endeavor that he felt compelled to warn them not to try to kill him or his companions because "they had People not far off to revenge their Deaths." Most Ochese towns offered tepid support for the visitors, but, according to Spanish reports, not even "the populace of Casista," Cussabo's own town, supported them with any conviction. Once again, Yamasees received timely warnings, but when the Ocheses saw how the returning warriors "had dipt their hands in [the Yamasees'] blood" and taken three scalps, they agreed to send out their own war parties.[76]

Or so they said, anyway. When Ouletta and a number of other Ochese headmen met with Nicholson in Charles Town that October of 1723, the governor chastised them for their failure to make war on the Yamasees. He also had little patience for their misrepresentations. Several months earlier, Ouletta had apparently warned several Cussitas on their way to Charles Town that "some of the Captains of the white people were for knocking you on the head." Tallapoosas were also surprised to hear him claim that the governor's talk regarding war on the Yamasees "was rotten at the root" and that the Cowetas could no longer count on Carolinian friendship.[77] The mistrust among Creeks did not stop with misinformation. Sometime in that same summer of 1723, Cussabo's warriors attacked a Yamasee peace delegation to the Cowetas.[78] The deaths of ambassadors under Coweta protection seemed to threaten fratricidal conflict: Brims's son Seepeycoffee himself visited Mobile with the hope of securing French support against Cussabo and Hastings, and when the Tuckabatchee Captain and other Tukabatchee warriors visited the Abeca town of Okfuskee on their return from the Yamasees, Cowetas in the town "threatened to put them to death, for breaking out with the Yamasees, among whom were some of [Ouletta's] people."[79] Eight months later, in June 1724, the Assembly asked the Tallapoosas with all earnestness, "How do the Cowetaws and Lower Towns take your falling on the Yawmasees? Do you think they intend to take the Yawmases' part against You?" Carolinians braced for a schism that might drive most of the Ocheses into the arms of the French and Spaniards.[80]

Ocheses and Tallapoosas did not come to blows because these disputes were actually knitting the Creeks together. Indeed, while Carolina sought to craft rules of exchange to foster their union, Creeks exchanged information in a way that encouraged unity on their terms. Despite (or perhaps because of) Tallapoosas' and Ocheses' disagreements, the Tukabatchee Captain informed Ocheses of his intentions before executing them. Officials in Charles Town recognized that such conversations also enabled Creeks to bridge differences and influence each other. Early in 1724, when Cowetas were considering inviting a French delegation to their towns, Carolinians asked Tallapoosas to dissuade them. When some Tallapoosas requested permission to move closer to the Carolinian settlements in mid-1725, the governor's council thought it best to wait until they first discussed the matter with Brims. These many conversations did not always yield consensus, but they maintained a crucial dialogue.[81]

In the frequently acrimonious dialogues of 1723–24 we see not just a growing Creek cohesion but also the dynamics of influence and exchange that defined it. Zamumo's legacy still lived: not only did intertown alliances and networks of exchange preserve local autonomy, but the leaders of these towns also employed material resources and information in their struggles with one another. Carolinian gifts enabled upstarts like Cussabo to challenge Brims and his sons Ouletta and Seepeycoffee for prominence in Charles Town's exchange network. It provided the Tukabatchee Captain the resources to stand at the head of a large body of Abeca and Tallapoosa warriors when he delivered an unwelcome message into Ochese square grounds. But in this brave new world where many could claim access to these symbols of elite power, not even Cussabo's mountain of gifts could convince his fellow Cussitas to support his raids on the Yamasees. Cussabo failed to turn Carolinian largesse into instant authority because the control of information also played a crucial role in the political fortunes of the ambitious. This is why even bitter opponents still conversed. But just as gifts could be tribute depending on the relative power of giver and recipient, so too did conversations occur within a complex calculus of power. Governor Nicholson provided Ouletta and Brims and eventually Cussabo himself with medals and commissions to "carry" talks from Charles Town, but these were only one mark of a distinguished speaker. In 1722, when Ouletta "sent for all the Towns of the Upper and lower Creek" to "hear the Talk he carried with him" from Charles Town, the Abecas declined to attend because they claimed "they had the Talk already," and the Alabamas "were not sent to" because they had not chosen a successor to their "King." In other words, while the Abecas presumed not to need Coweta's leaders to maintain their ties to Charles Town, Cowetas decided that no Alabama leader of stature cared to hear what the Carolinians had to say. Information went only to those whom the speakers considered appropriate and came only from those whom the listeners respected.[82]

But why would Ouletta demonstrate his ties to Charles Town by claiming that the governor's talk was "rotten at the root" and war with the colony seemed imminent? Why promise Carolinians and Tallapoosas to attack Yamasees and then fail to do so? Lying was a part of conversing, and it was especially effective at demonstrating power. Ouletta kept lines of communication with Charles Town open every time he promised to attack the Yamasees. He doubtlessly captured the attention of the gathering of "beloved men" in 1722 much as he upset confident Cussitas in 1723 by warning them not to trust Carolinian friendship. And he also demonstrated his power over these credulous listeners because they lacked the information (or perhaps just the power) to contest his assertions. As Brims explained two years later, yes, there were rumors among his people that the British planned to attack them with five hundred men. But according to Brims, "We that are head men give no Credit to these Stories But the Young Men may believe them." Lies demonstrated power; recognizing them as such required it. However duplicitous, it was this kind of control of information—of the past itself—that led Cherokeeleechee in 1715 to refer to a "stable and permanent" friendship with the Spaniards, Ocheses in 1717 to blame Yamasees for "having drawn them into a war with" Carolina, and, sixty years later, Lower Creeks to reassure Bartram of their "inviolable" alliance.[83]

Of course, too many lies undermined a leader's credibility, and so at the gathering of beloved men in 1722, when Ouletta presented the Okfuskee King with the second of the two medals Nicholson had given him in Charles Town, the Dog King of Okfuskee "and some others . . . said that they did not hear the Talk."[84] Leaders of greater influence than the Dog King acted more forcefully. Sometime after the meeting, the Tukabatchee Captain visited Charles Town himself and on his return "hid" the talk from Brims's son Ouletta. The conversation about who knew what and who should know it must have left Ouletta in an uncomfortable position of ignorance.[85] Talking conveyed influence and listening acknowledged that influence. Tukabatchees, Okfuskees, Cussitas, and Cowetas had long experience with each other as allies. They talked, lied, and argued with each other because wars of words promised influence within the alliance. This exchange of ideas also strengthened the bonds that kept them collectively strong.

And collective strength remained crucial. All towns, even those who lived with Cherokeeleechee on the southern limits of Ochese orbit, recognized the utility of British friendship even if they did not deeply trust the colonists. This leader, St. Augustine's staunchest ally on the Chattahoochee, still needed the Carolinians if he was to live up to his name, which meant "Cherokee killer."[86] And on the Cherokees, all could agree. Ocheses hoping to thwart the war party led by the Tukabatchee Captain attempted to divert the warriors with a "false report that the Cherokees were discovered in the Woods," and Tallapoosas reluctant to join the upstart Cussabo on his Yamasee raid dismissed him by saying they were instead headed north against the Cherokees.[87] Carolinians recognized as well as anyone the importance of the Cherokees to Creek unity. For them, news of the continuing war was "good news." Indeed, as one of Carolina's agents explained the strategy to the Board of Trade in 1717, the colony's security lay in determining "how to hold both as our friends, for some time, and assist them in Cutting one anothers throats without offending Either."[88] Through the Creek-Cherokee war that Carolinians promoted, Creeks would ideally see the Carolinians as a source of supplies rather than a target for raids. Furthermore, war promoted the conversations and intertown cooperation that the British preferred.

The agent's letter documented the parallel coalescence of two new southeastern identities. Carolinians, using Cherokee warriors, trader-diplomats like Hastings, gifts from Governor Nicholson, and the promise of trade and the threat of an embargo, were making Creeks. For their part, Creeks relied on intertown alliance and conversation as well as a reformed trade with Charles Town, Mobile, and St. Augustine to keep the Carolinians off balance. Seeking equilibrium, Carolinians reached out to London and reformed their colony. Quite unintentionally, then, Creeks were also making Britons. And a half century later, William Bartram heard one version of these mutual origins.

An undesirable answer to questions everyone hoped to avoid, the Yamasee War reoriented the Southeast. When a number of allies brought together by the wars for slaves realized with alarm that they needed to reform it, they destroyed their old relationship with Charles Town by killing the traders who embodied that relationship. The negotiations of Ocheses, Tallapoosas, Abecas, and Alabamas with officials in St. Augustine, Pensacola, Mobile, and, eventually, Charles Town, enabled them to shift the foundations of exchange from items acquired through violence to those procured from hunting and, to a lesser extent, farming. Old alliances of war became new bonds rooted in peace. These reformers did not end war in the region because Carolinians fostered a new Creek-Cherokee war, but their alliances with one another and friendship with all three colonial powers ensured that they remained centers of power and their towns persisted as centers of peace.

Indian powerbrokers put the British on the defensive and provided French and Spaniards with new opportunities for diplomatic and even territorial expansion. The Yamasee War provided the French with the confidence to finance and settle the new port of New Orleans after 1717 and develop the foundations of plantation agriculture in the Lower Mississippi Valley. Spaniards meanwhile gained an influence in the Chattahoochee Valley that they had not enjoyed since 1686. For Carolinians, survival required reform. To depend solely on commerce was to build an empire of matchsticks—unstable and explosive. So they introduced new trade regulations to structure their Indian relations, new regulators to oversee them and the Indians, and new forts to protect the regulators.

The new defensive posture evinced an unusual Carolinian humility, but it also made clear the Carolinians' belief that they had more to protect within the colony (namely rice and slaves) than they had to gain from without. Through these reforms Carolinians also acknowledged for the first time the importance of a closer partnership with London.

Carolinians were turning to one center of power at a time that Creeks were looking to many. Their new multilateralism marked a new dynamic in southeastern history, where Indians explicitly sought friendship with all of the competing colonial powers, but it also formed part of a larger development throughout eastern North America. As imperial rivalries intensified in the late seventeenth century and the early eighteenth, many Indian peoples positioned themselves among multiple empires rather than alongside one. They did so because they remained in control of these strategic imperial borderlands but also because they had learned that participation in imperial war could prove self-destructive. Much as the War of the League of Augsburg of 1689–97 had devastated England's Iroquois allies, the War of the Spanish Succession had left Yamasees, Ocheses, and their allies vulnerable. The Iroquois are perhaps most famous for their new role as neutral powerbrokers after the Great Peace signed in Montreal in 1701, playing rival empires off one another, but they were not alone in their pursuit of what one New York secretary of Indian affairs a half-century later called "the modern Indian politics." However innovative, this new policy built upon old interests in local autonomy and multiple sources of power. This multilateralism was, much as the Yamasee War itself had been, a new effort to seek shelter from the violence of empire.[89]

So profound were these changes that their Native architects had to reorganize themselves and their history. Debates divided towns and families because they were about the relationships that towns and families were to have with each other, with their new British friends, and, most disconcertingly, their new Yamasee enemies. Later political and military developments helped the Creeks resolve these debates, but the legacies and silences of this dislocation remained. Late in the nineteenth century, Ispahihta recounted how Yamasees avoided eventual European domination by walking "deep into the water very humbly, singing pretty songs, and so that tribe was lost."[90] The upheavals that made the Creeks had remade regional exchange networks and refashioned empires, but they had also required bloodshed and debate. In the case of the Yamasees, it also required Creeks to forget former friends, and their postwar commitment to autonomy, exchange, and the control of information allowed them to do just that. The mnemonic sleight of hand might lead some to call into question the reliability of Indian oral accounts. Instead, it should remind us that later generations often come to terms with their present by rethinking their past. Indeed, when later Carolinians blamed Indians for a war that colonial traders had spawned or took sole credit for an imperial order that Indians helped create, they were doing much the same thing.[91]

Chapter 7

Cries of "Euchee!": Imperial Trade in a Creek Southeast

[John Sharp] in the meantime made no resistance but asked them to Smoke tobacco and entreated them not to use him after that rude manner telling them that the White people and they were friends and a great many friendly Arguments he used to them in English but all availed him nothing, neither would any of them Speak a Word of English, Or if they could they would not let him know it, but whenever he spoke to them only laughed at him. One would come up to him and Shake him by the hand and tell him he was a Tallepoosa, and take off his Coat another would Cry out Euchee, and take off his Shirt and others two Egellahs Cowealahs and Yomahitahs till they had Stripped him out of all his Clothes leaving him nothing but his breeches on, they carried away all his Slaves except one which was his Slave man, who made his escape from them. In short they left him not a thread of Clothes to Cover him nor victuals to eat except a little Corn and Pumpkins which they could not carry off.

—William Hatton, 1724[1]

On November 9, 1724, John Sharp suffered for the empire he served. In the dark hour just before dawn, the English trader awoke to the sound of gunfire. The sound was familiar. Since 1716, Sharp's neighbors in the Cherokee towns of Tugaloo and Noyouwee had been at war with the Creeks. This time, however, Creeks were taking aim at his home rather than those of his Cherokee neighbors. Amid the pop and whine of flying bullets, Sharp was wounded in the leg. Moments later, his two hundred assailants stormed the house, overwhelming the hapless trader and his three slaves and stripping the house and store of nearly everything. The shivering and bewildered Carolinian took refuge among the nearby Cherokees, who, as he reported to his dismay, had "kept themselves Secure in their Forts" while the "Savage dogs" (as he called the Creeks) "went about their business." Rushing to Sharp's assistance a day after the attack, Sharp's fellow trader, William Hatton, wondered, "If the Creeks demolish our Stores, and rob us of Our Goods by the Indian town Sides, what may we expect from their hands when they meet us in the Woods with a Number capable to Over power us?"[2]

The answer was neither as simple nor as dark as Hatton imagined. Without a doubt, many Creeks harbored a deep resentment of the British, and the leader of Sharp's assailants, a Tallapoosa named Sleyamaseechee or Steyamasiechie and whom the British called Goggle Eyes, apparently exhorted his companions before the raid that if "they mett with white men they should use them as Cherokeys" because "the white men always gave the Cherokeys an account of their Setting out to war against them." So deep was the resentment against the Carolinians that Hoboyhatchee, a Carolinian ally who was "king" of the Abeca town of Abikudji, later acknowledged, "I Expected Nothing Less then a War." Hatton was even more pessimistic, conjuring the ghosts of the Yamasee War when he observed, "For my Part among all the destructions I beheld in the late War (which was a great deal of it) I saw none worse than this. . . . [Sharp's] House was like a Colander So full of Shot holes and the Yard perfectly plowed up wth bullets." But Steyamasiechie's anger and the destruction it wrought did not lead to war, and some of the reasons may have lain in what Hatton considered the "Miracle" that Sharp, inside a newly ventilated house, had received only a leg wound.[3] Creeks probably deliberately spared Sharp, for had they intended to "use [a white man] as Cherokeys," Sharp would have been dead.[4]

By leaving Sharp alive, his Tallapoosa, Yuchi, Egellah, Cowealah, and Yomahitah assailants asserted their understandings of trade and its meaning. The discussions were as old as Zamumo, but this contribution was punctuated with smoke and noise and sent via a messenger humiliated by his nakedness.[5] One root of the attackers' protest lay in the fact that at least five peoples humiliated Sharp, but he and his superiors saw—indeed, needed to see—only one. Creeks, a unitary people closely attached to Charles Town's trade, were a fundamental piece of British dreams of a secure Southeast. United in their friendship with the Carolinians, they could protect the colony from French invaders marching overland from Louisiana. United in their enmity against the Yamasees, they could prevent the colony from hemorrhaging slaves to St. Augustine. Carolinians recognized that Creek unity and loyalty continued to evade them, so they encouraged a Creek-Cherokee war that they hoped would foster a Creek military and material dependence on Charles Town. This war, combined with a trade regulated by Indian agents, trade embargoes, and new forts, could then mold these towns into a single nation within a well-ordered empire. The people of Charles Town, as well as those of St. Augustine and New Orleans, struggled to create something the Southeast had yet to see, even during the days of Moundville: polities that tied all towns and peoples into unitary empires linked by trade. French and Spaniards played secondary roles in this process east of the Alabama River because neither Louisiana nor La Florida possessed the trade volume or regulatory clout to finance colonial expansion and, by extension, exercise decisive influence among the Creeks. But in this period when all three empires sought influence via more closely regulated commerce, Britons distinguished themselves from their imperial rivals less in their commitment to commerce as a tool of empire than in their capacity to employ it.[6]

Exchange held much different meanings and ends for southeastern Indians. Trade did not build empires; it supported local interests and regional alliances. A number of Indian peoples had used the Yamasee War to end trade as an engine of war, and the new price agreements that they negotiated with the Carolinians revived some of the protocols of predictable exchange and also improved the purchasing power of Indians' deerskins, but British regulators, embargoes, and forts spoke of a new coercive interest. Some Creek allies, including Steyamasiechie, were becoming increasingly frustrated with the ways that Carolinians used exchange to make them imperial pawns, a singular people trapped by trade in a fruitless war with Cherokees. John Sharp, as a trader among the Cherokees who had served as an assistant factor, had direct ties to all three of Carolina's new tools for crafting Creek unity. He made a logical target for their frustration.

Steyamasiechie's attack and the talks that followed were ultimately struggles over whether the exchange of things would promote the growth of empire or the autonomy of towns. These struggles would come to include Sharp, Creeks, and Cherokees, but also Carolinians, Louisianans, and Floridians, as well as Yamasees, Chickasaws, and Choctaws. Although Creeks initially succeeded in insisting on local autonomy and parried Carolinian efforts to mete out their own justice upon Sharp's assailants, Carolinians were able to reassert their own interests at the end of the 1720s. They did so by relying increasingly on their own resources rather than the Indian alliances that had long been the foundations of colonial profits and power. Creeks responded to Britons' resurgent influence in the region by turning to Carolina's rivals in St. Augustine and New Orleans. Creeks' ability to forge regional relations largely on their own multilateral terms meant that a decade after his humiliation, Sharp and his countrymen still traded in a colonial Southeast defined by colonial ports and Native *talwas*.

1724–26: Towns Ascendant, an Empire Unbalanced

In the six years following the end of the Yamasee War, Carolinians erected a new regulatory and diplomatic structure for dealing with Indians. Steyamasiechie's attack highlighted the inadequacy of these efforts to craft a single people. Each of the five names that Sharp remembered amid the predawn chaos—Tallapoosa, Yuchi, Egellah, Cowealah, Yomahitah—had a history. Together, these five histories suggest the varied backgrounds and common interests that made Creeks so difficult for the British to manipulate. The most immediately recognizable name would have been that of Steyamasiechie, the Tallapoosa warrior. He was one of about twenty-five hundred people occupying a dozen or more *talwas* along the eponymous river. His ancestors had built temple mounds along its banks and then modified their societies with objects that Apalachicolas, Spaniards, and English had all carried from the coast. The term was obviously a very general one because one of the Tallapoosa's companions preferred to be more specific in his identification: the Cowealah, if his name was synonymous with Cheeawoole (also known as Hothliwahali). Although these two warriors came from groups with long-standing ties to the Tallapoosa Valley, the other three identified with peoples who knew the valley as a place of refuge. Yomahitas, more frequently known as Tamahitas, met English traders along the upper reaches of the Tennessee River during the early 1670s before Westo and Iroquois attacks from the east and north forced them south. Yuchis had inhabited the Tennessee Valley as early as de Soto's *entrada* in 1540, but by the 1670s, some had fled south to the upper Savannah River Valley and perhaps the Coosa and Tallapoosa Valleys. Some also joined the Ochese settlements after 1690. By the 1720s, about four hundred to six hundred of them lived in two towns on the Savannah and Chattahoochee Rivers, but some had also probably moved to the Tallapoosa Valley. The Yuchi probably had close ties to the man who called himself an Egellah. Egellahs, or Thawegilas, were a Shawnee group that joined the Yuchis during their migrations, perhaps from Ohio. These five peoples had sought each other in their disparate quests for strength and security. As Sharp might have realized, they cooperated in order to protect their local interests.[7]

However sensitive they were to the politics and histories behind Sharp's humiliation, Carolinians had recognized even before the attack on Sharp that if they were going to turn these many pasts into one Creek future, then they needed more than "agents," trade regulators like Thomas Nairne who had combined private profit with public service. Instead, they sought "a proper Person not concerned in the Indian Trade." They appointed Tobias Fitch as the colony's exclusive ambassador to and regulatory voice among the Creeks. Fitch was to obtain restitution for Sharp's losses, determine Creeks' interest in reconciling with the Cherokees, and ensure that Lower Creeks ended their friendship with the Yamasees. George Chicken set out with a similar status and the less daunting task of maintaining the Cherokees' ties with Charles Town and determining their inclinations toward peace with the Creeks. Cherokees and Creeks welcomed the new men and their new status, calling them "beloved men," or men of distinction charged with keeping peace between the colony and its Indian allies. Despite the power of these new emissaries, they failed to assert British authority in the interior because they neglected the protocols of exchange that anchored influence. Eventually, even Sharp would seek redress through the personal relations that defined the region.[8]

Things began promisingly for Carolina's new initiative when Fitch met with sixty Tallapoosa and Abeca headmen late in July 1725. Steyamasiechie initially denied responsibility for the attack, a maneuver the slippery Ouletta would have admired, but Fitch had the information to dismiss such dissembling. The other headmen recognized his command of facts and his Carolinian stature and convinced Steyamasiechie to concede that he was "heartily Sorry" for the incident. The war leader offered to return Sharp's three slaves—a woman and her young children—as partial compensation for the act. As for returning the stolen goods, though, he could do nothing: they had already been distributed.[9] At this point, the other headmen intervened. Since Steyamasiechie had made "so frank a Confession," they would all contribute to the repayment for Sharp's goods after their people returned from their winter hunts. Fitch accepted the offer, but he then attempted to turn the headmen's cooperative gesture into an acceptance of a shared Creek identity. "If you are not Punctual To the Promise you make me," he admonished the gathering, "then all this Talk is To No Purpose and I am of opinion that our King will look on you as Enemies and Treat you as such wherever He Meets You." By making all Creeks complicit in Steyamasiechie's crime and punishment, Fitch was trying to create the cohesive polity that Carolinians craved and that Creeks had explicitly challenged at Sharp's trading house. Charles Town's ally, the Abikudji *mico* Hoboyhatchee, parried Fitch's claim to Creek unity by warning Steyamasiechie that if he did not pay the promised skins, "I will then go Down to the English and let him know it And he may do with you as he thinks fit."[10] Where Fitch asserted singularity, Hoboyhatchee insisted that Creek cooperation did not outweigh individual and local autonomy.

Fitch understood Hoboyhatchee well enough to note his words, but he tenaciously clung to his point. Carolinians wanted Creek unity, and Fitch planned to use trade to get it. He pressed his point with a history lesson and a warning. Had it not been for the Carolinians and their trade, he chided the young men, "You would not have known how to War Nor yet Have anything To War with." Before the English, "You had no hoes or Axes than What you made of Stone. You wore nothing But

Skins." This was a different history of trade than the one that Creeks might have told of personal relationships and influential objects, but they were not in a position to haggle over such details. During a second meeting in late August, Fitch warned them that if they failed to make their promised payments, the government in Charles Town would cut off their supply of ammunition.[11] All could expect to suffer for the way-wardness of a few. As they had for decades, Carolinians were using the exchange of valuable objects to establish a more perfect union among their Indian trade partners. In contrast to the military alliances that Thomas Nairne and his contemporaries cobbled together before 1715, Fitch and his superiors in Charles Town were using their objects in explicit acts of Indian tribal formation, insisting that trade would continue only if Creeks reconfigured old alliances into a new unitary polity.

In that same summer of 1725, Fitch gained another opportunity to apply a different kind of pressure through exchange. While visiting Coweta at the end of July, he learned that Yamasees had recently killed Brims's "son" and successor, Ouletta. Fitch was hopeful that the killing might provoke the Creek-Yamasee war Carolinians had long sought, but he was also happy for the opportunity to have a direct hand in Lower Creek politics. Brims explained that his "son" Seepeycoffee would replace the deceased Ouletta and assured Fitch that his newly appointed successor would prove a faithful friend despite his years of close association with Britain's rivals in New Orleans and St. Augustine. Brims then asked that Seepeycoffee receive the commission that Ouletta had received from Carolina's governor, Francis Nicholson. More than medals and pieces of paper, commissions certified the bearers' special relationships with the leaders of Charles Town. When Fitch recommended to the council that Seepeycoffee receive the commission, he implied that his superiors would be prudent to attach this uncertain ally more closely to Carolina.[12]

With commissions and trade embargoes, Fitch and his superiors hoped that the exchanges that once linked towns in alliance or tribute could now subject the same towns to a vast commercial and imperial network. In pursuing such grand ambitions, though, Fitch lost much of the influence he had acquired when Steyamasiechie first offered to make amends. While Fitch was in Coweta, a small delegation of Spaniards and Yamasees arrived in the hopes of redressing Ouletta's death. Fitch stifled these plans when he led a menacing assemblage of Cussita warriors into Coweta's town square, but he could not prevent the Cowetas' "Kind Behaviour to the Yamasees." More troubling for him and his superiors, when he returned to the Abecas in late August, he learned that some warriors had resented his strong words regarding Sharp and that "if the Beloved man would have war They would give him war." Fitch suffered no violence, and Seepeycoffee and Steyamasie-chie both demonstrated their desire for Carolinian friendship when they led war parties against the Yamasees, but the bloodshed did not stop Seepeycoffee from visiting St. Augustine to reopen talks of peace.[13]

If, as Nairne had opined a decade and a half earlier, the Indians "Effect them most who sell best cheap," why then did the wealthy Carolinians and their beloved man Fitch fail to secure Creek contrition and compensation for Sharp's losses? Why was Carolina, the region's foremost trading power, struggling to maintain its footing in the interior? There were three reasons. First, Fitch often made a poor beloved man, speaking of peace but threatening war, giving talks but also mobilizing warriors. Second, neither Carolinians nor Creeks could control their supposed subordinates. Fitch himself recognized that traders minded "neither Law, nor nothing else," even trading at the town of the Hispanophilic Cherokeeleechee. Meanwhile, Brims struggled to maintain influence over the increasingly pro-Carolinian people of neighboring Cussita, and Charles Town's close ally, the "king" of Okfuskee, could not prevent his own warriors from joining those who threatened to give Fitch "war."[14]

Third, and most intractable of all, Fitch railed and leaders failed because the British were trying to regularize a vast, complex network of personal relations. Not even Fitch's promise of an English commission could turn Seepeycoffee against New Orleans and St. Augustine. As Seepeycoffee himself explained, his people had sent him to negotiate with the French and Spaniards during the Yamasee War, and he had specifically assured these colonial neighbors "of my Freindship in Particular." Such personal ties were not confined to leaders. In 1728, Fitch's successor, Charlesworth Glover, still failed to understand why Lower Creeks remained interested in Spanish trade when it was so paltry in comparison to Charles Town's. "When a small Spanish canoe is coming to your Towns the whoop will be carried to the Abecaws before she gets to the Cowetaws," he chided, "but I can never hear any of you talk of our Pack horses coming till you hear the Bells jingle."[15] What Glover and Fitch before him failed to realize was that the paths that carried enthusiastic messages between Cowetas and Abecas also allowed them to take advantage of the many personal connections that leaders like Seepeycoffee, Hoboyhatchee, Brims, and others had cultivated with the Europeans and with each other. They were, as Ouletta exhibited during his uncomfortable and sometimes mendacious shuttle diplomacy with Charles Town in 1723, the rocky routes to influence among the Creeks. They enabled Tallapoosas and Alabamas to tell Fitch, when he came looking for an escaped African slave, "For our part we are Indians and will Differ with no White people."[16] And they also enabled a devoted enemy of the Yamasees like Steyamasiechie to lead a violent protest against a servant of Carolina. Indians used trade to promote personal balance in a way that kept British imperialists perpetually off-balance.

As a trader, John Sharp knew as well as anyone that Indian exchange depended less on colonial regulators like Tobias Fitch and more on personal relations like his own with the Cherokees of Tugaloo. He shared his Cherokee neighbors' frustration with Carolina's inaction in punishing the Creeks who had attacked him and other traders among the Cherokees. So Sharp appealed to the Cherokees, who were already planning a large attack against the Creeks, that they do unto traders among the Creeks as Creeks had done to him. "See that you serve them so," he admonished their leaders, "and see what the English will say to you."[17] The leaders made no reply, but plenty of young warriors from Tugaloo hearkened to Sharp's words. And so in the spring of 1726, while the trader Miles MacIntosh was on the path from the Upper Creeks to Charles Town, Cherokees ambushed him and his partners, stole their horses and deerskins, and had them "stripped naked as ever they was born and beat them and told them they did that in revenge of Sharp." In the Southeast after the Yamasee War, even a former public servant like Sharp had more confidence in personal networks of influence and revenge than imperial networks of trade and justice. Not surprisingly, regulators like Chicken referred to him as a "Villain" and wondered whether he was "fit to be permitted to go into any Nation of Indians more."[18]

1726–33: Empire Reasserted

Unfortunately for Sharp, his talk and the actions of frustrated Cherokees opened a crisis so deep that it swallowed completely his own quest for retribution. Sharp had spoken at a meeting of Cherokees who were less concerned with his grievances than with their own frustration over Carolina's unwillingness to break with Creeks who attacked Cherokee towns and harassed Carolinian traders with impunity. So instead of seeking British traders among the Creeks, most of them chose a more provocative target. Shortly before MacIntosh and his unfortunate companions lost their shirts to disgruntled Tugaloos, five hundred Cherokees and Chickasaws, flying British flags and carrying British drums, attacked the prominent pro-Carolinian town of Cussita. Cherokees stoked the fires of Creek rage when they told some of their Cussita captives "that it was the English that set them on to come and cut them off." So great was Creeks' consternation that even the Carolinian stalwart, the Tukabatchee Captain, offered to make war on the Carolinians "if the Lower Creeks struck the blow first."[19]

Days after hearing the news, the alarmed Carolinian assembly resolved to warn the Cherokees and Creeks "that unless they forbear such insults We must discontinue the trade."[20] As much as they acknowledged the power of trade to influence their inland allies, they also recognized its inadequacy: some legislators spoke in heated terms about a military expedition against Cherokeeleechee's town, a known haven of Spanish sympathizers, while their more fiscally sensible colleagues sought more immediate redress by authorizing Fitch and Chicken to return inland to seek an end to the Creek-Cherokee War, a war that Carolinians had started.[21] Indians' unwillingness to conform to the regulations of empire forced Carolinians to redouble their efforts at crafting one. Sharp and his complaint, meanwhile, never reappeared in the records. Apparently, Britain's effort to consolidate power in the Southeast could not tolerate the personal efforts and agendas of others, even its own subjects.

Whatever the inadequacies of trade as a tool of imperial power in 1726, Creeks nonetheless appreciated its effectiveness. As long as Charles Town controlled the bulk of the things that southeastern people traded with and gave to one another, Carolinians could exert pressures beyond the limits of interpersonal influence. When Tallapoosas met Lower Creeks at Tukabatchee to discuss how best to respond to the Cherokees and their Carolinian supporters, all of them, including the same Tukabatchee Captain who had promised to support a war against Carolina, proclaimed a renewed desire for peace with the colony. Not even Spanish and Yamasee gifts could revive the fires of belligerence. Throwing the Spanish and Yamasee gifts in the council fire, Tallapoosas collectively vowed, according to one Carolinian trader, that "the Lower Creeks might do as they pleased, [but] they would stand by the English for they knew that the Spaniard could not supply them with what they wanted." Brims, Seepeycoffee, and a large Lower Creek delegation did affirm a new peace with the Spanish governor, Antonio Benavides, during a meeting at Fort San Marcos in May 1726, but Brims also made sure to mention that his people would appreciate some arms and ammunition. Benavides dodged the request with an offer to send several soldiers inland to serve as advisors and ambassadors.[22] Floridanos' obvious weakness probably convinced Cussitas and two other Lower Creek towns to oppose the new peace with La Florida and the Yamasees.[23]

Brims returned from Fort San Marcos at the end of July, just in time to meet Fitch. As he had the year before, Brims informed the beloved man of an untimely death: Seepeycoffee had recently drunk himself to death with a keg of rum. Now Brims requested a British commission for his brother, Chekilli, the very man who would lecture Georgia officials on Creek history and Coweta power in 1735. Fitch agreed, but Chekilli, whose name meant "rough," proved a formidable obstacle to a smooth peace with the Cherokees.[24] During a meeting at Tukabatchee in October 1726, Abeca enthusiasm for peace with the Cherokees failed to convince Chekilli, who doubted Cherokee intentions: "I see no Present with the Talk so that we have nothing but this beloved man's word for it." Fitch argued for a different interpretation of gifts, one that emphasized submission. "It may be customary amongst Indians to send presents as tokens of peace," he conceded, "but then these tokens are sent from a people submitting to those they send." Chekilli flatly rejected Fitch's equation of gifts as tribute, and he offered himself as an example. "Had the Talk come from here to them we should have sent some tokens of peace." To underscore his point, he proposed that Creeks confirm their own peace overture to the Cherokees with a white feather and a string of white beads. But the message and the gifts contained a warning as well. By including a string of red beads, Chekilli made clear his expectation that Cherokees kill or expel those who continued fighting. As it had been for centuries, words of friendship without gifts were meaningless.[25]

Of course, not all words and not all gifts carried equal weight. Chekilli was stalling for time, and he knew that many Creeks, especially among the Tallapoosas and Abecas, desired peace regardless of the Cherokees' oversight. When Creeks and Cherokees agreed to mend their differences at a joint conference in Charles Town, Chekilli's obstructionism became more obvious and less defensible. Although Charles Town's friend Hoboyhatchee and the Abecas arranged a firm peace with the Cherokees in mid-January 1727, Lower Creeks did not arrive in Charles Town until the end of the month, some six weeks later than expected. Neither the late arrival nor the small size of Chekilli's delegation dissuaded the acting governor, Arthur Middleton, from pushing for the two things he and all Carolinians had sought since the dark morning of April 15, 1715: Lower Creek war with the Yamasees and its concurrent affirmation of peace with the Carolinians. Since January 1716, Carolinians had counted on the Creeks' war with the Cherokees to force Lower Creeks to accept Carolinian friendship and military supplies. Now that Middleton was proposing to end this Cherokee-Creek war, he first needed assurances that Lower Creeks would not support Yamasees based in St. Augustine. He convinced the Long Warrior, the Cherokees' principal spokesman, to push for the same. Chekilli offered a captive Yamasee boy as a peace offering to Middleton and, despite Creeks' and Yamasees' kin ties, proclaimed, "We are Different Nations," but his offer for peace with the Cherokees—a white wing and brief words reluctantly addressed to the Long Warrior—remained insincere. When the Long Warrior warned that the peace would be "Spoilt" on first word of a

Cherokee death or Yamasee attack, Chekilli could only repeat his earlier brief words of peace.[26]

The Charles Town conference of January 1727 marked eleven years since the deaths at Tugaloo, when Carolinians had begun using the twin tools of trade regulation and Cherokee war to shape Creek politics and identity. Unfortunately, not even a meeting with Middleton could mold Creeks to fit a *pax Caroliniana* centered on Charles Town and its trade. Creeks remained confident in their own networks of exchange and ideas, and Chekilli's promises were as empty as Long Warrior and Middleton had feared. Yamasee attacks on South Carolina's southern plantations had become more brazen in the summer of 1726, after Brims's visit to Fort San Marcos, and Middleton's 1727 peace conference did nothing to stop them. Yamasees and escaped Carolina slaves regularly looted and burned plantations near Port Royal, killing residents and taking captives to St. Augustine. In July 1727, the Carolinian trader Matthew Smallwood and his four companions were killed on their way from Fort King George to their store at the forks of the Altamaha River. British colonists immediately suspected Lower Creeks, but they were only partially right. Lower Creeks, notorious among Carolinians for their duplicity, were certainly involved in the murders, but their war party's leader came from Abikudji, the home of the Abeca leader and Carolinian ally Hoboyhatchee. Creek multilateralism appeared to be slowly dissolving the trade and diplomacy that bound the region to Charles Town.[27]

But the old ties held because Carolinians mobilized in a way they had not since the Yamasee War. First, they moved the king's garrison from the Altamaha River to more a more practical location near Port Royal. In addition, they sent Colonel John Herbert to the Cherokees and Captain Charlesworth Glover to the Creeks. While Herbert persuaded the Cherokees to resume their attacks on Lower Creek "She Rogues," Glover headed for Okfuskee, the Creek town with perhaps the oldest and strongest ties to Charles Town. From this safe position, he ordered Carolinian traders among the Lower Creeks to remove to Okfuskee or Tukabatchee. He also demanded that Lower Creeks pay compensation for their attacks. In the summer and fall of 1727, however, Carolinian legislators sought more than the usual tools of beloved men, trade embargo, military garrison, and proxy war. They talked as well about raising two armies of Carolinian militia, one to proceed against the Yamasees and the other against the Lower Creeks. Money was no object. Despite the colony's financial straits, legislators defied royal orders and circulated more bills of credit to finance their costly plans.[28]

However much colonial leaders spoke of war, they knew that trade and talk remained the most effective tools. Glover pinned his hopes not on the militia but on Upper Creeks who might convince Lower Creeks to abandon their persistent friendship with the Yamasees and Spaniards. The Long Warrior of Coweta visited him in Okfuskee to say the Lower Creeks were deeply divided, with Cowetas and Apalachicolas alone in their support for the Spaniards. British anger and the resultant embargo encouraged the others' new disposition. "We have had white people come amongst us from several Parts," the Long Warrior explained. Regular visits from all three imperial rivals "was for the good of our Women and Children, But now we find it is a great affront." Despite his willingness to accede to British demands for singular friendship, even a British partisan like Long Warrior believed power and security should come from many sources. As he later contended, "Brims bid me ask you what harm it did to receive Spaniards, French or any white People, he could see no harm in it."[29] Hoboyhatchee, the *mico* of Abikudji, agreed, and he stalled as long as possible before finally accepting responsibility for not stopping Smallwood's attackers. In an effort to mend this breach, he joined Glover in encouraging Tallapoosas and Abecas to mount an attack against the Yamasees.[30]

Even as he worked to assemble the large Upper Creek war party, Glover also visited Coweta in an effort to thwart a series of Spanish, French, and Yamasee overtures. Glover's presence, combined with the complete lack of ammunition among the Lower Creek towns, began to influence Lower Creek sentiments. While fearful Spaniards refused to ascend the river and challenge Glover, a French traveler who claimed to be a "prince" arrived in Coweta in the middle of March, encouraging Lower Creeks "to be at Peace with all white People." His listeners appreciated the words, but Louisianans' continuing focus on the Mississippi Valley (and Bienville's recall to France in 1725) meant that they had few supplies to blunt the Carolinian embargo. Unfortunately, Louisianans directed their limited resources primarily to cultivating the Mississippi Valley and fortifying several western outposts. One week later, Spanish soldiers visiting Apalachicola town suddenly found themselves trussed up and taken upriver to the pro-Carolinian town of Osuche. Not only had Apalachicolas turned on their Floridano friends, but Chekilli himself endorsed the capture. Chekilli did not stop other Spanish sympathizers from freeing the captives, but the soldiers returned to St. Augustine well aware that Lower Creeks resented their failure to offer a secure alternative to the British.[31]

It was apparent to all that the comfort of women and children as well as the power of warriors depended on a reliable friendship with the Carolinians. For his part, Glover recognized that forts and other displays of force would advance British interests much less effectively than trade. "It's the trade governs these people. If there comes an Army they will fly to the French." Trade mattered, but Glover also recognized the power of a few well-placed gifts. For Brims, "who has all the Power and whose heart is for the Spaniards," Glover suggested some rum, sugar, and a silk sash. Although Glover overestimated the *mico*'s influence, he recognized that gifts might very easily (and cheaply) "win the old man's heart."[32] However much people like the Long Warrior, Chekilli, and Glover talked about trade, they never forgot the importance of gifts to their union; where the former provided profits to Charles Town's traders and needed strength for warriors and their women and children, the latter affirmed the mutual obligations that bound both peoples as allies.

There were also other bonds at work. Chekilli and other Lower Creeks accepted relations with Carolinians they still mistrusted in part because of growing ties with their neighbors to the west. Relations with the Talla-poosas, Abecas, and, to a lesser extent, the Alabamas, were decades old, but the crises and conversations of the 1720s fostered a new rhetorical kinship. During a conference in Okfuskee in early March 1728, Hoboy-hatchee urged Chekilli and the Lower Creeks to send their own war parties against the Yamasees. "If your people are killed," he assured them, "we will revenge it."[33] Vengeance for the deaths of individuals was nor-mally the responsibility of a murdered person's clan. In making his promise, the *mico* of Abikudji was asserting a common kinship with his Coweta counterpart. Hoboyhatchee and Glover would have disagreed sharply over the meaning of his expression of unity and cooperation, but the Abikudji leader was claiming that the peoples from the Chatta-hoochee to the Alabama Valleys were more than an alliance of *talwas*. He was urging them to recognize a common kinship in their negotia-tions with Carolinians and their wars with Yamasees. Such policies remained subject to debate, but that desire for debate also highlighted their common interest in resolving them.

Of course, these debates did not occur in a vacuum. The failure of Middleton's effort to end the Creek-Cherokee war in 1727 had inspired more than new rounds of diplomacy from Glover and Herbert. While Glover talked with Creeks in the winter and spring of 1728, seventy-nine colonists and ninety Indians under the command of Colonel John Palmer took war to St. Augustine's Yamasees. The invaders arrived in early March and caught La Florida's inhabitants completely unawares. While Spaniards took shelter behind the impregnable walls of their fort, Palmer's force spent three days razing the nearby towns of Yamasees and runaway African slaves. Although the raiders killed only fifteen and cap-tured but thirty, their success marked the end of Spanish-Yamasee dep-redations and the beginning of a new Carolinian assertiveness. Not since the Yamasee War had colonists ventured in such large numbers against Indian enemies. The Indians near St. Augustine, who had already lost nearly two hundred of their kin in an epidemic in 1727, were deeply demoralized by Spaniards' unwillingness to confront the invaders. The two Yamasee towns near Fort San Marcos left Apalachee, and many others of St. Augustine's four hundred Indian allies abandoned Spaniards to seek refuge among Florida's savannas and swamps.[34] Hundreds of miles to the northwest, Charlesworth Glover saw how Lower Creeks now understood from the news that Carolinians "were now in earnest." Glover pressed his advantage with calculated generosity and reopened Carolinian trade with the Lower Creeks.[35]

After years of diplomatic uncertainty, Carolinians had used their own resources to regain the initiative in the Southeast. Their words and their things were shaping events. During the summer after Palmer's success in St. Augustine, it was not hard for French in New Orleans to believe rumors that 160 British regulars were mobilizing Lower Creek support for attacks against La Florida and even Louisiana.[36] The reality was less dramatic but more consequential. In 1729, the Lords Proprietor retroceded their charter to the Crown, paving the way for the arrival of a new royal governor, Nathaniel Johnson, at the end of 1730. The same man overthrown by the anti-proprietary coup in 1719 returned to Charles Town with plans to secure the colony with a series of townships at strategic points along the colony's frontiers. Located about sixty miles from Charles Town, the proposed towns would simultaneously revive European immigration (which the proprietors had obstructed after the coup) and restrict the movements of invading Indians and escaping slaves. In some respects, the plan replaced Barnwell's garrisons with settler populations that could both defend and occupy territory. The colony's new plans maintained the colony's preeminence as a laboratory of British imperialism. Just as Barnwell in 1721 had prompted the Board of Trade to think about North American colonies as part of a continental rivalry with France, Johnson's plan was the first to expressly replace Indians with colonists as defenders of that empire.[37]

Relations with Indians figured prominently as both cause and consequence of the colony's good fortune. The dual successes of Palmer and Glover had resolved the last vexing vestiges of the Yamasee War: Yamasees no longer threatened Carolina, and Lower Creeks no longer supported them. Wider developments also played a role. Carolinians gained new room to maneuver when Natchez on the Mississippi River began a two-year war against their French neighbors and oppressors in 1729, and this was followed shortly by French discovery of a planned revolt of African slaves in the summer of 1731. In 1730, the Scottish nobleman and adventurer Alexander Cuming simultaneously revived metropolitan interest in the Southeast and Cherokee ties with the British by bringing a Cherokee delegation to London at his expense. The next year, Carolinians resumed long-standing efforts to open regular trade with the Choctaws.[38]

Charles Town possessed new power, and Creeks took notice. A group of Lower Creeks, calling themselves Yamacraws and including primarily Yamasees and Apalachicolas, abandoned the Chattahoochee for the lower reaches of the Savannah River about 1729, reaffirming old ties to the area even as they recognized and secured British control of the strategic and unpopulated lands. Tallapoosas joined Carolinians' efforts to improve relations with the Choctaws by establishing a small town on the new western trading path in 1731.[39] Charlesworth Glover, who spearheaded this new Choctaw initiative, also convinced Tallapoosas and Ocheses to return with him to Charles Town in 1732 to affirm a peace with the newly arrived Governor Johnson. Cowetas and Cussitas were notably absent from the ceremony, but the friendship that Upper and Lower Creek headmen ratified—and the new trade prices that would reaffirm it each trading season—demonstrated Carolinian ascendance.[40]

British confidence only grew the following year, when General James Oglethorpe established the colony of Georgia. Combining philanthropy with imperial strategy, the colony's patrons hoped to provide the worthy poor with a fresh start as small farmers who could simultaneously reinforce British North America's southern flank against future French and Spanish aggression. When Oglethorpe and other colonists arrived on the banks of the lower Savannah River in February 1733, Tomochichi and other Yamacraws welcomed them and agreed to cede a stretch of land downstream from their town. Three months later, Oglethorpe met with Lower Creeks, who asserted their influence over the emigrant Yamacraws, established norms for trade with the new colony, and acknowledged the Georgians' right to settle coastal lands south of the Savannah. As Oglethorpe exulted to Georgia's trustees, "We have concluded a peace with the lower Creeks who were the most Dangerous Enemies to South Carolina and formerly friend to the French and Spaniards."[41] With his eyes clouded by pride and inexperience, Oglethorpe believed he had achieved the firm Anglo-Creek alliance that had eluded Barnwell, Fitch, and Glover.

At the very least, his successes marked the rise of a new British confidence in the Southeast and the empire more generally. It was in the 1730s that long overdue political stability yielded what one of South Carolina's first historians called "a new era" of "freedom, security, and happiness," which included what another early historian called a nearly unprecedented "instance of public and private prosperity." Although Georgia remained utterly dependent on heavy subsidies from Parliament in London, Parliament's unprecedented support for Britain's newest colony also testified to the government's growing commitment to

overseas expansion.[42] Both the commitment and the pan-Atlantic sense
of the British empire that drove it were themselves the product of Anglo-
Americans, like Barnwell and Johnson. They recognized their need for
British support and championed the benefits that Britain would derive
from strong colonies bound to London by a trade that would simultaneously endow colonies and mother country with the resources to protect
themselves from Native and European rivals. Small wonder that Sharp
and his unresolved losses vanished from the record. His problems were
too small and his ambitions too personal for this newly confident
empire.[43]

1733–35: Stories of Origin, Claims of Interdependence

Whatever Nathaniel Johnson in Charles Town or James Oglethorpe in
Savannah might have thought about their colonies' future, Indians
remained decisive to Britain's imperial dream, and that fact would force
all Europeans to continue dealing with Creeks and other Indians in a
most localized way. Among the British, Charlesworth Glover knew perhaps better than anyone that trade remained Carolinians' best lever for
influence among inland peoples. Meanwhile, Louisianans and Floridanos lacked the populations or economies to rival the British, so they continued the generosity that secured their regional relevance. Even the
European most experienced with regional political norms, Louisiana's
Jean-Baptiste Le Moyne de Bienville, needed to be reminded. Forced out
of the colony in 1725, Bienville returned as a royal governor in 1733. He
came as a savior, intent on rebuilding a colony devastated by war with
the Natchez, but he quickly learned that Louisiana's straits, rather than
his prestige, conditioned Indians' attitudes toward his weakened colony.
"Hence comes likewise the insolence with which they pretend to consider as tribute the presents which the King is so kind as to grant them,"
he wrote in 1733.[44] Much as in 1686, when Mobilas and Tuanis had
sought Spanish gifts instead of English trade goods, European objects
remained symbols of relationships. Firearms were powerful, and wool
cloth was beautiful and practical, but, as Bienville lamented, the context
of their presentation still mattered just as much as the objects themselves. Creek *talwas* continued to assert this fact because they all benefited from the diverse activities of allies—whether kin, friends, or even
rivals—in other *talwas*. Bienville had to give "tribute" because he inhabited a region where he was not the center of power. Bienville's troubles
were in part the product of a colonial Southeast where local interests
could trump imperial ones and where multilateral diplomacy remained
the most effective route to influence.

In 1734 Patrick Mackay became the newest, if least able, student of this political reality. That spring, before Oglethorpe departed for London in the company of a delegation of Yamacraws and Lower Creeks, he sent the brusque Mackay inland to enforce Georgia's new regulations for traders among the Creeks. The direct challenge to South Carolina's long-standing claims to oversee southeastern Indian peoples presented Creeks with a new set of rivals with whom they could build their influence. As Mackay asserted an authority he did not possess, he demonstrated the fractious weakness of British imperialism and the fractious power of Creek localism.[45] Mackay arrived among the Lower Creeks in November 1734, and during his time among the Upper and Lower Creeks, he sought to establish control over the traders he considered too numerous and unruly. By revoking the licenses of some and attempting to discipline others physically, he attacked the personal relations that defined Creeks' trade relationship. His hosts responded accordingly. Hitchitis on the Chattahoochee River held a council of war in response to Mackay's confiscation of their trader's goods, and only the direct intercession by the trader protected Mackay from violence. When Mackay prepared to beat the trader William Edwards at Okfuskee, some recalled how an Okfuskee headman named the One-Handed King held the trader close "and said that if he would whip the said William Edwards they should whip him too." Edwards was freed without harm.[46]

In his own mind, at least, Mackay had grounds for such zeal. Oglethorpe had warned him that war might soon pit Britain against France and Spain. In March 1735, while among the Lower Creeks, he solicited their military support in case of war and then urged them to attack the Spaniards. Although they all apparently answered "that they would stand by him with their Lives, or Words to that Effect," the leaders of only two towns actually sent warriors south, and when Licka, the *mico* of the Yuchis, set out against the Spaniards, he did so in secret.[47] Two months later, Mackay met with Upper Creek leaders in Okfuskee to demand that the Upper Creeks either destroy Fort Toulouse or permit the construction of a British fort at a site of his choosing. If they refused either, he threatened an embargo. After a week of deliberation, the headmen agreed to allow a fort at Okfuskee.[48] The sources of such persuasive power were obvious to Mackay: "If it were not for [British] friendship," he chided the Lower Creeks, "they would be as in the past in leathers and clothes of skins." Like Oglethorpe, Mackay believed he had achieved British hegemony. When Creeks like Chekilli later admitted that he "never tired of hearing what Tomochichi tells . . . about" the wonders of the latter's journey with Oglethorpe to London, Mackay imagined two Indian leaders marveling at the great metropolis that now occupied the center of their world.[49]

Despite Mackay's successes with Licka and the new fort and Chekilli's fascination with London, Georgia's agent had little appreciation for the ways that Creeks forced him to accept relations built not on military or commercial force but on personal relationships and the exchanges that supported them. Besides the Okfuskees' protection of Edwards, Creeks demanded that Carolinians and Georgians return evicted traders. The portraits by the German traveler Philip George Friedrich von Reck of Senkaitschi and his wife illustrated much of what Mackay understood and overlooked (see fig. 2). The red and blue woolens were products of a British industry financed by European and Indian consumers in America. But such styles did not reflect the dependence that Mackay imagined because they were purchased according to price agreements that southeastern peoples had already negotiated with the Carolinians after 1715. Indeed, in 1732, Cherokees and Creeks both negotiated price reductions for Carolinian trade goods. And between 1716 and 1736, Carolinians increased the portion of their public expenditures devoted to gifts to Indians from 4 percent to 7 percent of their annual budgets. Furthermore, even as southeastern Natives remained in control of what the historian James Axtell has called a "consumer revolution," Native craftspeople continued to produce those items that they could endow with superior material quality, such as Senkaitschi's moccasins, or spiritual power, such as his buffalo robe.[50] When Mackay reminded them of their primitive past, Lower Creeks simply reminded him that Spaniards also gave them presents of clothes, tools, and firearms, and if the agent wanted to withdraw the British traders, he was more than welcome. Mackay recognized neither how British trade was a product of negotiation nor how personal bonds and generosity remained keys to influence. Consequently, he remained dumbfounded at how these Indians could admire London and yet remain "overawed by the silly place in possession of the French called fort Thoulouse and by [the Spanish fort] Saint Marks."[51]

Stories of London did not diminish Creek appreciation for two rotting stockades because the latter provided the French and Spanish gifts that reaffirmed the power of Creek leaders. And neither colony to the south was about to concede the deerskin trade or the political influence of gift giving entirely to the British. Until 1763, Fort Toulouse continued to supply Alabamas and Tallapoosas so well that roughly equal numbers of individuals were buried in the exclusive presence of either French or British goods. Although Spanish exchanges consisted almost entirely of gifts, in 1738 the governors of Florida and Cuba did attempt to establish a trading post at Fort San Marcos. Creeks professed interest, but Spaniards simply lacked the resources.[52] Creek interest was part of a larger pattern. In 1728, Glover complained about the ways Creeks celebrated the arrival of Spanish canoes and still welcomed (if less enthusiastically) the sound of bells on English pack horses; in 1735, Mackay should have recognized that Okfuskees like the One-Handed King had good reason to protect British traders as well as French forts. They had learned over generations that a single friend was a dangerous one.

Such considerations were perhaps most explicit three years earlier, when Alabamas decided not to join Charlesworth Glover and other Creeks on their journey to Charles Town in 1732. According to the commander at Fort Toulouse, one Alabama leader who strongly supported the French was "going to abide by what the others do" in Charles Town. It was a way for a close ally of Louisiana, a man the French commander called "our king," to simultaneously maintain access to the power of the British.[53] Of course, power relations among Creek *talwas* also influenced Alabamas' Francophilism. Because Alabamas were "stinking linguas," or speakers of a language that was significantly different from that spoken by the neighboring Tallapoosas and the majority of Creeks, they occupied a lower status in the eyes of their neighbors.[54] Perhaps close ties with the French could elevate the Alabamas in the eyes of their Tallapoosa friends upriver, much as trade with Henry Woodward and the English had augmented Cussita immigrants' prominence among the Hitchiti-speaking Apalachicolas. Bienville described the hopes of one Alabama chief in 1734: "If the French would supply the Talapoosas, Abihkas and Kawitas, which are villages of his nation among which the English have always traded, with the limbourg, guns, powder [and] bullets at the same prices only as those for which they are traded to the Choctaws, that would turn them completely away from the English." The Alabama offered his advice as a friend of the French but also as a leader who knew that an expanded French trade network could improve his stature among peoples whom he claimed as members of his "nation."[55] Common interest promoted conversation among Alabamas, Ocheses, Tallapoosas, and Abecas even as rivalries kept them searching for the upper hand. European goods were crucial to both agendas.

Like John Sharp, Tobias Fitch, and Charlesworth Glover before him, Patrick Mackay did not understand that influence came from many paths and many kinds of exchange. Or rather, like them, he did not want to understand. After the Yamasee War, Carolinians and then Georgians increasingly believed that regional influence depended on a well-organized empire spearheaded by confident emissaries and bound by a vast network of British trade. When Creeks asserted their local autonomy—whether violently with Sharp or deliberately with Mackay—they only intensified British efforts to restrict this independence and assert through embargoes, gifts, and forts the unitary control of an emerging empire. Georgia's very existence, which was predicated on securing the debatable lands between South Carolina and La Florida, was in many respects an extension of this struggle between British imperialism and Creek localism. From John Barnwell to the Board of Trade to James Oglethorpe, Britons in America and the home island increasingly believed that their power in the Southeast depended not on unstable alliances with partners pursuing multilateral agendas but instead on their efforts alone. Mackay listened to Creeks with a tin ear in part because of the empire he served.

This is not to say that Creeks abandoned their efforts to educate, for they had much to gain from traders who recognized the imperatives of kinship and governors who acknowledged the power of many friends. In June 1735, Chekilli and a large assembly of Lower Creek headmen and warriors visited Savannah to receive the gifts that Oglethorpe had sent along with Tomochichi back to Georgia. Chekilli at the least had much more than gifts on his mind, for it was during this meeting that he offered Georgians his two-day lesson in Cussita history. As the historian Steven Hahn has noted in an extended examination of Chekilli's talk, the Coweta *mico* told sacred history as political ideology. His story of the Cussitas, their cooperation with Abecas, Alabamas, and Chickasaws, their assistance to the Coosas, and their union with the Apalachicolas justified his claim to membership in the Lower Creeks' "eldest town," legitimated his "Strong Mouth," and ultimately established his capacity to speak with the British on behalf of Upper and Lower Creeks.[56]

But Chekilli staked out more than the ideological foundations of his prominence. He also explained the nature of influence among the Creeks. By describing how Cussitas and Apalachicolas exchanged white wings, how Alabamas, Abecas, and Chickasaws shared medicines and fires, and even how the four competing friends compared the scalps they had taken, Chekilli noted how Creeks, however contested their unity or his leadership, depended on exchanges that bound them in complex relations. Cussita might enjoy a strong enough friendship with the Chickasaws to justify including them in the story in a way that an Alabama teller might not, but Chekilli was also asserting a generality that focused on timelessness, on the "eldest" and hence most powerful and sacred bonds. However new these ties were, however new the story, the roots stretched back before Zamumo's meeting with de Soto. The exchange of things and ideas brought Creeks together. As Ouletta had shown a decade earlier, sometimes Creeks were joined by lying; as Apalachicolas suggested when they told the secretary Thomas Causton that they had a different story from Chekilli's ("which they say will be an Improvement to his") they were frequently joined by debating.[57]

And these many exchanges helped them build common stories in the most unexpected ways. In the fall of 1737, Cherokee emissaries arrived among the Alabamas in an effort to end their continuing war. The Alabamas rejected the offer, according to the French commander at Mobile, because the Alabamas wanted to avenge themselves for the treason that they suffered more than twenty years ago from Cherokees, "who massacred [them] without mercy [presuming] on the good faith of a peace of the firmest kind."[58] Alabamas had incorporated an Ochese story to spurn an old common enemy. In the exchange of ideas and stories, Creeks had adapted ancient practices to confront new challenges to local autonomy. Europeans sought to be singular centers of exchange and influence in the region, an objective that had eluded even the great chiefs of Moundville. In 1735, though, the bonds among Creeks remained strong enough that, even if Georgians did not understand or believe Chekilli's story, they still had to listen.

Two years before Chekilli's lesson in Creek history and political science, Patrick Mackay met with the elusive Cherokeeleechee. It was part of his effort to cajole and coerce all Lower Creeks into an exclusive relationship with the British. In Cherokeeleechee, a regular visitor to Fort San Marcos and a man whom Mackay considered "the craftiest, most cunning and the boldest-spoken Indian I have had as yet occasion to converse with," the Georgia agent faced a difficult task. When he accused the *mico* of hiding his continuing visits to St. Augustine, Cherokeeleechee vehemently denied it: "I am a Mico and Micos scorn to speak lies." Mackay was not convinced: when it came to the British and Spaniards, he wrote, "It is my opinion he will endeavour to deceive both parties." In the exchange of information (however accurate) and of gifts (however willingly given), Cherokeeleechee retained a position of influence. And there was little Mackay could do about it. However much he might imagine that his people could easily conquer St. Augustine or Mobile, however much he believed Creeks were cowed by Tomochichi's descriptions of London's power and populace, Cherokeeleechee was not worried. "Your King always threatens to demolish Augustine and conquer the French at Moville," he told Mackay. "And the Cut Cheek King (meaning the Governour of Augustine) threatens to destroy Charles Town and the King of Moville says he will destroy both, but I shall never see the day that the one shall conquer the other."[59]

Cherokeeleechee was right, but barely. The wily leader died in the 1740s, less than a generation before Britain signed the peace accords sealing its victory over France and Spain in the Seven Years' War and gaining undisputed imperial claim to North America east of the Mississippi River.[60] Creeks' capacity to maintain the multilateral relationships that had anchored their local autonomy and their regional influence faced significant problems after the Treaty of Paris of 1763, but at least for the remainder of Cherokeeleechee's life, the multiple colonial centers meant that the British could not make the Southeast into a region of their choosing. The colonists of South Carolina and Georgia were very influential in the affairs of the entire region, but that influence still rested on networks of exchange based on the particularities of the local. John Sharp served an empire with grand ambitions rooted in commercial dominance, but he still faced humiliation at the hands of people shouting Yuchi, Tallapoosa, Egellah, Cowealah, and Tamahita. Patrick Mackay could take pride in the power of his people, their transatlantic connections, and their growing territorial control, but he still had to listen to a *mico* whose claims to power and truth faced no effective challenge.

Despite the snubs they suffered, Sharp and Mackay drew reassurance from the power of their respective colonies and the empire to which they belonged. They also knew that the power of their empire and the security of their colonies depended increasingly on Britons' capacity to mobilize their own resources. For his part, Sharp suffered the censure of his countrymen for failing to use these resources. Mackay remained safely ensconced in his arrogance because he relied on them. In a region in which power still rested mostly on the connections of individuals, Carolinians and Georgians were looking to their connections with each other, whether in the form of more plantations, more forts, or better leaders (governors as well as beloved men). The efforts formed part of a larger trend in Indian affairs and the consolidation of the British empire. Beginning in the 1720s, Carolinians, Virginians, Pennsylvanians, and New Yorkers increasingly sought help from Britain for dealing with their respective "Indian problems." Such overtures fostered the construction of new forts, the planning of new frontier communities, and even the creation of a new colony. These efforts joined Britons' growing sense on both sides of the Atlantic in the 1720s and 1730s that they shared a stake in the creation of a British empire.[61] As a result of colonial pressures, in 1755 the Board of Trade in London introduced a new system of Indian administration with superintendents who would be responsible for entire segments of North America and would report directly to London rather than colonial capitals. Colonists' inability to influence adequately the Indian polities on their western frontiers convinced some colonists to promote what they hoped would be a larger and hopefully more effective imperial system.[62] Together, all of these improvements would ideally secure what alliances alone could not. Cherokeeleechee's truth faced few European challenges in his town, but he had little capacity to stop the changes that threatened someday to overwhelm it.

In the meantime, however, the rules of the region remained more Creek than Carolinian; more rooted in exchange than extraction. If Mackay and Sharp did not acknowledge this fact explicitly, other Indians did. In 1734, Choctaws continued their long-standing efforts to establish regular trade relations with the British. The establishment of Georgia had further inspired their efforts, and one leader, Red Shoes, made several efforts to visit Savannah in the years after it was founded. The British believed they were on the verge of splitting the Choctaws from their old French allies, but Red Shoes had a different set of expectations rooted more in a town's multiple paths to power and the many trading partners who supported it. "He told an Alabama that although he had been among the English and carries to his nation an English flag he would not abandon at all the word of the French; that he knew well that the Alabamas saw the Englishman and the Frenchman; that that was good."[63]

Conclusion
Gifts and Trade, Towns and Empires

A decade and a half after Red Shoes offered his words of praise for Creek multilateralism, the French philosopher Charles Secondat, baron de Montesquieu, wrote admiringly of Britain's empire. In Montesquieu's eyes, Britain achieved power without resorting to tyranny by planting overseas colonies "to extend its commerce more than its domination." Britain, in the eyes of its people and its admirers, had created an empire that avoided the pitfalls of decadence and tyranny by devoting itself not to the control of people and territory as much as of trade and the sea. As Montesquieu wrote later in the same work, "A naval empire has always given the peoples who have possessed it a natural pride, because, feeling themselves able to insult others everywhere, they believe that their power is as boundless as the ocean."[1] With its control of the seas anchored by a thriving commerce and Europe's most powerful navy, Britain's pride was hardly a hollow one. Montesquieu's observations were published more than three thousand miles away from where Red Shoes uttered his, and the two men never met, but we should not ignore the connections that made their two statements possible.

In some respects, the ties are obvious. By the time de Soto offered his feather to Zamumo, Indian and European histories in the colonial Southeast were inseparable because their survival in the region depended on exchange. Gifts and trade enabled Indians to survive the "floods" of disease and dislocation that had swallowed towns like Coosa. Indian leaders' expectations of gifts conditioned the expansion of Franciscan missions and shaped the emergence of trade that eventually stalled the evangelical experiment. Far from the peal of mission bells, Indian peoples who had exchanged Spanish goods in the early and mid-seventeenth century followed the same trading paths to flee the slave raids of the late seventeenth century. After 1660, exchange enabled refugees to find shelter and new power as allies. They adapted their understandings to the English, blending gifts and trade to profit but not perish from the exchange of people. They forced the French to provide some of the alternatives that helped them maintain networks among *talwas*, even when this complicated French investors' efforts to create a colony of plantations and slaves. As Indians modified these trade practices in the early 1700s, they formed new alliances first to take best advantage of trade and then to reform it. European gifts and trade helped unite the allies called Creeks. Throughout the two centuries that separated Zamumo from Senkaitschi and de Soto from Mackay, Indians and Europeans had reconfigured their relations of exchange. Gifts and commodities both played continuous roles, but their measure and meanings continuously changed. This is not to say that innovation divorced eighteenth-century Creeks and their neighbors from their Mississippian forebears. Creek insistence on older patterns of reciprocity and multilateralism forced their colonial neighbors to accept the fact that partners in exchange could not dictate, only influence. The webs of empire had many strands in the Southeast, but Creeks and their neighbors ensured that it was often difficult to find where the center lay.

Southeastern trade patterns did not serve the British or other European empires in a way that Montesquieu celebrated because exchange relations promoted the interdependent and competing efforts to survive in the Southeast. The act of offering deerskins for wool cloth, for instance, simultaneously fit within the mutual need for profit and for alliance. It supported the autonomy of a town and promoted the hegemony of an empire. In some respects, Creeks were themselves born from trade. From the time the Yamasees visited the Chattahoochee Valley with Henry Woodward in 1685 (and perhaps as early as the Cussitas' migration to the Chattahoochee itself), the peoples who became Creeks built their alliances with trade in mind. In the history that some told Bartram, they "sat down" at the Ocmulgee Old Fields just in time to take advantage of the new British colony of Charles Town. And Carolinians were neither the first nor the last to oblige this interest. Beginning in the mid-seventeenth century, Floridanos linked their colony's fortunes to trade for Apalachee corn and Apalachicola deerskins. And although French and British traders wrested control of most of this trade after the early 1700s, even the Spaniards did not cease pursuing Creek consumers.

But as much as Europeans and Indians all recognized the benefits of trade, no one depended upon it entirely. Creeks had little power without recourse to the ties of kinship and gifts that their Mississippian predecessors had pioneered. Ties of Yamasee-Apalachicola kinship provided both peoples with trustworthy allies during their budding English partnership in the 1680s, and these bonds doubtless anchored Cherokeeleechee's connections to St. Augustine when he defied the inquisitorial Patrick Mackay. Such ties spanned decades and the region as a whole, but they resided in the relationships of individuals. Perhaps no one embodied this fact more than Brims, the man whom Europeans called "Emperor." He extricated Lower Creeks from the Yamasee War by meeting with leaders from Mobile, Pensacola, St. Augustine, and Charles Town, as well as pursuing other undocumented negotiations with leaders from Tallassee, Tukabatchee, and his Chattahoochee Valley neighbors, among others, but his success also depended on the efforts of kin like his son Seepeycoffee, who visited Mobile and St. Augustine, and his daughter Coosaponakeesa, who married the Carolinian trader John Musgrove. Of course, Brims struggled mightily to maintain these personal links to regional influence during the 1720s, as upstarts like Cussabo challenged his leadership. Nonetheless, Brims's influence over these and other kin ties prompted officials like Charlesworth Glover to recommend in 1728 a few choice gifts to "win the old man's heart." Europeans' willingness to offer such gifts highlights how they, too, recognized that power rested on foundations besides profit. Gifts and trade together bound the fates of towns and empires; they justified Red Shoes's admiration for the Creeks as well as Montesquieu's for the British.

And British administrators in London did well to heed the relationships that inspired this admiration. Although Indians might appear incidental to the architecture of empire, they were unavoidable, if not central, instigators behind London's increasingly regulatory turn after 1720. Members of the Board of Trade first considered a larger regulatory apparatus in part at the insistence of Carolinians like John Barnwell, who contended that only support from London could secure the colony and empire from the ambitions of France and its Indian allies. The frustrations of colonial agents like Tobias Fitch and Patrick Mackay only amplified the requests for the centralized administration that Britain assembled in the 1740s and 1750s. However firmly Britons believed that they oversaw an empire bound by the gentle ties of trade, Creeks forced Britons to acknowledge that this "original great tie" was a slippery knot. Precisely because exchange could simultaneously serve divergent interests, Britons had to develop more coercive measures to regulate trade and the relations it sealed. Montesquieu was in the end only partly right: trade was a foundation of empire because Britain's expanding commerce justified an expanding administrative control.

Perhaps, then, the sagacious Red Shoes was betting on the wrong strategy, the defiant Cherokeeleechee was whistling in the dark, and the well-dressed Senkaitschi was purchasing his own submission. Such suppositions, however, depend upon an awareness of the nearly three centuries of dispossession that followed Red Shoes's meeting with the unnamed Alabama, and Red Shoes and his contemporaries lived as we all do, in a world conditioned more by the lived past than the unknowable future. From the vantage point of 1734, Red Shoes would have looked back upon more than three centuries of communities securing their power through exchange relations and alliances with many partners. The violence of colonization had certainly shaken and destroyed many of these very towns, but those that survived and prospered in the Southeast did so because they had remodeled old practices for new times. And they would continue to do so long after Red Shoes and his contemporaries died. Exchange did not lose its relevance as a source of power just because Britons and their European American successors devised new tools of empire. Through the traumas of removal and dispossession during and after the nineteenth century, southeastern Natives shared stories, so that accounts bore strong resemblances across towns and time. Even as they came to appreciate all that they held in common, *talwas* and clans nonetheless retained some of their distinctiveness, which they proclaimed through stories of independence and primacy. This indomitable autonomy of *talwas*, clans, and the larger Creek nation was the product of centuries of exchanges, of lies and truth, of power and submission, of gifts and commodities. Creeks remain colonized, but they are still capable of exchanging stories. This exchange, and the sovereignty that it asserts, is perhaps Zamumo's greatest gift. But then again, if a history of exchange teaches us anything, it is that it was never entirely his to begin with.

Notes

Introduction

1. Most scholars believe that Altamaha was located at what is now the Shinholser site in the Oconee Valley. John E. Worth, "Late Spanish Military Expeditions in the Interior Southeast, 1597–1628," in *The Forgotten Centuries: Indians and Europeans in the American South, 1521–1704*, ed. Charles Hudson and Carmen Chaves Tesser (Athens, Ga., 1994), 108; Mark Williams, "Growth and Decline of the Oconee Province," in *The Forgotten Centuries*, ed. Hudson and Tesser, 190–92. For more details on the Shinholser site, see Mark Williams, *Archaeological Excavations at Shinholser Site (9BL1): 1985 & 1987*, LAMAR Institute Publication 4 (Watkinsville, Ga.: LAMAR Institute, 1990), 19–22, 201, PDF file accessed July 17, 2006 from http://shapiro.anthro.uga.edu/Lamar/reports.htm. For travel times, see Charles Hudson, *Knights of Spain, Warriors of the Sun: Hernando de Soto and the South's Ancient Chiefdoms* (Athens, Ga., 1997), 160–64.

2. Rodrigo Rangel, "Account of the Northern Conquest and Discovery of Hernando de Soto," trans. and ed. John E. Worth, in *The de Soto Chronicles: The Expedition of Hernando de Soto to North America in 1539–1543*, ed. Lawrence A. Clayton, Vernon James Knight Jr., and Edward C. Moore, 2 vols. (Tuscaloosa, Ala., 1993), 1: 272.

3. Williams, *Excavations at Shinholser*, 34, 232–33.

4. Rangel, "Account," 272; Vernon James Knight Jr., "The Institutional Organization of Mississippian Religion," *American Antiquity* 51.4 (October 1986): 675–87.

5. Thomas Nairne, *Nairne's Muskhogean Journals: The 1708 Expedition to the Mississippi River*, ed. Alexander Moore (Jackson, Miss., 1988), 75.

6. John Stuart, quoted in Kathryn E. Holland Braund, *Deerskins and Duffels: The Creek Indian Trade with Anglo-America, 1685–1815* (Lincoln, Neb., 1994), 26.

7. For examples of this line of analysis in the Southeast, see Verner W. Crane, *The Southern Frontier, 1670–1732* (Ann Arbor, Mich., 1929), 117; James H. Merrell, *The Indians' New World: Catawbas and Their Neighbors from European Contact through the Era of Removal* (Chapel Hill, N.C., 1989), 49–91; Braund, *Deerskins and Duffels*, 63; James Axtell, *Natives and Newcomers: The Cultural Origins of North America* (New York, 2001), 104–41; Steven C. Hahn, *The Invention of the Creek Nation, 1670–1763* (Lincoln, Neb., 2004), 75–77. The characterization also appears in the more expansive literature on the fur trade in northeastern North America, such as Denys Delâge, *Bitter Feast: Amerindians and Europeans in Northeastern North America, 1600–1664*, trans. Jane Brierley (Vancouver, 1993); Eric Hinderaker, *Elusive Empires: Constructing Colonialism in the Ohio Valley, 1673–1800* (New York, 1997), 66–77.

8. A number of works from northern North America have provided the foun-

dations for my general understandings of exchange, but several works from the Southeast offer perceptive glimpses into such dynamics. In the case of this latter group, though, limitations of space or topical focus prevent authors from examining how pre-contact norms evolved over the course of colonization. See David Murray, *Indian Giving: Economies of Power in Indian-White Exchanges* (Amherst, Mass., 2000); Richard White, *The Middle Ground: Indians, Empires, and Republics in the Great Lakes Region, 1650–1815* (New York, 1991), 94–141; Arthur J. Ray and Donald B. Freeman, *"Give Us Good Measure": An Economic Analysis of Relations between the Indians and the Hudson's Bay Company before 1763* (Toronto, 1978); Kathleen DuVal, *The Native Ground: Indians and Colonists in the Heart of the Continent* (Philadelphia, 2006); Joel W. Martin, "Southeastern Indians and the English Trade in Skins and Slaves," in *The Forgotten Centuries*, ed. Hudson and Tesser; William L. Ramsey, " 'Something Cloudy in Their Looks': The Origins of the Yamasee War Reconsidered," *Journal of American History* 90.1 (2003): 44–75; Daniel H. Usner, *Indians, Settlers, and Slaves in a Frontier Exchange Economy: The Lower Mississippi Valley before 1783* (Chapel Hill, N.C., 1992).

9. Timothy Silver, *A New Face in the Countryside: Indians, Colonists, and Slaves in South Atlantic Forests, 1500–1800* (New York, 1990), 7–34; Bruce D. Smith, "Variation in Mississippian Settlement Patterns," in *Mississippian Settlement Patterns*, ed. Bruce D. Smith (New York, 1978); Judith A. Bense, *Archaeology of the Southeastern United States: Paleoindian to World War I* (San Diego, 1994), 184–90; Helen Hornbeck Tanner, "The Land and Water Communications of the Southeastern Indians," in *Powhatan's Mantle: Indians in the Colonial Southeast*, ed. Peter H. Wood, Gregory A. Waselkov, and M. Thomas Hatley (Lincoln, Neb., 1989).

10. Among the many who support this idea, see R. Barry Lewis and Charles Stout, "The Town as Metaphor," in *Mississippian Towns and Sacred Spaces: Searching for an Architectural Grammar*, ed. R. Barry Lewis and Charles Stout (Tuscaloosa, Ala., 1998); Joshua Piker, *Okfuskee: A Creek Indian Town in Colonial America* (Cambridge, Mass., 2004), 7–9.

11. John Brewer, *The Sinews of Power: War, Money, and the English State, 1688–1783* (New York, 1989); James Pritchard, *In Search of Empire: France in the Americas, 1670–1730* (New York, 2004); Henry Kamen, *Empire: How Spain Became a World Power, 1492–1763* (New York, 2003).

12. Marcel Mauss, *The Gift: Forms and Functions of Exchange in Archaic Societies*, trans. Ian Cunnison (New York, 1967); Marshal Sahlins, *Stone Age Economics* (Chicago, 1972), esp. 157–68, 185–86; C. A. Gregory, *Gifts and Commodities* (London, 1982); Timothy Earle, *How Chiefs Come to Power: The Political Economy in Prehistory* (Stanford, Calif., 1997); Natalie Zemon Davis, *The Gift in Sixteenth-Century France* (Madison, Wis., 2000); Murray, *Indian Giving*.

13. Thomas J. Pluckhahn, Robbie Ethridge, Jerald T. Milanich, and Marvin T. Smith, Introduction to *Light on the Path: The Anthropology and History of the Southeastern Indians*, ed. Thomas J. Pluckhahn and Robbie Ethridge (Tuscaloosa, Ala., 2006), 1. Some of the most important exceptions to this trend are Patricia Galloway, *Choctaw Genesis, 1500–1700* (Lincoln, Neb., 1995); Marvin T. Smith, *Coosa: The Rise and Fall of a Southeastern Mississippian Chiefdom* (Gainesville, Fla., 2000); Vernon J. Knight Jr., "The Formation of the Creeks," in *The Forgotten Centuries*, ed. Hudson and Tesser. All of them highlight the importance of bridging the chronological divide between Mississippian and colonial periods, but none of them shows the relevance of their connections for the history of the colonial region. James Taylor Carson, *Searching for the Bright Path: The Mississippi Choctaws from Prehistory to Removal* (Lincoln, Neb., 1999) offers one useful approach by

noting the persistence of certain Mississippian practices among the Choctaw of the eighteenth and nineteenth centuries, but he still avoids the intermediate period that links his two periods of comparison.

14. Merrell's work on the formation of the Catawbas remains invaluable, but as a comparative work, it lacks the chronological depth and the discussion of French and Spanish influences that a Creek history can provide. Merrell, *The Indians' New World.*

15. Joshua Piker's excellent study of the Creek town of Okfuskee demonstrates that Creeks were first and foremost members of their towns. Steven Hahn's wide-ranging study of the Creeks contends that these many townspeople did develop a collective sense of themselves after about 1730, when their leaders began claiming southeastern lands on the basis of a Creek "national" territory. Because of their particular foci, though, neither explains how individual towns remained autonomous even as particular leaders mobilized large groups of Creeks along lines of common identity and interest. Hahn, *Invention;* Piker, *Okfuskee.*

16. Alan Gallay, *The Indian Slave Trade: The Rise of the English Empire in the American South, 1670–1717* (New Haven, Conn., 2003). This point regarding violence is made eloquently in Ned Blackhawk, *Violence over the Land: Indians and Empires in the Early American West* (Cambridge, Mass., 2006).

17. For the reiteration of an old lament regarding the disconnection between Indian history and colonial history more generally, see James H. Merrell, "Indian History during the English Colonial Era," in *A Companion to Colonial America,* ed. Daniel Vickers (Malden, Mass., 2003), 133. Among those that belong to a growing list of exceptions, see Fred Anderson, *Crucible of War: The Seven Years' War and the Fate of Empire in British North America, 1754–1766* (New York, 2000), 22–65; Mary Beth Norton, *In the Devil's Snare: The Salem Witchcraft Crisis of 1692* (New York, 2002); Peter Silver, *Our Savage Neighbors: How Indian War Transformed Early America* (New York, 2008). Regarding the negotiated power of empires, see Jack P. Greene, "Negotiated Authorities: The Problem of Governance in the Extended Polities of the Early Modern Atlantic World," in *Negotiated Authorities: Essays in Colonial Political and Constitutional History* (Charlottesville, Va., 1994); Kamen, *Empire;* Hinderaker, *Elusive Empires;* Blackhawk, *Violence over the Land.*

18. White, *The Middle Ground;* Evan Haefeli and Kevin Sweeney, *Captors and Captives: The 1704 French and Indian Raid on Deerfield* (Amherst, Mass., 2003), 4.

19. Steven Oatis, *A Colonial Complex: South Carolina's Frontiers in the Era of the Yamasee War, 1680–1730* (Lincoln, Neb., 2004), presents these ideas in a somewhat different light. Where he sees Anglo-Indian relations as a product of ultimately incompatible systems, I argue that Indians forced Europeans to accept a series of changing norms of town-based exchange until the middle of the eighteenth century, when Europeans (especially the British) organized an empire capable of circumventing these local pressures.

20. All sources cited in this work are my own translation unless cited as an English translation. I have checked quotations of published translations with original sources to verify their accuracy. I have modernized the spellings and punctuation of English texts to suit modern conventions except regarding capitalization and the spelling of proper names. I have left the former in the interests of reminding the reader that the texts have been changed and the latter in the hopes that readers might understand the sources for some of my interpretations of those names. Regarding Muscogee (Creek) oral traditions, see an excel-

lent collection by Bill Grantham, *Creation Myths and Legends of the Creek Indians* (Gainesville, Fla., 2002). The transcripts of my interviews are deposited with the Muscogee (Creek) Nation's Cultural Preservation Office, Okmulgee, Oklahoma.

Chapter 1

1. Edgar Legare Pennington, "Some Ancient Georgia Indian Lore," *Georgia Historical Quarterly* 15.2 (1931): 197.

2. Mauss, *The Gift*; Sahlins, *Stone Age Economics*, esp. 157–68; Gregory, *Gifts and Commodities*; Davis, *The Gift.*

3. Traditions regarding the foundational, or mythic, past might speak of timelessness, but their tellers and listeners adapt material to address contemporary concerns. On the different types of oral tradition and their links to one another and lived experience, see Jan Vansina, *Oral Tradition as History* (Madison, Wis., 1985), 20–32; William Bascom, "The Forms of Folklore: Prose Narratives," in *Sacred Narratives: Reading in the Theory of Myth*, ed. Alan Dundes (Berkeley, Calif., 1984); Bruce Lincoln, *Theorizing Myth: Narrative, Ideology, and Scholarship* (Chicago, 1999), 147–59; Peter Nabokov, *A Forest of Time: American Indian Ways of History* (New York, 2002), 85–104.

4. Pennington, "Georgia Indian Lore," 194.

5. Ibid., 197. Besides the transcription of Chekilli's account that Pennington published, a similar one appears in Talk of Creek Leaders, Savannah, June 11, 1735, in *The Colonial Records for the State of Georgia*, ed. Kenneth Coleman and Milton Ready, vol. 20 (Athens, Ga., 1982), 381–87. I have drawn my summary from both.

6. Charles Hudson, *The Southeastern Indians* (Athens, Ga., 1976), 184–96, 235, 365–75; Benjamin Hawkins, *A Combination of "A Sketch of the Creek Country, in the Years 1798 and 1799"* (1848) *and "Letters of Benjamin Hawkins"* (1916) (Spartanburg, S.C., 1974), 75–78; James Adair, *The History of the American Indians, Particularly Those Nations Adjoining to the Mississippi, East and West Florida, Georgia, South and North Carolina, and Virginia* (1775; New York, 1968), 104–15, 129–31.

7. Thomas Causton to Trustees, June 20, 1735, in *Colonial Records for the State of Georgia*, ed. Coleman and Ready, 20: 401. Steven C. Hahn provides a more expansive discussion of this closing point in "The Cussita Migration Legend: History, Ideology, and the Politics of Mythmaking," in *Light on the Path*, ed. Pluckhahn and Ethridge.

8. John R. Swanton, "Social Organization and Social Usages of the Indians of the Creek Confederacy," in *Forty-Second Annual Report: The Indians of the Southeastern United States*, Bureau of American Ethnology Bulletin 137 (Washington, D.C., 1928), 51–52, 64, 71–72.

9. Wilbur Gouge, interview by author, Okmulgee, Okla., June 25, 1997. In another interview from 1937, the Tukabatchees are considered the "mother" of the Muskogees, with Abecas second and the Cussitas and Cowetas after them. Sandy Fife, interview by Grace Kelley, December 13, 1937, *IPH* 24: 250; John R. Swanton, *Early History of the Creek Indians and Their Neighbors*, Bureau of American Ethnology Bulletin 73 (Washington, D.C., 1922), 191–92.

10. Swanton, *Early History*, 173; James R. Gregory, "The Hee-chee-tees of the Creeks," *The Indian Journal* (Eufala, Indian Territory), April 19, 1901. Thanks to Buddy Cox for the article by Gregory.

11. Timothy R. Pauketat, *Ancient Cahokia and the Mississippians* (New York,

2004), 69. For an excellent introduction to the changing understandings of the mounds, see Robert Silverberg, *The Mound Builders* (1970; Athens, Ohio, 1986).

12. Although some scholars have contended that forty thousand people inhabited Cahokia, George Milner's more modest estimate of three thousand to eight thousand and Timothy R. Pauketat and Neal H. Lopinot's estimate of ten thousand to fifteen thousand are based on systematic study of settlement data. I find Pauketat and Lopinot's estimate slightly more convincing. Milner, *The Cahokia Chiefdom* (Washington, D.C., 1998), 123–24; Timothy R. Pauketat and Neal H. Lopinot, "Cahokian Population Dynamics," in *Cahokia: Domination and Ideology in the Mississippian World*, ed. Timothy R. Pauketat and Thomas E. Emerson (Lincoln, Neb., 1997).

13. Pauketat, *Ancient Cahokia*, 75–95 (quote 80).

14. Ibid., 120–24.

15. Biloine Whiting Young and Melvin L. Fowler, *Cahokia: The Great Native American Metropolis* (Urbana, Ill., 2000); Pauketat, *Ancient Cahokia*, 145–53.

16. The concept of the chiefdom is one that scholars have employed for societies ranging from pre-Roman Gaul to contemporary New Guinea. My understanding of the chiefdom draws in part upon the definitions and debates among the following works: Robert L. Carneiro, "The Chiefdom: Precursor of the State," in *Transition to Statehood in the New World*, ed. Grant D. Jones and Robert R. Krautz (Cambridge, 1981); Christopher S. Peebles and Susan M. Kus, "Some Archaeological Correlates of Ranked Societies," *American Antiquity* 42.3 (1977): 421–48; Paul D. Welch, *Moundville's Economy* (Tuscaloosa, Ala., 1991); David G. Anderson, *The Savannah River Chiefdoms: Political Change in the Late Prehistoric Southeast* (Tuscaloosa, Ala., 1994), 12–52; Morton H. Fried, *The Evolution of Political Society: An Essay in Political Anthropology* (New York, 1967); Timothy Earle, *How Chiefs Come to Power: The Political Economy in Prehistory* (Stanford, Calif., 1997); Robin A. Beck, "Consolidation and Hierarchy: Chiefdom Variability in the Mississippian Southeast," *American Antiquity* 68.4 (2003): 641–61. For an important reappraisal of the term and Mississippian history in particular, see Timothy R. Pauketat, *Chiefdoms and Other Archaeological Delusions* (Lanham, Md.: Altamira Press, 2007). Scholars also disagree on the meaning of "Mississippian," but my definition relies on Claudine Payne and John F. Scarry, "Town Structure at the End of the Mississippian World," in *Mississippian Towns and Sacred Spaces: Searching for an Architectural Grammar*, ed. R. Barry Lewis and Charles Stout (Tuscaloosa, Ala., 1998), 22–24; Pauketat, *Ancient Cahokia*, 10–14; Vernon James Knight Jr., "The Institutional Organization of Mississippian Religion," *American Antiquity* 51.4 (1986): 678; Anderson, *The Savannah River Chiefdoms*, 126–29.

17. Jon Muller, *Mississippian Political Economy* (New York, 197), 193–201.

18. Archaeologists disagree whether Mississippian culture spread from Cahokia or developed throughout the Southeast at roughly the same time, but most chronologies seem to point convincingly to the former. See David G. Anderson, "Examining Chiefdoms in the Southeast: An Application of Multiscalar Analysis," in *Great Towns and Regional Polities in the Prehistoric American Southwest and Southeast*, ed. Jill E. Neitzel (Albuquerque, N. Mex., 1999), 225–27; Pauketat, *Chiefdoms and Other Archaeological Delusions*, 105–9.

19. Jeffrey P. Brain and Philip Phillips, *Shell Gorgets: Styles of the Late Prehistoric and Protohistoric Southeast* (Cambridge, Mass., 1996), 360–94; Vernon James Knight Jr., James A. Brown, and George E. Lankford, "On the Subject Matter of Southeastern Ceremonial Complex Art," *Southeastern Archaeology* 20.2 (2001): 129–41.

20. Vernon J. Knight Jr. and Vincas P. Steponaitis, "New History of Mound-ville," in *Archaeology of the Moundville Chiefdom*, ed. Vernon James Knight Jr. and Vincas P. Steponaitis (Washington, D.C., 1998), 14–20; Vincas P. Steponaitis, "Population Trends at Moundville," in ibid., 21–25; Paul D. Welch, "Control over Goods and the Political Stability of the Moundville Chiefdom," in *Political Structure and Change in the Prehistoric Southeastern United States*, ed. John F. Scarry (Gainesville, Fla., 1996); Welch, *Moundville's Economy*; Peebles and Kus, "Archaeological Correlates," 441.

21. Adam King, *Etowah: The Political History of a Chiefdom Capital* (Tuscaloosa, Ala., 2003), 123–26.

22. John H. Blitz and Karl G. Lorenz, *The Chattahoochee Chiefdoms* (Tuscaloosa, Ala., 2006), 105–18.

23. King, *Etowah*, 79–80; Blitz and Lorenz, *The Chattahoochee Chiefdoms*, 133–35; Pauketat, *Ancient Cahokia*, 156–62.

24. Vernon J. Knight Jr., "Some Developmental Parallels between Cahokia and Moundville," in *Cahokia: Domination and Ideology*, ed. Pauketat and Emerson, 246; Pauketat, *Ancient Cahokia*, 160.

25. Knight, "Institutional Organization," 675–87; Peter Martyr D'Anghera, *De Orbe Novo: The Eight Decades of Peter Martyr D'Anghera*, ed. and trans. Francis A. MacNutt, 2 vols. (New York, 1912), 2: 262–63 (quote).

26. Fray Andrés de San Miguel, *An Early Florida Adventure Story*, trans. John H. Hann (Gainesville, Fla., 2000), 70–71 (quote). For comparative discussions, see Robert L. Hall, *An Archaeology of the Soul: North American Indian Belief and Ritual* (Urbana, Ill., 1997), 3; Mary W. Helms, *Ulysses' Sail: An Ethnographic Odyssey of Power, Knowledge, and Geographical Distance* (Princeton, N.J., 1988). On the likelihood that neighbors were principal partners in exchange, see Muller, *Mississippian Political Economy*, 355–84.

27. For discussions of Spanish examples, see Chapters 2 and 3. British and French examples appear in Chapters 6 and 7, respectively.

28. Luys Hernández de Biedma, "Relation of the Island of Florida," trans. and ed. John E. Worth, in *The De Soto Chronicles: The Expedition of Hernando de Soto to North America in 1539–1543*, ed. Lawrence A. Clayton, Vernon James Knight Jr., and Edward C. Moore, 2 vols. (Tuscaloosa, Ala., 1993), 1: 239 (quotes about serving de Soto); Rodrigo Rangel, "Account of the Northern Conquest and Discovery of Hernando de Soto," trans. and ed. John E. Worth, in ibid., 1: 303; Gentleman of Elvas, "True Relation of the Hardships Suffered by Governor Don Hernando de Soto and Certain Portuguese Gentlemen in the Discovery of the Province of Florida," trans. and ed. James Alexander Robertson with footnotes and updates by John H. Hann, in ibid., 1: 120 ("unite his blood"). For another example of Natives offering slaves to the Spaniards, see Biedma, "Relation," in ibid., 1: 232. For a general discussion of these points, see Marvin T. Smith and David J. Hally, "Chiefly Behavior: Evidence from Sixteenth-Century Spanish Accounts," in *Lords of the Southeast: Social Inequality and the Native Elites of Southeastern North America*, ed. Alex W. Barker and Timothy Pauketat, Archaeological Papers of the American Anthropological Association 3 (1992): 99–110.

29. Bense, *Archaeology of the Southeastern United States*, 187; John P. Hart and C. Margaret Scarry, "The Age of Common Beans (Phaseolus vulgaris) in the Northeastern United States," *American Antiquity* 64.4 (1999): 653–58.

30. James W. Hatch, "Mortuary Indicators of Organizational Variability among Late Prehistoric Chiefdoms in the Southeastern U.S. Interior," in *Chiefdoms in the Americas*, ed. Robert D. Drennan and Carlos A. Uribe (Lanham, Md.,

1987); Mary Lucas Powell, "In the Best of Health? Disease and Trauma among the Mississippian Elite," in *Lords of the Southeast*, ed. Barker and Pauketat, 81–98.

31. Vernon J. Knight Jr., *Tukabatchee: Archaeological Investigations at an Historic Creek Town, 1984*, Report of Investigations, no. 45 (Moundville, Ala., 1985), 116–18; Thomas Nairne, *Nairne's Muskhogean Journals: The 1708 Expedition to the Mississippi River*, ed. Alexander Moore (Jackson, Miss., 1988), 48; John Lawson, *Lawson's History of North Carolina*, (1714; Richmond, Va.: Garrett and Massie, 1951), 198–201.

32. Antoine Simon Le Page du Pratz, *The History of Louisiana, or of the Western Parts of Virginia and Carolina: Containing a Description of the Countries That Lie on Both Sides of the River Mississippi: With an Account of the Settlements, Inhabitants, Soil, Climate, and Products*, ed. and trans. Joseph G. Tregle Jr. (1774; Baton Rouge, La., 1975), 312.

33. Documents generally mentioned male "caciques," with the "Empress" of Cofitachequi, whom I discuss further below, and "Cacica María," whom I mention in Chapter 2, being two notable exceptions. For evidence on warriors being buried near or in some mounds, see David J. Hally, "The Chiefdom of Coosa," in *The Forgotten Centuries*, ed. Hudson and Tesser, 244–45.

34. My discussion of women's public influence remains speculative and draws largely on examples from the colonial Cherokees and Iroquois, whose strong clans provided an important public role for the senior women. Theda Perdue, *Cherokee Women: Gender and Culture Change, 1700–1835* (Lincoln, Neb., 1999), 49–54; Daniel K. Richter, *The Ordeal of the Longhouse: The Peoples of the Iroquois League in the Era of European Colonization* (Chapel Hill, N.C., 1992), 42–44. See also my discussion of women's political influence in Chapter 6.

35. David J. Hally and Hypatia Kelly, "The Nature of Mississippian Towns in Georgia: The King Site Example," in *Mississippian Towns and Sacred Spaces*, ed. Lewis and Stout, 60–63; Bense, *Archaeology of the Southeastern United States*, 207.

36. Gouge, interview by author, Okmulgee, Okla., June 25, 1997; Valeria Littlecreek, interview by author, Okmulgee, Okla., June 27, 1997. It is worth noting that the published stories describing clan origins do not make any mention of emergence from the earth. There is only mention of peoples encountering their totemic animals or the process by which clans aggregated or splintered. Swanton, "Social Organization," 107–14; George E. Lankford, comp. and ed., *Native American Legends: Southeastern Legends; Tales from the Natchez, Caddo, Biloxi, Chickasaw, and Other Nations* (Little Rock, Ark., 1987), 118–20.

37. George Stiggins, *Creek Indian History: A Historical Narrative of Genealogy, Traditions, and Downfall of the Ispocoga or Creek Indian Tribe of Indians* (Birmingham, Ala., 1989), 64; Nairne, *Muskhogean Journals*, 32–34, quote from 60; Hudson, *The Southeastern Indians*, 185–95.

38. Charles Hudson, *The Juan Pardo Expeditions: Exploration of the Carolinas and Tennessee, 1566–1568* (Washington, D.C., 1990), 62–63.

39. Gentleman of Elvas, "True Relation," 1: 85 (quote); Rangel, "Account," 1: 284–88; James B. Langford Jr. and Marvin T. Smith, "Recent Investigations in the Core of the Coosa Province," in *Lamar Archaeology: Mississippian Chiefdoms in the Deep South*, ed. Mark Williams and Gary Shapiro (Tuscaloosa: University of Alabama Press, 1990), 115.

40. Knight, "Developmental Parallels between Cahokia and Moundville," 245. Muller, *Mississippian Political Economy*, 386, criticizes the "exaggerationalist" tendencies of those who see political complexity despite the absence of such data. I offer the following discussion to address his legitimate concerns that scholars not create the illusions we wish to see.

41. Swanton, *Early History*, 236; Hally, "The Chiefdom of Coosa," 244–45; David H. Dye, "Warfare in the Sixteenth-Century Southeast: The De Soto Expedition in the Interior," in *Columbian Consequences*, vol. 2, *Archaeological and Historical Perspectives on the Spanish Borderlands East*, ed. David Hurst Thomas (Washington, D.C., 1990); Chester B. DePratter, *Late Prehistoric and Early Historic Chiefdoms in the Southeastern United States* (New York, 1991), 34.

42. Swanton, *Early History*, 231–39. Regarding the location of the Napochies that Coosas and Spaniards attacked, see Charles M. Hudson, *Knights of Spain, Warriors of the Sun*.

43. Gentleman of Elvas, "True Relation," 99–104; Biedma, "Relation," 235; Rangel, "Account," 294; Garcilaso de la Vega, the Inca, "La Florida," trans. Charmion Shelby, ed. David Bost and Vernon James Knight Jr., in *The De Soto Chronicles*, ed. Clayton, Knight, and Moore, 2: 350.

44. Lawson, *History*, 184 ("Fairs and Markets"); William P. Cumming, ed., *The Discoveries of John Lederer* (Charlottesville, Va., 1958), 41–42 ("higgling"); Merrell, *The Indians' New World*, 28–30; On the ball game, see Hudson, *The Southeastern Indians*, 408–21; Adair, *History*, 428–30.

45. For a similar point, see Greg Keyes, "Myth and Social History in the Southeast," in *Perspectives on the Southeast: Linguistics, Archaeology, Ethnohistory*, ed. Patricia B. Kwachka (Athens, Ga., 1994).

46. Adair, *History*, 39.

47. William Bartram, *Travels through North and South Carolina, Georgia, East and West Florida* (1792; Savannah, Ga., 1973), 35.

48. Hawkins, *A Sketch of the Creek Country*, 81–83.

49. Swanton, "Social Organization," 54–55. Gregory related a beautiful and more detailed version of this same story, which he concluded with the caveat, "Being for verbal transmission only." The document has no addressee, signatory, or date, but other available evidence indicates that Gregory wrote it to Emmett Starr, perhaps in 1910, James R. Gregory Papers, OHS.

50. Hawkins, *A Sketch of the Creek Country*, 81–83; Hudson, *The Southeastern Indians*, 234–36; Mary R. Haas, "Creek Inter-Town Relations," *American Anthropologist* 42 (1940): 479–89.

51. Swanton, "Social Organization," 200–202; Joel Martin, *Sacred Revolt: The Muskogees' Struggle for a New World* (Boston, 1991), 22–27.

52. Vernon J. Knight Jr., "Symbolism of Mississippian Mounds," in *Powhatan's Mantle: Indians in the Colonial Southeast*, ed. Peter H. Wood, Gregory A. Waselkov, and M. Thomas Hatley (Lincoln, Neb., 1989), 279; Silverberg, *The Mound Builders*, 11, 38–39, passim; Gregory to Emmett Starr, Inola, Indian Territory (Oklahoma), August 20, 1900, James R. Gregory Papers, OHS. For another assessment of Creeks being different from the Mound-builders, see Charles Gibson, "Gibson's Indian Lore: Unpublished History by Charles Gibson," *Cherokee Advocate*, August 20, 1904, 1.

53. Such different theories do not mean that the two traditions have not borrowed extensively from one another. When Gregory rejected the current archaeological theories that the ancestors of the Creeks, Choctaws, Cherokees, and Chickasaws built the mounds of the Southeast, he actually drew upon the nineteenth-century science of phrenology. The Creek doctor noted that his people's skulls were similar in shape to those of the nineteenth-century's paragons of civility, the British, and concluded Creeks were too free to consent to such onerous construction work. Gregory to Starr, August 20, 1900, James R. Gregory Papers, OHS. For a related discussion of the links between white and Indian

historians, see Claudio Saunt, "Telling Stories: The Political Uses of Myth and History in the Cherokee and Creek Nations," *Journal of American History* 93.3 (2006): 673–97. For an excellent discussion of a set of Cherokee traditions that may also deal with their links to and breaks with a Mississippian past, see Raymond D. Fogelson, "Who Were the Aní Kutáni? An Excursion into Cherokee Historical Thought," *Ethnohistory* 31.4 (1984): 255–63.

54. Keeper Johnson, interview by author, Okmulgee, Okla., June 18, 1997.

55. Craig Womack, *Red on Red: Native American Literary Separatism* (Minneapolis, 1999), 29. For supporting discussions on the need to understand Native intellectual history through their oral and written traditions, see Nabokov, *A Forest of Time*, 237; Donald Fixico, *The American Indian Mind in a Linear World: American Indian Studies and Traditional Knowledge* (New York, 2003), 79–80.

56. Myron Bartlett, "Macon Land Sales—Antiquities," Macon *Telegraph*, November 1, 1828, 1.

57. Adair, *History*, 39.

58. Myron Bartlett, "Macon Land Sales—Antiquities," 1.

59. Randall Floyd, "Indian Mound Haunts Grovetown Home," Augusta (Georgia) *Chronicle*, November 8, 1998, E2.

Chapter 2

1. Swanton, "Social Organization," 71–72. According to Swanton, 71, Proctor was "one of the leading 'reactionaries' among the Creek at this time."

2. This cooperative relationship has received limited attention among Florida scholars. Amy Turner Bushnell notes the ties among Native leaders, Spanish officials, and Franciscans, but she does not discuss Natives' role in fostering them. Similarly, although Jerald Milanich and John Worth acknowledge the voluntary nature of Indians' association with the Spanish, Indians in their view were accepting a colonial system of Spanish manufacture. Paul Hoffman presents a more nuanced picture when he notes that by 1608 "Spaniards . . . had reached accommodation with the caciques that limited Spanish demands on Indian societies just as fully, perhaps even more fully, than Imperial laws did." But his details do not always support this more balanced assessment. For instance, he describes the Spanish response to the Guale revolt of 1597, which I discuss below, as "swift, brutal, prolonged, and effective," and believes Franciscans gained converts by using "shrewd tactics whose general tenor was to support the authority of the caciques." In neither of these latter instances does he show how Indians were forcing Spaniards to accept a cooperative relationship. This chapter is partly devoted to redressing this oversight. Amy Turner Bushnell, *Situado and Sabana: Spain's Support System for the Presidio and Mission Provinces of Florida* (Athens, Ga., 1994); Jerald T. Milanich, *Laboring in the Fields of the Lord: Spanish Missions and Southeastern Indians* (Washington, D.C., 1999); John E. Worth, *The Timucuan Chiefdoms of Spanish Florida*, vol. 1, *Assimilation*, and vol. 2, *Resistance and Destruction* (Gainesville, Fla., 1998); Paul E. Hoffman, *Florida's Frontiers* (Bloomington, Ind., 2002), 99, 83, 95 (pages listed in order of quotations' appearance).

3. As David Weber has noted, "[Spanish] missionaries failed to advance permanently, defend effectively, or Hispanicize deeply North American frontiers in the seventeenth century." Unfortunately, this cogent observation says little about Spaniards' unintended influences on the lands around and beyond their missions. Scholars of the Southeast continue to believe that Spain's regional

influence was small primarily because they have not examined it. Paul Hoffman's recent history of the colony's frontiers, for example, confines itself primarily to the state boundaries of Florida, and John Worth's admittedly "very preliminary exploration" of Spanish and English relations with southeastern Indians before 1700 has little to say about the Natives of the deep interior, whom he notes "remained in virtually complete isolation from direct European contact." Consequently, it is no surprise that Charles Hudson believes that the Spanish mission system was unable "to shape Indian societies at a distance," and that Alan Gallay asserts, "After the initial forays of Spanish explorers, Spain's influence did not reach much farther into the South than Florida." What follows here should suggest the limitations of these assessments. David J. Weber, *The Spanish Frontier in North America* (New Haven, Conn., 1992), 121; Hoffman, *Florida's Frontiers*; John E. Worth, "Spanish Missions and the Persistence of Chiefly Power," in *The Transformation of the Southeastern Indians, 1540–1760*, ed. Charles Hudson and Robbie Ethridge (Jackson, Miss., 2002), 45, 47; Charles Hudson, Introduction to *The Transformation of the Southeastern Indians*, ed. Hudson and Ethridge, xxv; Gallay, *The Indian Slave Trade*, 33. For examples of works that discuss Spanish missions in their regional contexts, see Cynthia Radding, *Wandering Peoples: Colonialism, Ethnic Spaces, and Ecological Frontiers in Northwestern Mexico, 1700–1850* (Durham, N.C., 1997); James F. Brooks, *Captives and Cousins: Slavery, Kinship, and Community in the Southwest Borderlands* (Chapel Hill, N.C., 2002); Susan M. Deeds, *Defiance and Deference in Mexico's Colonial North: Indians under Spanish Rule in Nueva Vizcaya* (Austin, 2003).

4. Matthew Restall, *Seven Myths of the Spanish Conquest* (New York, 2003), 33–44.

5. For this summary and the events that follow, see Weber, *The Spanish Frontier*, 33–70; Hoffman, *Florida's Frontiers*, 20–43.

6. The accounts disagree on the ruling woman/women of the province. Gentleman of Elvas, "True Relation," 1: 82; Biedma, "Relation," 1: 278–80; Garcilaso, "La Florida," 2: 293.

7. Gentleman of Elvas, "True Relation," 1: 80–95 (quote 84); Biedma, "Relation," 1: 230–32; Rangel, "Account," 1: 277–88.

8. The chroniclers disagree on the numbers, but all coincide on the devastation. Indian deaths vary widely from 2,500 to 7,000. The lower numbers seem more reasonable since few towns reached half that number. Three accounts claim that 18–22 Spaniards were killed and 148–250 wounded. Garcilaso is alone in claiming 82 deaths. Gentleman of Elvas, "True Relation," 1: 99–104; Biedma, "Relation," 1: 234–35; Rangel, "Account," 1: 294; Garcilaso, "La Florida," 2: 336, 345, 350.

9. For a summary of the expedition, see Hudson, *Knights of Spain*. Hudson mentions that 257 of the survivors are known by name and that Elvas's figure of 311 is probably close. Hudson, *Knights of Spain*, 412; Gentleman of Elvas, "True Relation," 1: 165.

10. Kamen, *Empire*, 248–49.

11. For descriptions of Spaniards' appetites, see Gentleman of Elvas, "True Relation," 1: 77; Rangel, "Account," 1: 279. Of the four accounts, Rangel mentions de Soto chastising the chief of Ocute for an unspecified grievance. The other three mention only a warm reception. In 1597, however, missionaries were forced to cut short their journey to Ocute because the chief threatened to kill them if they arrived in his town. Rangel, "Account," 1: 272; Governor Méndez de Canzo to King, St. Augustine, February 4–6, 1600, AGI SD 224.

12. No sixteenth-century eyewitness accounts offer conclusive evidence of diseases. Hoffman notes that Coosa's supposed decline between 1540 and 1560 has been attributed to witnesses who had no interest in colonizing the region; other contemporary reports suggest that the chiefdom suffered little, if any population loss. Hoffman, *Florida's Frontiers*, 40–43, esp. nn. 63, 64. Paul Kelton has pointed out that there is no documentation of epidemics in the interior Southeast before 1696. He further asserts that trade between Spaniards and non-mission Indians was too infrequent to spread infection inland. Although I find plenty of evidence for the seventeenth-century trade ties that could have carried diseases from Spanish communities to Native towns, Kelton is right to question the prevalence of acute infectious diseases in the sixteenth century. More important, he makes clear why scholars must find better proof before they unquestioningly assert the ubiquity of post-contact epidemics. For my discussion of Native-Spaniard contacts, see below in this chapter and Chapter 3 especially. Paul Kelton, *Epidemics and Enslavement: Biological Catastrophe in the Native Southeast, 1492–1715* (Lincoln, Neb., 2007).

13. Ann F. Ramenofsky, *Vectors of Death: The Archaeology of European Contact* (Albuquerque, N. Mex., 1987), 55–63; Marvin T. Smith, *Archaeology of Aboriginal Culture Change in the Interior Southeast: Depopulation during the Early Historic Period* (Gainesville, Fla., 1987), 84–85; Smith, *Coosa*, 100–107; Ann F. Ramenofsky and Patricia Galloway, "Disease and the Soto Entrada," in *The Hernando de Soto Expedition: History, Historiography, and "Discovery" in the Colonial Southeast*, ed. Patricia Galloway (Lincoln, Neb., 1997); Robert L. Blakely and Bettina Detweiler-Blakely, "The Impact of European Diseases in the Sixteenth Century Southeast: A Case Study," *Midcontinental Journal of Archaeology* 14.1 (1989): 62–89.

14. John H. Hann, *Apalachee: The Land Between the Rivers* (Gainesville, Fla., 1988), 7–12; John F. Scarry, "Stability and Change in the Apalachee Chiefdom," in *Political Structure and Change in the Prehistoric Southeastern United States*, ed. John F. Scarry (Gainesville, Fla., 1996); Marvin T. Smith, "Aboriginal Depopulation in the Postcontact Southeast," in *The Forgotten Centuries*, ed. Hudson and Tesser, 266; Smith, *Aboriginal Culture Change*, 98–103; Mary Lucas Powell, "Human Skeletal Remains from Ocmulgee National Monument," in *Ocmulgee Archaeology: 1936–1986*, ed. David J. Hally (Athens, Ga., 1994), 129; DePratter, *Late Prehistoric and Early Historic Chiefdoms*, 163–65. Gerald F. Schroedl, "Cherokee Ethnohistory and Archaeology from 1540 to 1838," in *Indians of the Greater Southeast: Historical Archaeology and Ethnohistory*, ed. Bonnie G. McEwan (Gainesville, Fla., 2000), notes that some early historic Cherokees began building their first council houses on top of the old mounds, explicitly symbolizing the ways in which more popular political forms had replaced the control of an individual.

15. Grantham, *Creation Myths and Legends*, 204–9 (quote 206). See also ibid., 24–26, 199–227 for additional context.

16. Adair, *History*, 166. For a history of Coosa after 1600, see Smith, *Coosa*, 68–81, 91–117.

17. René Laudonnière, *Three Voyages*, trans. and ed. Charles E. Bennett (1975; Tuscaloosa, 2001), 60, 62.

18. Worth, *The Timucuan Chiefdoms*, 1: 13–18, 2: 2–8; John H. Hann, *A History of the Timucuan Indians and Missions* (Gainesville, Fla., 1996), 73–84, 257–61; Jerald T. Milanich, "Native Chiefdoms and the Exercise of Complexity in Sixteenth-Century Florida," in *Chiefdoms and Chieftaincy in the Americas*, ed. Elsa M. Redmond (Gainesville, Fla., 1998); Grant D. Jones, "The Ethnohistory of the Guale Coast through 1684," in *The Anthropology of St. Catherines Island*, vol. 1, *Nat-*

ural and Cultural History, by D. H. Thomas, G. D. Jones, R. S. Durham, and C. S. Larsen, Anthropological Papers of the American Museum of Natural History 55 (1978): 155–210; John E. Worth, *The Struggle for the Georgia Coast: An Eighteenth-Century Spanish Retrospective on Guale and Mocama*, American Museum of Natural History, Anthropological Papers 75 (Athens, Ga., 1995), 12. The estimate of fifty thousand Timucuas comes from Worth, *The Timucuan Chiefdoms*, 2: 8, but he acknowledges it as speculation "virtually incapable of proof."

19. Luís Gerónimo de Oré, *The Martyrs of Florida, 1513–1616*, trans. and ed. Maynard Geiger (New York, 1936), 33–38; Charles Hudson, *The Juan Pardo Expeditions: Exploration of the Carolinas and Tennessee, 1566–1568* (Washington, D.C., 1990), 23–46, 175–76; Bushnell, *Situado and Sabana*, 38–41, 61–62; Paul E. Hoffman, *A New Andalucia and a Way to the Orient: The American Southeast during the Sixteenth Century* (Baton Rouge, La., 1990), 266; Hann, *A History of Timucuan Indians*, 50–72.

20. Eugene Lyon, "The Enterprise of Florida," in *Columbian Consequences*, ed. Thomas, 2: 291.

21. Kamen, *Empire*, 255.

22. David Beers Quinn, ed., *New American World: A Documentary History of North America to 1612*, 5 vols. (New York, 1979), 2: 192.

23. Hoffman, *Florida's Frontiers*, 69–70. Officials in La Florida did not act in isolation. Imperial developments in northwestern Mexico and eastern Paraguay suggest that Spaniards recognized the benefits of moderation in the late sixteenth century. Daniel T. Reff, "The Jesuit Mission Frontier in Comparative Perspective: The Reductions of the Río de la Plata and the Missions of Northwestern Mexico, 1588–1700," in *Contested Ground: Comparative Frontiers on the Northern and Southern Edges of the Spanish Empire*, ed. Donna J. Guy and Thomas E. Sheridan (Tucson, 1998), 25. For a discussion of the inadequacy of Spanish military strategy, see Richard W. Slatta, "Spanish Colonial Military Strategy and Ideology," in ibid., 83–96.

24. Joseph del Prado to King, December 30, 1654, AGI SD 229; Francisco Morgado to King, July 27, 1597, AGI SD 231; Weber, *The Spanish Frontier*, 107; Bushnell, *Situado and Sabana*, 44. Regarding Spanish goods in elite burials, the following examples come from Alabama and South Carolina: Knight, *Tukabatchee*, 169–85; Cameron B. Wesson, "Prestige Goods, Symbolic Capital, and Social Power in the Protohistoric Southeast," in *Between Contacts and Colonies: Archaeological Perspectives on the Protohistoric Southeast*, ed. Cameron B. Wesson and Mark A. Rees (Tuscaloosa, Ala., 2002); Hudson, *The Juan Pardo Expeditions*, 138–40.

25. Rebecca Saunders, *Stability and Change in Guale Indian Pottery, A.D. 1300–1702* (Tuscaloosa, Ala., 2000), 177. For a different example of stress on craft production possibly caused by disease, Marvin Smith notes the decline of craft specialization during the early seventeenth century. It could be that, as he surmises, diseases were disrupting chiefly hierarchies and the craftspeople they supported. It could also be that the arrival of Spanish goods supplanted these indigenous crafts. In either case, Spanish goods perhaps caused and certainly filled a crucial gap in the iconography of power. Smith, *Aboriginal Culture Change*, 108–12.

26. Franciscans took pride in their ability to impress Native leaders, and later historians consider it important to the Franciscans' success in New Mexico as well as Florida. Fr. Francisco de Marrón to King, January 23, 1597, AGI SD 235; Fr. Luís Gerónimo de Oré to King, Santo Domingo, [1617?], AGI SD 235; Weber, *The Spanish Frontier*, 115–16. On Franciscans' familiarity with disease, see

Daniel T. Reff, *Disease, Depopulation, and Culture Change in Northwestern New Spain, 1518–1764* (Salt Lake City, 1991), 260–64.

27. Amy Turner Bushnell, "The Sacramental Imperative: Catholic Ritual and Indian Sedentism in the Provinces of Florida," in *Columbian Consequences*, ed. Thomas, vol. 2; John E. Worth, "Spanish Missions and the Persistence of Chiefly Power," in *Transformation*, ed. Ethridge and Hudson; Worth, *The Timucuan Chiefdoms*, 1: 36–43; Hoffman, *Florida's Frontiers*, 79.

28. Alonso de Escobedo, *La Florida*, excerpted in *Relación histórica de la Florida, escrita en el siglo XVII*, ed. Atanacio López (Madrid, 1931), 1: 27–28 (quotes). For a summary of this *entrada*, see Worth, "Late Spanish Military Expeditions in the Interior Southeast, 1597–1628," in *The Forgotten Centuries*, ed. Hudson and Tesser, 105–8. For Salas's linguistic abilities, see Maynard Geiger, O.F.M., *The Franciscan Conquest of Florida (1573–1618)* (Washington, D.C., 1937), 82–83.

29. Testimony of Gaspar de Salas, February 2, 1600, AGI SD 224, N. 35. Escobedo, *La Florida*, 28–30. Two lines from Escobedo, *La Florida*, 28 ("y luego se pusieron en presencia / de toda la familia endemoniada") suggest that Chozas first sought the approval of the members of Altamaha's closely related elite before meeting with the entire town.

30. The cause for Ocute's reticence is difficult to determine, but the best clues come from Escobedo. Although he mistranscribes Ocute as Quaque, he elliptically refers to Chozas's failure there by listing Quaque along with Tama (alias Altamaha) and two other towns of Fatufas (also known as Catufa or Patofa) and Usatipass and then saying that Chozas "converted three kingdoms, but not the first." Escobedo, *La Florida*, 28–29. For the quotes about Ocute's obstructionism, see Testimony of Salas, February 2, 1600, AGI SD 224, N. 35. Regarding Chozas's hasty departure, see Escobedo, *La Florida*, 31–32.

31. Juan probably shared these ambitions. Unlike the many Indian escorts who deserted Chozas, Juan remained with the expedition—and he collected on this loyalty when he returned to St. Augustine and he requested gifts from the governor for his service. He probably imagined that such loyalty would secure him similar Spanish generosity in the future, a generosity he might share with trips inland along the new path from Tolomato to the Oconee Valley. Alvárez de Castrillón to King, September 14, 1597, AGI SD 231.

32. Oré, *The Martyrs of Florida*, 73.

33. For summaries of the revolt, see Geiger, *The Franciscan Conquest*, 86–115; Hoffman, *Florida's Frontiers*, 82–86; Bushnell, *Situado and Sabana*, 60–66. For a documentary overview, see Quinn, *New American World*, 5: 69–92 (quote 5: 69).

34. Quinn, *New American World*, 5: 87.

35. Joseph M. Hall Jr., "Making an Indian People: Creek Formation in the Colonial Southeast, 1590–1735" (Ph.D. diss., University of Wisconsin, Madison, 2001), 87–93; Bushnell, *Situado and Sabana*, 66. Hoffman describes the Spanish response as "swift, brutal, prolonged, and effective in restoring Spanish control in Guale." Although Spaniards did respond effectively, they could not have pacified the province without the assistance of Indians who exacted their own concessions, such as a reduction in tribute or, as I describe below, Spanish gifts. Hoffman, *Florida's Frontiers*, 83. On the labor draft, see Hoffman, *Florida's Frontiers*, 85; Bushnell, *Situado and Sabana*, 121–23.

36. Bartolomé de Argüelles to King, August 3, 1598, AGI SD 229. Argüelles's statement is difficult to parse, but it offers intriguing insight into the politics of power, gifts, and tribute. It reads, "les alço El dho gobernador el tributo y aunque no era de mucha ynportancia parece que era una manera de Reconocimie-

nto con lo qual se ganaba opinion con los de la tierra adentro q no estiman en mas de quanto ben que a cada uno se le tributa." I translate the passage literally and loosely as, "The said governor raised their tribute and although it was not of much importance, it seems that it was a form of acknowledgment [of authority] with which we gained [a good] opinion from those from the inland who do not esteem those except according to how much they exact as tribute."

37. Argüelles to King, October 31, 1598, AGI SD 229.

38. Méndez to King, February 28, 1600, AGI SD 224, N. 35. Between 1583 and 1723, soldiers were paid 115 ducats a year. Bushnell, *Situado and Sabana*, 45.

39. Alonso de Cano to King, February 23, 1600, AGI SD 229.

40. Méndez to King, February 23, 1598, AGI SD 224, N. 31. Among the beneficiaries of his largess were the Spaniards themselves, who by 1595 had apparently received some nine thousand reales' (over one thousand pesos') worth of supplies from the cacique and his people. Fray Andrés de San Miguel, *An Early Florida Adventure Story*, trans. John H. Hann (Gainesville, Fla., 2000), 7.

41. Governor Méndez de Canzo feared that Guale resistance to a Mocama leader would, as he put it, "undercut what I have done with so much work to attract and reduce the province [to Spanish allegiance]." Méndez to King, February 28, 1600, AGI SD 224, N. 35; Méndez to King, June 26, 1600, AGI SD 224, N. 36.

42. Diego Dávila to King, June 26, 1606, AGI SD 235.

43. Testimony of Juan de Lara, excerpted and translated in Worth, "Late Spanish Military Expeditions," 109.

44. "Relación del viage que hizo el señor Pedro de Ibarra, gobernador y Capitán General de la Florida, á visitar los pueblos indios de las provincias de San Pedro y Guale," in *Documentos históricos de la Florida y la Luisiana, siglos XVI al XVIII*, ed. Manuel Serrano y Sanz (Madrid, 1913), 183–84 (quote). People began moving into scattered farmsteads in the second half of the fifteenth century, probably as a result of relative peace and the growing population that accompanied it. Although such population dispersal probably did not induce people to abandon the mounds, it certainly accelerated the mounds' declining role toward the end of the century. Mark Williams, "Chiefly Compounds," in *Mississippian Communities and Households*, ed. J. Daniel Rogers and Bruce D. Smith (Tuscaloosa, Ala., 1995), 124–34; James W. Hatch, "Lamar Period Upland Farmsteads of the Oconee River Valley, Georgia," in ibid., 135–55.

45. Smith, *Aboriginal Culture Change*, 77–80; Marvin T. Smith, "Aboriginal Population Movements in the Postcontact Southeast," in *Transformation*, ed. Ethridge and Hudson, 10–12; Williams, "Growth and Decline," 191–93; Mark Williams, personal communication, May 13, 2004.

46. So little is known about the Santa Isabel mission and a contact-period archaeological site on the upper Altamaha River known as the Pine Barrens site that any conclusions must be tentative. Although Frankie Snow thinks the mission population was from the Oconee Valley, John Worth believes it was Timucuan. Frankie Snow, "Pine Barrens Lamar," in *Lamar Archaeology*, ed. Williams and Shapiro, 82–89; Oré, *The Martyrs of Florida*, 129, 135, n. 22; Worth, *The Timucuan Chiefdoms*, 1: 73; John E. Worth, "The Timucuan Missions of Spanish Florida and the Revolt of 1656" (Ph.D. diss., University of Florida, 1992), 68–69, 76 n. 14.

47. Fernández de Olivera to King, October 13, 1612, AGI SD 225, N. 4.

48. According to Amy Turner Bushnell, traveling the two hundred miles between St. Augustine and the center of the province of Apalachee took roughly

twelve days. The cape, today's Cape St. George, is located where the Apalachi-cola River empties into the Gulf of Mexico and would probably have been about another week's travel distant. Two and a half months' travel could mean that the visitors had arrived from a location as much as four times farther away than Apalachee. Bushnell, *Situado and Sabana*, 114; Bushnell, personal communication, November 28, 2007.

49. In 1600 the population of the colonial city was about 500, and perhaps as large as 700. Hoffman, *Florida's Frontiers*, 75–76. Estimating the population of southeastern Indians is much more difficult, but two benchmarks might serve as rough guides. An unsigned report on Florida's Indians written before 1571 lists a total population of 47,000 in the peninsula's provinces of Tocobaga, Calusa, Apalachee, and Noroco. John Worth believes some 50,000 to 150,000 people inhabited the peninsula and panhandle of Florida at the time of contact. Memoria de lo que en la florida pasa de los yndios de la misma tierra, n.p., n.d., AGI Indiferente 1571, N. 40; Worth, *The Timucuan Chiefdoms*, 2: 2–8.

50. Fr. Francisco Pareja et al. to King, January 17, 1617, AGI SD 235.

51. Comparisons to other colonial exchange situations suggest the likelihood of widespread disruption from contact with Europeans, whether in the seventeenth-century Jesuit missions of northern Mexico or Paraguay or in the nineteenth-century trade in the Pacific Northwest of North America. The details from Florida are less conclusive. Reff, "Jesuit Mission Frontier," in *Contested Ground*, ed. Guy and Sheridan; David Igler, "Diseased Goods: Global Exchanges in the Eastern Pacific Basin, 1770–1850," *American Historical Review* 109.3 (2004): 693–719; Hoffman, *Florida's Frontiers*, 105.

52. Smith, *Aboriginal Culture Change*, 46–51; Knight, *Tukabatchee*, 107.

53. Clark Spencer Larsen, Margaret J. Schoeninger, Dale L. Hutchinson, Katherine F. Russell, and Christopher B. Ruff, "Beyond Demographic Collapse: Biological Adaptation and Change in Native Populations of La Florida," in *Columbian Consequences*, ed. Thomas, 2: 409–28; Bushnell, "The Sacramental Imperative," in ibid., 2: 475–90

54. Milanich, *Laboring*, xiii.

55. As the English colonial agent argued before the Creeks in 1725, "I must tell your Young Men that if it had not Been for us, you would not have known how to War Nor yet Have anything To War with. You have had nothing But Bows and Arrows To kill Deer; You had no hoes or Axes then What you made of Stone." Tobias Fitch, "Captain Fitch's Journal to the Creeks, 1725," in *Travels in the American Colonies*, ed. Newton Mereness (New York, 1916), 181. For more recent reprises of Fitch's theme, see Steven C. Hahn, "The Mother of Necessity: Carolina, the Creek Indians, and the Making of a New Order in the Colonial Southeast, 1670–1763," in *Transformation*, ed. Ethridge and Hudson; Braund, *Deerskins and Duffels*.

Chapter 3

1. Mose Wiley, interviewed by Grace Kelley, Dustin, Okla., November 22, 1937, *IPH* 49: 383–84.

2. Although commerce expanded throughout Spain's American empire during the seventeenth century, Florida historians have understood this transformation primarily as a response to irregular royal support. They have paid much less attention to the ways the trade grew from the wider economy of the empire or the relations that Native and Spanish leaders negotiated and renewed. Hoffman,

Florida's Frontiers, 62–64, 120; Bushnell, *Situado and Sabana*, 56. Bushnell has more recently noted the importance of appreciating the dynamics of Spain's seventeenth-century empire and the consequences of Indian negotiation in "Gates, Patterns, and Peripheries: The Frontier in Latin America," in *Negotiated Empires: Centers and Peripheries in the Americas, 1500–1820*, ed. Christine Daniels and Michael V. Kennedy (New York, 2002), 21–23.

3. Gregory A. Waselkov, "Seventeenth-Century Trade in the Colonial Southeast," *Southeastern Archaeology* 8.2 (Winter 1989): 117–33, discusses archaeological evidence for this process.

4. Richard Boyer, "Mexico in the Seventeenth Century: Transition of a Colonial Society," *Hispanic American Historical Review* 57.3 (1977): 455–78; John Lynch, *The Hispanic World in Crisis and Change, 1598–1700* (Oxford, U.K., 1992), 289; José Morilla Critz, "Crisis y transformación de la economía de Nueva España en el siglo XVII: Un ensayo crítico," *Anuario de Estudios Americanos* [Spain] 45 (1988): 241–72; Alejandro de la Fuente and Cesar Garcia del Pino, "Havana and the Fleet System: Trade and Growth in the Periphery of the Spanish Empire, 1550–1610," *Colonial Latin American Review* 5.1 (1996): 95–116.

5. On the uses and abuses of the *situado*, see Amy Bushnell, *The King's Coffer: Proprietors of the Spanish Florida Treasury, 1565–1702* (Gainesville, Fla., 1978), esp. 118–36 (quote 127); Bushnell, *Situado and Sabana*, esp. 36–59. On St. Augustine's surprising wealth, see Eugene Lyon, "Richer Than We Thought: The Material Culture of Sixteenth-Century St. Augustine," *El Escribano: The St. Augustine Journal of History* 29 (1992): 1–17.

6. Bushnell, *Situado and Sabana*, 48 ("*expectation*," emphasis in original); Nicolás Ponce de León to King, June 30, 1637, AGI SD 225, N. 38 ("gaming"); Governor Damián de Vega Castro y Pardo to King, August 29, 1644, AGI SD 225, N. 42; Engel Sluiter, *The Florida Situado: Quantifying the First 80 Years, 1571–1651* (Gainesville, Fla., 1985); Hoffman, *Florida's Frontiers*, 114, 118.

7. Worth, *The Timucuan Chiefdoms* 1: 196–97; Bushnell, *Situado and Sabana*, 111–16; Spanish Crown, Cédula to Governor Don Andrés Rodríguez de Villegas, Madrid, May 18, 1629, AGI México 1066, Libro 9, folio 39 (quote). Thanks to Patricia Meehan for bringing this document to my attention. Although Worth points out that the mission known as Tocoy was depopulated by the late 1610s, missionaries did move other converts to the area to found the mission of San Diego de Helaca and maintain a population to ferry passengers across the St. Johns River. This new site may still have been known popularly as Tocoy in 1628. Worth, *The Timucuan Chiefdoms*, 1: 71.

8. Oré, *The Martyrs of Florida*, 118 (quote); Governor Damián de Vega Castro y Pardo to King, August 22, 1639, AGI SD 225, N. 39; Hann, *Apalachee*, 5, 13–14; Amy Bushnell, "That Demonic Game: The Campaign to Stop Indian Peolota Playing in Spanish Florida, 1675–1684," *The Americas* 35.1 (1978): 4. On the significance of Apalachee's corn as a motivator for Apalachee evangelization, see also Governor Luis Horruytiner to King, November 15, 1633, AGI SD 233.

9. Worth, *The Timucuan Chiefdoms*, 1: 110–14.

10. Brooks, *Captives and Cousins*, 1–55; Barbara Ganson, *The Guarani under Spanish Rule in the Rio de la Plata* (Stanford, Calif., 2003), 30–51.

11. Worth, *The Timucuan Chiefdoms*, 1: 178, 182–83, 193–97; David Hurst Thomas, "The Archaeology of Mission Santa Catalina de Guale: Our First 15 Years," in *The Spanish Missions of La Florida*, ed. Bonnie McEwan (Gainesville, Fla., 1993), 13–16; Bonnie G. McEwan, "Hispanic Life on the Seventeenth-Century Florida Frontier," in ibid., 316.

12. Francisco Ramírez, Juan de Cueva, and Francisco Menéndez Márquez to King, January 30, 1627, AGI SD 229. For comparison of expenses for gifts across various years, see Sluiter, *The Florida Situado*. Knight, *Tukabatchee*, 176, believes that Spaniards were already indiscriminate in their gift giving by the early 1600s.

13. Order of Sergeant Major Eugenio de Espinosa to Sergeant Major Antonio Herrera López y Mesa, September 9, 1633, enclosed in Relation of merits of Antonio Herrera López y Mesa, April 22, 1649, AGI Indiferente 114, N.23 (quote). For corroborating evidence of trade goods moving in both directions, see Waselkov, "Seventeenth-Century Trade," 117; Joseph Hall, "Between Old World and New: Oconee Valley Residents and the Spanish Southeast, 1540–1621," in *The Atlantic World and Virginia, 1550–1624*, ed. Peter Mancall (Chapel Hill, N.C., 2007).

14. Governor Francisco de Riano y Gamboa to King, Havana, August 29, 1637, in Quaderno detodas las cartas delos distritos delas cinco Audiencias del año de 1637 ecepto las del Virrey questan en quaderno aparte, AGI Indiferente 186; Testimonio del descubrimiento de Apalache, in Quaderno detodas las cartas . . . , AGI Indiferente 186; Governor Luis de Horruytiner to King, June 24, 1637, AGI SD 225, N. 35.

15. For population figures, see Alejandro de la Fuente, "Población y crecimiento en Cuba (Siglos XVI y XVII): Un estudio regional," *Revista europea de estudios latinoamericanos y del Caribe* 55 (1993): 65; Hoffman, *Florida's Frontiers*, 116. Hann, *Apalachee*, 174, cites figures of fourteen hundred for Apalachee's most prominent town of San Luís in 1675, but he is not certain how many of these people would have inhabited a town center as opposed to dispersed farmsteads. For travel times and distances, see Testimony of Benito López in Testimonio sobre el descubrimiento de Apalache, enclosed in Riano y Gamboa to King, August 29, 1637, enclosed in Quaderno de todas las cartas, AGI Indiferente 186; Governor Damián Vega Castro y Pardo to King, August 22, 1639, AGI SD 225, N. 39.

16. Vega Castro y Pardo to King, July 9, 1643, AGI SD 225, N. 41; Order of Vega Castro y Pardo to Nicolás Estévez de Carmentatis, September 23, 1643, enclosed in Relation of services of Estévez de Carmentatis, June 22, 1680, AGI Indiferente 128, N. 124. For a discussion of weather and harvest patterns, see Hoffman, *Florida's Frontiers*, 117–20.

17. Order of Governor Luis Horruytiner, November 3, 1638, enclosed in Antonio de Herrera López y Mesa, April 22, 1649, AGI Indiferente 114, N. 23; Governor Damian de Vega Castro y Pardo to King, August 22, 1639, AGI SD 225, N. 39; Worth, *The Timucuan Chiefdoms*, 2: 19; John H. Hann, *The Native American World beyond Apalachee: West Florida and the Chattahoochee Valley* (Gainesville, Fla., 2006), 55. It is worth noting that in spite of the similarity of names, Chacatos and Choctaws were not related.

18. Bushnell, *Situado and Sabana*, 126 (quote). Governor Damian de Vega Castro y Pardo to King, July 9, 1643, AGI SD 225, N. 41; Juan Diez de la Calle, *Memorial y noticias sacras, y reales del imperio de las Indias Occidentales . . . Esciuiale por el año 1646 Iuan Diez de la Calle*, 2 vols. (n.p., n.d.), vol. 1, f. 25 v, R/3080, Rare Books and Manuscripts Collection, Biblioteca Nacional, Madrid; Testimony of Sergeant Pedro de la Vera, December 10, 1688, AGI Escribanía de Cámara 156C, pieza 25; John H. Hann, ed. and trans., "Translation of Governor Rebolledo's 1657 Visitation of Three Florida Provinces and Related Documents," *Florida Archaeology* 2 (1986): 92; Francisco de Florencia to Governor Pablo de Hita Salazar, n.p., May 25, 1675, enclosed in Hita Salazar to King, June

8, 1675, AGI SD 839; Governor Pedro Aranda y Avellaneda to King, November 10, 1688, AGI Escribanía 156C, pieza 25 (quote); Hann, *Apalachee*, 152.

19. English and French traders also married women in the towns where they traded. Lawson, *History*, 25; Le Page du Pratz, *The History of Louisiana*, 312; Andrés González de Barcia Carballido y Zúñiga, *Barcia's Chronological History of the Continent of Florida*, trans. Anthony Kerrigan (Gainesville, Fla., 1951), 362 (quote).

20. Testimony of Diego de Peña, October 18, 1717, enclosed in Benavides to King, September 28, 1718, AGI SD 842. For a fuller discussion of Ayala, see Chapter 6. For a more detailed discussion of a similar blending of European and indigenous norms in the fur trade, see White, *The Middle Ground*, 94–139.

21. Knight, *Tukabatchee*, 175–77. More quantitative analysis from the Tallapoosa Valley supports Knight's conclusions. Where only 27 percent of burial sites included burial goods during 1400–1550 C.E., some 65 percent of burials included goods of some kind during 1600–1715 C.E. Cameron B. Wesson, "Creek and Pre-Creek Revisited," in *The Archaeology of Traditions: Agency and History before Columbus*, ed. Timothy R. Pauketat (Gainesville, Fla., 2001), 103. See also Wesson, "Prestige Goods, Symbolic Capital." Gregory A. Waselkov, "The Macon Trading House and Early European-Indian Contact in the Colonial Southeast," in *Ocmulgee Archaeology*, ed. Hally, reminds us that most of this trade was probably small-scale and carried on by Indians.

22. Vega Castro y Pardo to King, July 9, 1643, AGI SD 225, N. 41 (quote). The last document to suggest *doctrinas* in Altamaha is Fr. Lorenzo Martínez to King, October 22, 1636, AGI SD 235.

23. Francisco Menéndez Márquez and Pedro Benedit Horruytiner to King, March 18, 1647, AGI SD 229 ("as frequently"); Governor Benito Ruiz Salazar y Vallecilla to King, May 22, 1647, AGI SD 229; Menéndez Márquez and Horruytiner to King, July 27, 1647, AGI SD 235; Hann, *Apalachee*, 16–19; Bushnell, *Situado and Sabana*, 128; Ives Goddard, Patricia K. Galloway, Marvin D. Jeter, Gregory A. Waselkov, and John E. Worth, "Small Tribes of the Western Southeast," in *Handbook of North American Indians*, ed. William C. Sturtevant, vol. 14, *Southeast*, ed. Raymond D. Fogelson (Washington, D.C., 2004), 176–77.

24. Menéndez Márquez and Horruytiner to King, July 27, 1647, AGI SD 235.

25. Hoffman, *Florida's Frontiers*, 124; Sluiter, *The Florida Situado*; Governor Benito Ruíz de Salazar Vallecilla to King, July 5, 1650, AGI SD 225, N. 54 (quote); Captain Domingo de Leturiondo to Governor Manuel de Cendoya, San Luís, October 30, 1672, AGI SD 864; Worth, *The Timucuan Chiefdoms*, 1: 201. Worth cites documentation indicating that Ruiz's visit was in 1645, but Leturiondo thinks it was in 1649 "more or less."

26. Governor Diego de Rebolledo to Antonio de Argüelles, March 10, 1655, enclosed in Report on Antonio de Argüelles, [1662], AGI SD 23, N. 8 ("great contagion"); Don Alonso Meléndez, Don Francisco de Ibarra, Don Juan de Zapala, Don Bernabé de Aluste, and Don Thomas de Yor to King, October 26, 1657, AGI SD 235 ("more people"); Hoffman, *Florida's Frontiers*, 126–28.

27. Worth, *The Timucuan Chiefdoms*, 2: 41.

28. Ibid., 2: 38–87 (quote 2: 58); Worth, *The Struggle for the Georgia Coast*, 13; Hann, *Apalachee*, 22.

29. A similar process was occurring in Nueva Vizcaya, north of New Spain. When Spaniards reduced their gift offerings to Native leaders and simultaneously drafted more converts for the silver mines, they laid the groundwork for growing Indian resistance in and beyond the missions. Susan M. Deeds, *Defiance*

and Deference in Mexico's Colonial North: Indians under Spanish Rule in Nueva Vizcaya (Austin, Tex., 2003), 62–65, passim.

30. Hann, *Apalachee*, 44.

31. For a specific example of this cultural shift, see Keyes, "Myth and Social History," in *Perspectives on the Southeast*, ed. Kwachka.

Chapter 4

1. Pennington, "Georgia Indian Lore," 197.

2. Governor Alonso Aranguiz y Cotes to the King, October 21, 1659, AGI SD 839.

3. Swanton, *Early History*, 23.

4. Stephen Bull to Lord Ashley, Albemarle Point, September 12, 1670, in *The Shaftesbury Papers and Other Records Relating to Carolina and the First Settlement on Ashley River Prior to the Year 1676*, ed. Langdon Cheves, South Carolina Historical Society *Collections* 5 (1897): 194.

5. Bishop Gabriel Díaz Vara Calderón to King, Havana [?], 1675, AGI SD 151.

6. Díaz to King, 1675, AGI SD 151.

7. White, *The Middle Ground*, 1; Robbie Ethridge, "Creating the Shatter Zone: Indian Slave Traders and the Collapse of the Southeastern Chiefdoms," in *Light on the Path*, ed. Pluckhahn and Ethridge.

8. Auto contra Atanacio, indio apalachino, St. Augustine, February 12, 1677, AGI EC 156A. This document is also published and translated by John H. Hann, ed. and trans., "Murder of the Tama-Yamasee 1675," in "San Pedro y San Pablo de Patale: A Sixteenth-Century Spanish Mission in Leon County, Florida," ed. B. Calvin Jones, John Hann, and John F. Scarry, *Florida Archaeology* 5 (1991): 152–58.

9. For a study that challenges White's characterization of a "shattered" Ohio Valley, see Heidi Bohaker, "The Significance of Algonquian Kinship Networks in the Eastern Great Lakes Region, 1600–1701," *William and Mary Quarterly* 63.1 (2006): 23–52.

10. For other discussions that link exchange and migration, see Karen Vieira Powers, *Andean Journeys: Migration, Ethnogenesis, and the State in Colonial Quito* (Albuquerque, N.Mex., 1995); Merrell, *The Indians' New World*, 114–17.

11. For a survey of the current scholarship on the Mississippian period, see David G. Anderson, "Examining Chiefdoms in the Southeast: An Application of Multiscalar Analysis," in *Great Towns and Regional Polities in the Prehistoric American Southeast*, ed. Jill E. Nietzel (Albuquerque, N.Mex., 1999); for an assessment of the historic evidence, see Marvin T. Smith, "Aboriginal Population Movements in the Postcontact Southeast," in *Transformation*, ed. Ethridge and Hudson.

12. Pennington, "Georgia Indian Lore," 192–98; quote from 197. For a different version, see "Talk of Creek Leaders, Savannah, June 11, 1735," in *Colonial Records for the State of Georgia*, ed. Coleman and Ready, 20: 381–87. Many historians have referred to this account as a "Creek" origin story. Although many peoples known as Creeks appear in the story, Chekilli was clear throughout that this was the story of his people, the Cussitas, and their alliance with, and superiority over, the Apalachicolas.

13. Testimony of Nicolas Ramirez, December 10, 1688, AGI Escribanía 156C, pieza 25, f. 109. For summaries of the available evidence, see Knight, "The Formation of the Creeks," 375–85; Hann, "Late Seventeenth-Century Forebears," 68; Steven C. Hahn, *The Invention of the Creek Nation, 1670–1763* (Lincoln, Neb.,

2004), 27; John H. Blitz and Karl G. Lorenz, *The Chattahoochee Chiefdoms* (Tuscaloosa, Ala., 2006), 193–96.

14. James R. Gregory, "The Hee-Chee-Tees of the Creeks," *Indian Journal* (Eufala, Indian Territory), April 19, 1901. For background on what Gregory called "the most critical period of the Creek Nation," see Claudio Saunt, *Black, White, and Indian: Race and the Unmaking of an American Family* (New York, 2005), 151–68, 186–91.

15. Knight, "The Formation of the Creeks," 380; John E. Worth, "The Lower Creeks: Origins and Early History," in *Indians of the Greater Southeast: Historical Archaeology and Ethnohistory*, ed. Bonnie G. McEwan (Gainesville, Fla., 2000), 268–69; Blitz and Lorenz, *The Chattahoochee Chiefdoms*, 82–83.

16. Governor Damián de la Vega Castro y Pardo to King, August 12, 1639, AGI SD 225; Knight, "The Formation of the Creeks," 383–84; Blitz and Lorenz, *The Chattahoochee Chiefdoms*, 82–83.

17. Lord Shaftesbury to Henry Woodward, May 23, 1674, in *The Shaftesbury Papers*, ed. Cheves, 440–41; Díaz to King, 1675, AGI SD 151. Such statements fit with a later report from 1690, when an English trader reported that the "kings" of Cussita and Coweta had 2,500 "fighting men." John Stewart to William Dunlop, April 27, 1690, *South Carolina Genealogical Society Magazine* 32.1 (1931): 30. By way of comparison, the undeniably populous province of Apalachee had approximately 1,920 families (and perhaps a similar number of warriors) and about 9,600 total inhabitants in 1689. Hann, *Apalachee*, 166.

18. Paul E. Lovejoy, *Transformations in Slavery: A History of Slavery in Africa*, 2nd ed. (Cambridge, U.K., 2000), esp. 68–70. For a dissenting opinion that argues that Africans retained significant control over these developments, see John Thornton, *Africa and Africans in the Making of the Atlantic World, 1400–1800*, 2nd ed. (Cambridge, U.K., 1998), esp. 125.

19. Lawson, *History*, 213. Centuries later, speakers of Muskogee preserve the linguistic equivalence between slaves and dogs when they use the term *estevpuekv*, which translates literally as "domesticated animal-person." Jack Martin and Margaret McKane Mauldin, *A Dictionary of Creek/Muskogee with Notes on the Florida and Oklahoma Seminole Dialects of Creek* (Lincoln, Neb., 2000), q.v. "slave." For a similar definition from Cherokee, see Theda Perdue, *Slavery and the Evolution of Cherokee Society* (Knoxville, Tenn., 1979), 4, 12. Despite the growing interest in Indian slavery in the colonial Southeast, no works from the region discuss the meaning of the institution before the beginning of the English-sponsored slave trade. I base this discussion on my own contentions in Chapter 1 regarding the power of trade with distant peoples and the work of Brooks, *Captives and Cousins*, esp. 10–19, 34–35; Richter, *The Ordeal of the Longhouse*, 35; Haefeli and Sweeney, *Captors and Captives*, 58–59, 152–55. For a discussion of clans, see Hudson, *The Southeastern Indians*, 193–96; Nairne, *Muskhogean Journals*, 32–34, 60–61. I borrow the term "social death" from Orlando Patterson, *Slavery and Social Death: A Comparative Study* (Cambridge, Mass., 1982).

20. Lawson, *History*, 51–52. Lawson was describing a Seneca practice, but he did not distinguish this northern practice from those of his hosts in the North Carolina piedmont.

21. Relation of services of Martín Alcaide de Cordova, Madrid, April 30, 1649, AGI Indiferente 113, N. 100; Order of Governor Benito Ruíz de Salazar Vallecilla to Juan Domínguez, July 20, 1648, enclosed in Relation of services of Juan Domínguez, Madrid, November 20, 1670, AGI Indiferente 119, N. 143.

22. Order of Governor Nicolas Ponce de León to Antonio de Argüelles, May

17, 1651, enclosed in Relation of services of Antonio de Argüelles, [1662], AGI SD 23, N. 8; Order of Ponce de León to Argüelles, June 20, 1651, enclosed in Relation of services of Antonio de Argüelles, [1662], AGI SD 23, N. 8 (quote). The slave raids that Spaniards recorded in the middle of the seventeenth century likely reflected Mississippian norms because Spaniards were incapable of altering them. See Chapter 3 for a discussion of Spaniards' inability to shape the southeastern slave trade before 1660.

23. Gentlemen of Elvas, "True Relation," 1: 60–62. For a more famous account of enslavement related to the Narváez expedition, see Alvar Núñez Cabeza de Vaca, *Alvar Núñez Cabeza de Vaca: His Account, His Life, and the Expedition of Pánfilo de Narváez*, ed. and trans. Rolena Adorno and Patrick Charles Pautz, vol. 1 (Lincoln, Neb., 1999).

24. Nairne, *Muskhogean Journals*, 62 (quote). For examples of prisoner exchanges, see Hann, *Apalachee*, 10–11; George Chicken, "Colonel Chicken's Journal to the Cherokees, 1725," in *Travels in the American Colonies*, ed. Newton D. Mereness (New York, 1916), 115–21. For a discussion of the diplomatic role of captives in the Southwest, see Brooks, *Captives and Cousins*, esp. chap. 1.

25. Eric E. Bowne, *The Westo Indians: Slave Traders of the Early Colonial South* (Tuscaloosa, Ala., 2005), 37–53, 57–65, 72–75.

26. Carla Gardina Pestana, *The English Atlantic in an Age of Revolution, 1640–1660* (Cambridge, Mass., 2004), 157–82, 220–21; Michael J. Braddick, "The English Government, War, Trade, and Settlement, 1625–1688," in *The Oxford History of the British Empire*, vol. 1, *The Origins of Empire: British Overseas Expansion to the Close of the Seventeenth Century*, ed. Nicholas Canny (Cambridge, U.K., 1998); Nuala Zahedieh, "Overseas Expansion and Trade in the Seventeenth Century," in ibid.; Denys Delâge, *Bitter Feast: Amerindians and Europeans in Northeastern North America, 1600–1664*, trans. Jane Brierley (Vancouver, 1993), 23 (quote); Merrell, *The Indians' New World*, 30–32; Maija Jansson, "Measured Reciprocity: English Ambassadorial Gift Exchange in the Seventeenth and Eighteenth Centuries," *Journal of Early Modern History* (Netherlands) 9.3–4 (2005): 348–70.

27. On the relative merits of firearms, see Bowne, *The Westo Indians*, 65–69. For a recent dissent, see Gallay, *The Indian Slave Trade*, 41. For quote, Lawson, *History*, 23.

28. Worth, *The Struggle for the Georgia Coast*, 15–17.

29. Henry Woodward, "A Faithfull Relation of My Westoe Voiage," in *Narratives of Early Carolina, 1650–1708*, ed. Alexander S. Salley Jr. (New York, 1911), 134; Instructions for Mr. Henry Woodward, May 23, 1674, in *The Shaftesbury Papers*, ed. Cheves, 446 ("more powerfull Nation"); Governor Alonso Aranguiz y Cotes to King, September 8, 1662, AGI SD 225, N. 75; Worth, *The Struggle for the Georgia Coast*, 15–18 ("put to the knife").

30. William Owen to Lord Ashley, Ashley River, September 15, 1670, in *The Shaftesbury Papers*, ed. Cheves, 200–201 ("Bull beggars"); Swanton, *Early History*, 67 ("Hiddy doddy").

31. Quoted in Robert M. Weir, *Colonial South Carolina: A History* (Millwood, N.Y., 1983), 57.

32. M. Eugene Sirmans, *Colonial South Carolina: A Political History, 1663–1763* (Chapel Hill, N.C., 1966), 20–22; Bushnell, *Situado and Sabana*, 136–38; Peter H. Wood, *Black Majority: Negroes in Colonial South Carolina from 1670 through the Stono Rebellion* (New York, 1974), 25–34; Auto, March 22, 1678, enclosed in Governor Pablo de Hita Salazar to Queen, November 10, 1678, AGI SD 839.

33. On early hostilities, see July 2 and July 11, 1672, *TJGC* 1: 40–41. Carolina's

initial alliances with the Kiawahs and other coastal peoples brought them into occasional conflict with the Westos. Shortly before Woodward traveled to the Westos in October 1674, he had received word from England that he should try to ally with the Apalachicolas in order to root out the Westos. Shaftesbury to Woodward, May 23, 1674, in *The Shaftesbury Papers*, 439–46.

34. Gallay, *The Indian Slave Trade*, 63; Bowne, *The Westo Indians*, 94–95.

35. Brett Rushforth, "'A Little Flesh We Offer You': The Origins of Indian Slavery in New France," *William and Mary Quarterly* 60.4 (2003): 793–95; Brooks, *Captives and Cousins*, 1–40. Rushforth and Brooks both explore some of Indians' motives for trading slaves, but such considerations are much less clear for the Southeast. We should nonetheless not assume wholehearted acceptance of the Carolinian trade. The preponderance of female captives suggests that Indians did not respond with alacrity to English demands for men.

36. For a discussion of the lives of Indian slaves in the colony, see William L. Ramsey, "'All & Singular the Slaves': A Demographic Profile of Indian Slavery in Colonial South Carolina," in *Money, Trade, and Power: The Evolution of South Carolina's Plantation Society*, ed. Jack P. Greene, Rosemary Brana-Shute, and Randy J. Sparks (Columbia, S.C., 2001). For a detailed discussion of south-central African references to the European slave trade as a commerce that, like cannibalism, consumed people, see John Thornton, "Cannibals, Witches, and Slave Traders in the Atlantic World," *William and Mary Quarterly* 60.2 (2003): 273–94.

37. For overviews of Yamasee history, see William Green, Chester B. DePratter, and Bobby Southerlin, "The Yamasee in South Carolina: Native American Adaptation and Interaction along the Carolina Frontier," in *Another's Country: Archaeological and Historical Perspectives on Cultural Interactions in the Southern Colonies*, ed. J. W. Joseph and Martha Zierden (Tuscaloosa, Ala., 2002); John E. Worth, "Yamasee," in *Southeast*, ed. Raymond D. Fogelson, *Handbook of North American Indians*, vol. 14, gen. ed. William Sturtevant (Washington, D.C., 2004).

38. Hann, *Apalachee*, 35; Worth, *The Timucuan Chiefdoms* 2: 134–37; Worth, *The Struggle for the Georgia Coast*, 22. For reference to Yamasees, including Altamahas among the Apalachicolas, see Caleb Westbrooke to Lord Cardross [?], St. Helena, February 21, 1685, in *BPROSC* 2:8.

39. Mark F. Boyd, ed. and trans., "Diego Peña's Expedition to Apalachee and Apalachicolo in 1716," *Florida Historical Quarterly* 28.1 (1949): 26 refers to a group of "diamaza" among the Apalachicolas. The "dia" sound offers a clear indication of the way in which one transcriber could use a "y" for a sound that another thought would be better represented by a "d" or "t."

40. Worth, *The Struggle for the Georgia Coast*, 199–200; Hann, *Apalachee*, 33–37; Antonio Matheos to Governor Juan Márquez Cabrera, San Luis, February 8, 1686, enclosed in Autos sobre la entrada de los enemigos ingleses en las provincias de timucua, apalachicoli, y caveta, y obstilidades que yntentan hazer, enclosed in Márquez Cabrera to King, March 19, 1686, AGI SD 839 ("Ocutis"); Serrano y Sanz, *Documentos históricos*, 195 ("siblings").

41. Smith, *Coosa*, 73–74, 112–17.

42. Craig T. Sheldon Jr., Introduction to *Southern and Central Alabama Expeditions of Clarence Bloomfield Moore*, ed. Sheldon (Tuscaloosa: University of Alabama Press, 2001), 20.

43. Ibid., 26.

44. Weber, *The Spanish Frontier*, 149–52.

45. Bishop Gabriel Díaz Vara Calderón to King, Havana [?], 1675, AGI SD 151; Marcos Delgado to Governor Juan Márquez Cabrera, Miculasa, September

19, 1686, enclosed in Márquez to Viceroy Conde de Paredes, November 14, 1686, AGI México 616. Delgado to Márquez, the River of Concepción, October 15, 1686, enclosed in Márquez to Viceroy Conde de Paredes, November 14, 1686, AGI México 616. Translations of these letters can be found in Mark F. Boyd, ed. and trans., "The Expedition of Marcos Delgado from Apalache to the Upper Creek Country in 1686," *Florida Historical Quarterly* 16.1 (1937): 3–32. Because Boyd did not have access to the originals, his translations are not always accurate. Consequently, I will cite the original documents and note some of my more significant disagreements with Boyd in my notes.

46. Delgado to Márquez, October 30, 1686, enclosed in Márquez to Conde de Paredes, January 4, 1687, AGI México 616. My population estimates come from Delgado's estimates of men in each town. I have altered the spelling of some towns for the sake of consistency with other references in the text, but I provide Delgado's spellings in the following list, which follows the order that Delgado visited them: "more than 500 warriors" in Qusate, "more than 100 warriors" in Pagna, "more than 200 warriors" in Qulasa, "up to 30 warriors" in Aymamu, and "more than 200 warriors" in Tubani. I then employ the standard practice of multiplying the number of warriors by four to reach my estimate. I do not alter the names "Chichimeco" or "Chalaque" because it is possible that the former name did not refer to the Westos, who were destroyed in 1680, and the latter may not have been the Cherokees because "Chalaque," like "Cherokee," derived from the Muskogean word "este-celokke," meaning speakers of another tongue. See Jack B. Martin and Margaret McKane Mauldin, *A Dictionary of Creek/Muskogee: With Notes on the Florida and Oklahoma Seminole Dialects of Creek* (Lincoln, Neb., 2000), q.v. "este-celokke."

47. Delgado to Márquez, September 19, 1686, AGI México 616; Delgado to Márquez, October 15, 1686, AGI México 616; Account of the caciques of these provinces, enclosed in Márquez to Conde de Paredes, November 14, 1686, AGI México 616. This last document is not among those that Boyd translated. It is also undated and unsigned, but the handwriting is similar to Delgado's other writings and is undoubtedly the "small sheet" to which Delgado referred in his letter of October 15, 1686, when he wrote of the peace between "the caciques of La Mobila and the caciques from these provinces which are listed in a small sheet that is included within." The caciques listed were from Guta, Oqchaio, Chicachuti, Osuchit, Pasqi, Tuani, Umansi, Atassi, and Tiquipachi.

48. Delgado to Márquez, October 30, 1686, AGI México 616. I am uncertain about Aymamu's affiliation. It is listed among the newly arrived towns in the region and comes right after Qulasa, which is "of the Pagna nation." Aymamu, though, is "de la propia nación," which could be translated as "of the same nation" as Qulasa, or it could mean "of the self-same nation," which I would take to mean that the Aymamus were their own independent nation. Since Delgado mentions that all three fled Choctaw attacks, either affiliation would make sense.

49. Delgado to Márquez, October 30, 1686, AGI México 616.

50. Delgado to Márquez, October 15, 1686, AGI México 616; Delgado to Márquez, October 30, 1686, AGI México 616. The reference to the Mobila translator comes from the later letter and is mistranslated in Boyd, "The Expedition of Marcos Delgado," 27–28. The passage is written as follows: "Para este caso fue dha Grande el haver llevado el indio xptiano de la movila que en ella le thenian por muerto de los indios chiscas el qual hallo dos hermanos que le vinieron a ber." I translate, "In this case the said talk was immensely helped by having

brought the Christian Indian from Movila whom they thought dead at the hands of Chisca Indians and who found two brothers who came to see him." Delgado to Márquez, October 30, 1686, AGI México 616.

51. Delgado to Márquez, October 30, 1686, AGI México 616. Boyd, "The Expedition of Marcos Delgado," 28, translates the passage regarding the trading path to Mobila to say that "the chief of Mobila was ordered" to open a route along the coast, but the original reads as follows: "Sera facil la comunicaçion abriendo el camino por tierras mas çercanas y vecinas ala mar como el Casique Grande de la movila le encarga a Vss.a y selo suplica." My translation: "The communication [between Apalachee and Mobila] will be easy by opening a route through lands close to the sea, as the great cacique of Movila charges Your Excellency and begs it of you."

52. Governor Juan Márquez Cabrera to Conde de Paredes, Viceroy of New Spain, July 22, 1686, AGI México 616. Later English writers also mentioned that they traded among the residents of Mobile Bay before the arrival of the French. Nairne, *Muskhogean Journals*, 76.

53. Delgado to Márquez, October 30, 1686, AGI México 616. This passage is especially garbled in Boyd, "The Expedition of Marcos Delgado," 27, and my corrected translation makes clear that some Indians saw the Spanish missions or the gifts they provided as the key to their security, even as late as the 1680s. Delgado's secondhand account refers to Tuanis and Apalachicolas in the third person, but context clearly indicates when Delgado is reporting Apalachicola as opposed to Tuani arguments. The relevant Spanish text follows:

que aunque estavan ya Poblando y otros Poblados estavan Para bolverse asustierras Porlo que sucedio enla provincia de apalachecoli con los Yngleses y Por no thener luz de Poderse ver conlos españoles ni xptianos, Porque aunque seavian Puesto avenir a dar la obediencia en la provincia de apalachecoli les hacian bolver diciendoles q la amistad delos españoles y xptianos no era Buena que los Resgates que traian les resgatavan ellos y que no Pasaran ala provincia de apalache que no eran buenos Resgates que mejores eran los Resgates delos Ingleses que Por una cosa davan mucho y Polvora y balas y escopettas y les respondieron ellos que como Podria ser si por causa delos Ingleses y chichumecos se avian venido huyendo y dejado sus tierras y que si ellos querian seguirla amistad delos yngleses que ellos no que no avian venido sino buscando la amistad delos españoles que siallavan luz delos españoles sequedarian como ansi loan hecho que todos sealegraron mucho en haver visto alos españoles y atodosGen.lmente.

Chapter 5

1. Swanton, "Social Organization," 67. Swanton, in ibid., 64, referred to Alindja as "an old and well-informed Tukabahchee Indian."

2. Despite the importance of these intertribal relationships and the internal debates that shaped them, scholars have paid them very little attention. Daniel K. Richter and James H. Merrell, Preface to the Paperback Edition, in *Beyond the Covenant Chain: The Iroquois and Their Neighbors in Indian North America, 1600–1800*, ed. Richter and Merrell (1987; University Park, Pa., 2003), xiv. For recent exceptions to this trend, see Wendy St. Jean, "Trading Paths: Mapping Chickasaw History in the Eighteenth Century," *American Indian Quarterly* 27.3–4 (2003): 758–80; Steven Oatis, *A Colonial Complex: South Carolina's Frontiers in the Era of the Yamasee War, 1680–1730* (Lincoln, Neb., 2004); Gilles Havard, *The Great Peace of Montreal of 1701: French-Native Diplomacy in the Seventeenth Century*, trans. Phyllis Aronoff and Howard Scott (Montreal, 2001); Daniel K. Richter, *Facing*

East from Indian Country: A Native History of Early America (Cambridge, Mass., 2001).

3. Swanton, "Social Organization," 65, n. 47; Swanton, "Religious Beliefs and Medical Practices of the Creek Indians," in *Forty-Second Annual Report of the Bureau of American Ethnology* (Washington, D.C., 1928), 607–8, 655, 657. He mentions their respective Latin names as "a species of *Salix*" and "Benzoin aestivale."

4. Braddick, "The English Government"; K. O'Brien and S. L. Engerman, "Exports and the Growth of the British Economy from the Glorious Revolution to the Peace of Amiens," in *Slavery and the Rise of the Atlantic System*, ed. Barbara Solow (Cambridge, U.K., 1991), 180–82; Ian K. Steele, *The English Atlantic, 1675–1740: An Exploration of Communication and Community* (New York, 1986), 33.

5. Gallay, *The Indian Slave Trade*, 48–68; Bowne, *The Westo Indians*, 99–100.

6. Márquez to King, January 25, 1682, AGI SD 226, N. 73; Bishop Ebelino de Compostela to King, Havana, September 28, 1689, AGI SD 151; Bowne, *The Westo Indians*, 99–100; Hann, *Apalachee*, 47–49. For fuller discussions of Apalachicolas' relations with Westos, Spaniards, and English, see Joseph M. Hall Jr., "Anxious Alliances: Apalachicola Efforts to Survive the Slave Trade, 1638–1705," in *Indian Slavery in Colonial America*, ed. Alan Gallay (Lincoln, Neb., forthcoming); Hahn, *Invention*, 30–39.

7. Fray Rodrigo de Barrera to Governor Juan Márquez Cabrera, San Antonio de Bacuqua, December 8, 1681, enclosed in Márquez to King, October 7, 1682, SD 226, Mary Ross Papers, Folder 59, Document 65, Georgia Department of Archives and History, Atlanta, Ga. Barrera was likely aware that commoners in the missions were the sources of most low-level discontent. Few chiefs, for instance, fled the missions even as many followers did. In 1700, one Spanish official came upon numerous scattered hamlets (*rancherías*)—communities without ceremonial grounds and thus without political and religious leaders—that had been occupied by runaways from the missions "for many years." Juan de Ayala Escobar, relación de méritos, Madrid, December 7, 1702, AGI Indiferente 136, N. 55.

8. Antonio Matheos to Governor Juan Márquez Cabrera, Casista, September 21, 1685, enclosed in Autos sobre la entrada, enclosed in Márquez Cabrera to King, St. Augustine, March 20, 1686, AGI SD 839. On the meaning of a cleared path, see also Nairne, *Muskhogean Journals*, 57.

9. Matheos to Márquez, San Luís, February 8, 1686, enclosed in Autos sobre la entrada, AGI SD 839 ("their word"); Matheos to Márquez, San Luís, March 14, 1686, enclosed in Autos sobre la entrada, AGI SD 839. Because the records of these Anglo-Apalachicola meetings make no mention of the five captives being an issue in 1685, it is possible that slave raiders captured the five in the autumn following the Carolinians' visit. Granting this possibility, however, does not diminish the grounds for and evidence of Apalachicola ambivalence. In fact, a seizure of captives after the embassy would highlight more starkly the incompleteness of the English overtures.

10. Peter Mathias, "Risk, Credit, and Kinship in Early Modern Enterprise," in *The Early Modern Atlantic Economy*, ed. John J. McCusker and Kenneth Morgan (Cambridge, U.K., 2000); Fr. Juan Mercado to Antonio Matheos, "today Sunday," enclosed in Autos sobre la entrada, AGI SD 839.

11. Caleb Westbrooke to Lord Cardross[?], St. Helena, February 21, 1685, *BPROSC* 2: 8; Governor Diego Quiroga y Losada to King, May 8, 1691, AGI SD

227B, N. 77; Quiroga y Losada to King, April 18, 1692, AGI SD 227B, N. 93; Lords Proprietors to Governor and Council, Whitehall, March 7, 1681, *BPROSC* 1: 117 (quote); Gallay, *The Indian Slave Trade*, 84–86; Worth, "Yamasee," 426–27. Regarding the Yamasees on Woodward's expedition, see Testimony of Nicolás, December 29, 1685, enclosed in Autos sobre la entrada, AGI SD 839. For population, see George C. H. Kernion, trans., "Documents Concerning the History of the Indians of the Eastern Region of Louisiana," *Louisiana Historical Quarterly* 8 (1925): 37. The French tally of 1,400 Yamasee men is undated, but probably comes from 1702. The total population was probably three times the number of men. I base this calculation on an English census of the Yamasees in 1715 that listed 413 men, 345 women, and 462 children. Governor Nathaniel Johnson to Board of Trade, Charlestown, January 12, 1720, *TRBPROSC* 7: 237–38.

12. Matheos to Márquez, San Luís, February 8, 1686, enclosed in Autos sobre la entrada, AGI SD 839; Matheos to Márquez, San Luís, March 14, 1686, enclosed in Autos sobre la entrada, AGI SD 839 (quote). Regarding English-sponsored raids, there is some evidence that suggests that the Apalachicolas' conflict with the English may have continued as late as 1688. In 1693, officials in Spain cited letters from Governor Quiroga y Losada dated February 24, and April 1, 1688, as evidence that the English and their Indian allies had "at different times and occasions made prisoners of some Christian and pagan Indians of the Guale and Yamasee languages in the province of Guale and also slaves of those of Apalachicola, taking them prisoner and carrying them to Charles Town." Given the Apalachicolas' ability to mislead the Spanish, such reports should be treated with caution, but the fact that the Apalachicolas are not included among those *attacking* these Christians and non-Christians is at least suggestive of their rocky relationship with the English. Council of State to King, Madrid, August 18, 1693, Estado 3968, Archivo de Simancas, Simancas, Spain.

13. Matheos to Márquez, May 21, 1686, enclosed in Márquez to King, May 29, 1686, AGI SD 839. The town of Ocuti (a likely alias for Ocute) joined Apalachicolas and other Hitchiti towns at the tense meeting with Matheos during his second *entrada*, so they were probably at this later assembly as well. Matheos to Governor Márquez Cabrera, San Luis, February 8, 1686, enclosed in Autos sobre la entrada, enclosed in Márquez Cabrera to King, March 19, 1686, AGI SD 839. For a discussion of linguistic similarities, see John H. Hann, "St. Augustine's Fallout from the Yamasee War," *Florida Historical Quarterly* 68.2 (1989): 189. These ties may have encouraged the town of Apalachicola to move to within fifty miles of the Yamasees' coastal settlements. On the later location of Apalachicola town, see below.

14. Governor James Colleton to Governor Diego Quiroga y Losada, Charles Town, April 1, 1688, AGI SD 839 (quote). Yamasee-Apalachicola cooperation was close enough that in 1703, when Carolinians heard rumors of a Spanish and French attack against the Apalachicolas, officials in Charles Town expected that their fearful allies would seek protection among their Yamasee friends. Much later, when the two peoples began fighting each other after 1717, one Apalachicola raid was foiled by an Apalachicola warrior who warned his Yamasee wife and family, who promptly spread the alarm to the remaining Apalachicolas and Yamasees in the town. *JCHA (1703)*, 95–97; John Barnwell to Governor Robert Johnson, n.p., n.d., *TRBPROSC* 8: 1–10.

15. Gallay, *The Indian Slave Trade*, 82–84; Hahn, *Invention*, 49–51.

16. Hahn has demonstrated that Coweta and Cussita likely moved east a year ahead of the others, but there is conflicting evidence regarding the timing of

the events and whether any towns remained along the Chattahoochee River. Spanish efforts to repopulate the valley make me believe that Apalachicolas abandoned it entirely. Angelo to Quiroga y Losada, May 24, 1690, enclosed in Quiroga y Losada to King, June 8, 1690, AGI SD 227B, N. 68; Auto, September 18, 1691, enclosed in Governor Diego de Quiroga y Losada to King, April 10, 1692, AGI SD 227B, N. 89; Hahn, *Invention*, 49–50; Hann, "Late Seventeenth-Century Forebears of the Lower Creeks and Seminoles," *Southeastern Archaeology* 16.1 (1996): 77; Worth, "The Lower Creeks," 279. Although there is no mention of the Apalachicola town's new location until 1708, they must have been neighbors for some time because, in 1712, Carolinian officials considered the two peoples politically and geographically close enough to merit a single colonial trade agent. Governor Nathaniel Johnson, et al., to Board of Trade, Charlestown, September 17, 1708, *BPROSC* 5: 203–9; *JCIT*, 29; Johnson to Board of Trade, January 12, 1720, *TRBPROSC* 7: 237–38. Regarding the establishment of the trading house, see Waselkov, "The Macon Trading House."

17. Assembly to Governor Seth Sothell, Charles Town, 1691[?], in William J. Rivers, *A Sketch of the History of South Carolina* (1856; Spartanburg, S.C., 1972), 424.

18. Anonymous [John Barnwell] untitled map of Southeast, [1721–27], Map Division, LOC; Herman Moll, untitled map of Southeast, [1712? 1717?], Map Division, LOC; *JCHA (1702)*, 6; *JCHA (1703)*, 95–97.

19. Captain Juan Jordan de la Reina to Conde de Galve, Viceroy of New Spain, Santa María de Galve, December 17, 1698, AGI México 617. Both quotes from Alférez Diego de Florencia to Governor Laureano de Torres y Ayala, Bahía de Santa María de Galve, October 19, 1698, enclosed in Torres y Ayala to King, January 1, 1699, AGI México 618.

20. For the Okfuskee settlement, see Piker, *Okfuskee*, 19–20; Thomas Nairne, A Map of South Carolina Shewing the Settlements of the English, French, and Indian Nations from Charles Town to the River Missisipi by Capt. Tho. Nairn. [1711], MS 152679, Huntington Library, San Marino, California. For mention of Atasis' and Tukabatchees' contacts with the Apalachicola towns of Coweta and Cussita, see Matheos to Márquez, San Luís, February 8, 1686, enclosed in Márquez to King, March 20, 1686, AGI SD 839. "Tiquipache" was one of the towns that Apalachees attacked in the fall of 1694 to avenge the Apalachicolas' sacking of San Carlos earlier that year. "Adaste" appears among the Ocmulgee River towns in an English map from the 1710s. English maps and Spanish documents also note the continuing existence of both towns on the Tallapoosa. Moll, Map of Southeast, [1712? 1717?], Maps Division, LOC; Torres y Ayala to King, St. Augustine, March 11, 1695, AGI SD 840; Declaration of Pedro Manuel Cavello, November 30, 1707, enclosed in Sebastian de Moscoso to Duque de Albuquerque, Santa María de Galve, February 10, 1708, AGI México 633. For the Coweta settlement, see Vernon J. Knight Jr., and Sherée L. Adams, "A Voyage to the Mobile and Tomeh in 1700, with Notes on the Interior of Alabama," *Ethnohistory* 28.2 (1981): 181, 191. Chickasaws also employed a similar practice in their efforts to secure their long trading paths to Charles Town. St. Jean, "Trading Paths," 766.

21. On English reaching the Mississippi River, see Verner W. Crane, *The Southern Frontier, 1670–1732* (Ann Arbor, Mich., 1929), 46.

22. Auto of September 18, 1691, enclosed in Governor Diego Quiroga y Losada to King, April 10, 1692, AGI SD 227B, N. 89; Governor Diego Torres y Ayala to Governor of Carolina, August 5, 1695 and March 3, 1695, enclosed in

Torres y Ayala to King, March 11, 1695, AGI SD 840; Testimony of the Junta de Guerra, November 3, 1694, enclosed in Torres y Ayala to King, March 11, 1695, AGI SD 840 (quote).

23. Of the Apalachees' thirteen towns, five had populations of one thousand or more. Bishop Diego Ebelino de Compostela to King, Havana, September 28, 1689, AGI SD 151. Apalachee power may help explain Apalachicola ferocity. Hahn points out that Apalachicola attacks following their move to the Oconee Valley probably owed much to their desire for "revenge" against the Christians, as one missionary put it. I agree, but it is instructive to remember that slave raiders' reputed savagery also owed much to their fears of losing too many of their own warriors. Bloodthirsty reputations that cowed defenders could save many raiders' lives. Hahn, *Invention*, 54–55; Fr. Jacinto de Barrera to Governor Diego Quiroga y Losada, April 28, 1692, enclosed in Quiroga y Losada to King, April 30, 1692, AGI SD 227B, N. 97.

24. Junta de Guerra, November 3, 1694, enclosed in Governor Laureano Torres y Ayala to King, March 3, 1695, AGI SD 840.

25. Francisco Menéndez Márquez and Pedro Benedit Horruytiner to King, March 18, 1647, AGI SD 229 (quote); André Pénicault, *Fleur de Lys and Calumet, Being the Pénicault Narrative of French Adventure in Louisiana*, ed. and trans. Richebourg Gaillard McWilliams (Tuscaloosa, Ala., 1981), 133–34.

26. Kelton, *Epidemics and Enslavement*, 143–88.

27. Knight and Adams, "Voyage to the Mobile and Tomeh," 182; Nairne, *Muskhogean Journals*, 47–48; Testimony of Juan de Roxas, January 9, 1710, enclosed in Governor Francisco Córcoles y Martínez to King, January 22, 1710, AGI SD 841. Roxas reported six hundred Tallapoosa "musketeers" (*escopeteros*) and four hundred archers, three hundred Abeca "musketeers" and six hundred archers, and five hundred Alabama "musketeers."

28. Usner, *A Frontier Exchange Economy*, 16–31; Diron D'Artaguette to Jerome Phelypeaux, Count of Pontchartrain, Fort Louis, August 18, 1708, *MPAFD* 2: 34 (quote); Bienville to Pontchartrain, Fort Louis, September 14, 1703, *MPAFD* 3: 34; Bienville to Pontchartrain, Fort Louis, February 25, 1708, *MPAFD* 3: 116.

29. Richebourg Gaillard McWilliams, ed. and trans., *Iberville's Gulf Journals* (Tuscaloosa, Ala., 1981), 171–74; Jean Baptiste Bernard de La Harpe, *Historical Journal of the Settlement of the French in Louisiana*, trans. Virginia Koenig and Joan Cain, ed. Glenn R. Conrad (Lafayette, La., 1971), 59.

30. La Harpe, *Journal*, 62–63, 70–71; Crane, *The Southern Frontier*, 95.

31. Don Patricio Hinachuba to Alferez Don Antonio Ponce de León, Ivitachuco, April 10, 1699, enclosed in Ponce de León to King, Havana, January 29, 1702, AGI SD 864 ("It is certain"); Don Juan de Ayala to Governor Joseph de Zúñiga y Cerda, San Luís, February 22, 1701[?], AGI SD 858; Zúñiga y Cerda to King, September 30, 1702, AGI SD 858 ("cruelly killed"). Hahn contends that these killings were in response to Spaniards' ill treatment of Hafuluque, an *inija* or second-in-command, of Apalachicola town who had helped broker the recent Apalachicola-Apalachee accords. The document he cites, however, describes how Hafuluque was "taken captive in a skirmish [*refriega*]" of Chacatos against Apalachicolas and Yamasees in 1701. If my reading is correct, it suggests that Hafuluque did not consider Chacatos to be part of the recent peace and/or that Apalachicolas and Apalachees knew few firm boundaries between peace and war at the beginning of the eighteenth century. Hahn, *Invention*, 58–60.

32. *JCHA (1702)*, 64.

33. Zúñiga y Cerda to King, September 30, 1702, AGI SD 840; Testimonio de

autos sobre el sitio que tenia puesto ala C[iuda]d y Presidio dela florida el Gov.or de San Jorge Ingles con los Yndios Y naz.es Ynfieles . . . , March 27, 1703, AGI SD 840; Francisco Romo de Uriza to Zúñiga y Cerda, San Luís, October 22, 1702, AGI SD 858; Zúñiga y Cerda to Governor of Havana, September 1, 1702, AGI SD 858; *JCHA (1703)*, 121 ("endeavour"). Regarding Carolinians' fears of the Apalachees, see *JCHA (1702)*, 6; *JCHA (1703)*, 95–97.

34. Hann, *Apalachee*, 264–83, 305–8; Gallay, *The Indian Slave Trade*, 144–49; Mark F. Boyd, trans. and ed., with Hale G. Smith and John W. Griffin, *Here They Once Stood: The Tragic End of the Apalachee Missions* (Gainesville, Fla., 1951), 48–49, 92; Manuel Solana to Andrés de Arriola, San Marcos, June 10, 1704, AGI México 618; Bienville to Pontchartrain, Fort Louis, September 6, 1703, *MPAFD* 3: 26 (quote).

35. A census from 1708 listed 250 men. Seven years later, another census counted 275 men and 638 men, women, and children. Johnson, et al., to Board of Trade, September 17, 1708, *BPROSC* 5: 208; Johnson to Board of Trade, January 12, 1720, *TRBPROSC* 7: 237–38; Governor Francisco Córcoles y Martínez to King, November 30, 1706, AGI SD 841. Regarding Carolinian fears, see April 26, 1704, *TJCHA* 2: 232.

36. Gallay believes the Apalachees relocated under duress. Given the presence of Apalachee warriors in the second Apalachicola attack on Apalachee in the summer of 1704, some Apalachees and Apalachicolas likely shared a hatred of the Spanish mission system. Gallay, *The Indian Slave Trade*, 148–49.

37. Testimony of Pedro Manuel Cavello, November 30, 1707, enclosed in Testimonio de los Autos hechos s.re Providenzias Dadas Por Su Ex.a Para la Bahia y P[uert]o de s[an]ta M.a de Galve, Año de 1708, No. 33, AGI México 633; Governor Francisco de Córcoles y Martínez to King, January 17, 1710, and enclosed testimony, AGI SD 841; Hahn, *Invention*, 79; La Harpe, *Journal*, 51, 54; Sebastián de Moscoso to Duque de Albuquerque, February 10, 1708, AGI México 633.

38. Duque de Albuquerque to King, México City, February 5, 1708, AGI México 633; Testimony of Cavello, November 30, 1707, enclosed in Testimonio de los Autos hechos sobre lo que nuebamente a acaezido en el Prezidio de Santa María de Galve . . . , enclosed in Duque de Albuquerque to King, Mexico City, February 5, 1708, AGI México 633; Crane, *The Southern Frontier*, 88; Oatis, *A Colonial Complex*, 70–71; Gallay, *The Indian Slave Trade*, 288–94. Gallay attributes the paucity of English sieges and invasions during the War of Spanish Succession to Carolinians' preference for slave raids and their quick profits. I believe that Indians shared this preference, especially after Pensacola.

39. Eric Hinderaker, "The Four 'Indian Kings' and the Imaginative Construction of the First British Empire," *William and Mary Quarterly*, 3rd ser., 53.3 (1996): 487–526; Gallay, *The Indian Slave Trade*, 209–10.

40. South Carolina Treaty with the Creeks at Coweta, in *Early American Indian Documents: Treaties and Laws, 1607–1789*, ed. Alden T. Vaughan, vol. 13, *North and South Carolina Treaties, 1654–1756*, ed. W. Stitt Robinson (Bethesda, Md., 2001), 90–91.

41. The complete list of signatories is as follows: "Hoboyetly, King of the Cowetas; Squire, King of the Ockmulges; Holowigah, Captain of the Cushitaes; Hoboietly, King of the Toquebatches; Hoboiutkay, King of the Shueshatches; Cooseste, Great Capt. of the Ocphuscas; Hoboyheetly, The Great Holbahmah Captain; Tuskastanaga haucha, Head Warriour of Kialegy; Tuskahenia, Head Warriour of Pooseshatche; Tuskastanaga Whetleboa, D[itt]o of Holbahmahs; Epha Micko, General; Tuskesanaga, Cowetas." Treaty with Creeks at Coweta, in

American Indian Documents, 13: 91. On the meaning of the name, see Swanton, "Social Organization," 103. There is the possibility that the title Hoboyetly is derived not from Hopayi ("seeker," or "far away") but instead comes from Hoboihithli ("good child"). Both are distinguished war titles, but Tim Thompson of the Muscogee Nation Cultural and Historic Preservation Office believes it is the former. Tim Thompson, personal communication with author, February 14, 2006.

42. It is worth noting that another version of the story of Coweta-Tukabatchee alliance mentions the medicines *miko hoyani-dja* and *pasa*. *Pasa*, or buttonsnake root, was also used at the busk but had been known as "the war physic" in the late eighteenth century. In other words, it is not hard to see that these medicines could have both red and white functions. Swanton, "Social Organization," 65; Swanton, "Religious Beliefs," 656.

43. Waselkov, "The Macon Trading House," 195; Gregory A. Waselkov and Marvin T. Smith, "Upper Creek Archaeology," in *Indians of the Greater Southeast*, ed. McEwan, 247, 253; Charles H. Fairbanks, "Excavations at Horseshoe Bend, Alabama," *Florida Anthropologist* 15.2 (1962): 53–64; Carol I. Mason, "Eighteenth-Century Culture Change among the Lower Creeks," *Florida Anthropologist* 16.1 (1963): 65–80; Adair, *History*, 147, 462; Philip Georg Friedrich von Reck, *Von Reck's Voyage: Drawings and Journal of Philip Georg Friedrich von Reck*, Kristian Hvidt, ed. and trans. (Savannah, Ga., 1980), 38; Kathryn E. Holland Braund, "Guardians of Tradition and Handmaidens to Change: Women's Roles in Creek Economic and Social Life during the Eighteenth Century," *American Indian Quarterly* 14 (1990): 239–58; Knight, *Tukabatchee*, 178; Waselkov and Smith, "Upper Creek Archaeology," 253; Lawson, *History*, 199; Nairne, *Muskhogean Journals*, 48. A similarly gendered involvement in the trading economy occurred among the Choctaws as well. Carson, *Searching for the Bright Path*, 52.

44. Alexander Longe, "A Small Postscript on the Ways and Manners of the Indians Called Cherokees," ed. David H. Corkran, *Southern Indian Studies* 21 (1969): 31 ("breechess"); Lawson, *History*, 25 ("Bed-fellow"); Nairne, *Muskhogean Journals*, 44–45 ("scandalous libertys," 44); Le Page du Pratz, *The History of Louisiana*, 41 ("our women"); Braund, *Deerskins and Duffels*, 23, 36, 74–75.

45. Nairne, *Muskhogean Journals*, 32–39 ("contemptable," 32; "Counterpoise" and "dwindled," 38). For similar insights on native leadership, see Lawson, *History*, 16–17.

46. Francis Le Jau, *The Carolina Chronicle of Francis Le Jau*, ed. Frank J. Klingberg (Berkeley, Calif., 1956), 132.

47. Nairne did appreciate some connection between beauty and peace when he commented on the Chickasaws' "songs belonging to the pipe of peace, which are several and the best the Chickasaws have." Nairne, *Muskhogean Journals*, 53, 57.

48. Ibid., 40; Piker, *Okfuskee*, 22–25.

49. Nairne, Map of South Carolina, MS 152679, Huntington Library; Nairne, *Muskhogean Journals*, 35 ("coronation"), 73 ("Crampt"), 75 ("cheap"); Gallay, *The Indian Slave Trade*, 166; Oatis, *A Colonial Complex*, 65–66.

50. Nairne, *Muskhogean Journals*, 56 ("better"), ("2 old men"); Bienville to Pontchartrain, Louisiana, February 25, 1708, *MPAFD* 3: 113 ("more attached"); Bienville to Maurepas, April 20, 1734, *MPAFD* 3: 670–71 ("good faith"); Abstract of letters from Bienville to Pontchartrain, Louisiana, July 28, 1706, *MPAFD* 2: 23 ("all the Indians"). On the nature of Louisiana's economy and the value of slaves, see Usner, *A Frontier Exchange Economy*, 26–28; Juliana Barr, *Peace Came in*

the Form of a Woman: Indians and Spaniards in the Texas Borderlands (Chapel Hill, N.C., 2007), 84–86.

51. Abstract of letters from Bienville to Pontchartrain, Louisiana, July 28, 1706, *MPAFD* 2: 25 (quote); Crane, *The Southern Frontier*, 90–95; Gallay, *The Indian Slave Trade*, 288–89.

52. Duque de Albuquerque to King, Mexico City, February 5, 1708, AGI México 633.

53. Regarding the hierarchical political organization of the Nahuas, also known as Aztecs, during the early eighteenth century, see James Lockhart, *The Nahuas after the Conquest: A Social and Cultural History of the Indians of Central Mexico, Sixteenth through Eighteenth Centuries* (Stanford, Calif., 1992), 47–58, 130–40. Regarding the military capacities of the Tarahumaras of New Spain's northern frontier during this time and Spanish efforts to construct the centralized leadership they considered appropriate and necessary for subject Indians, see Deeds, *Defiance and Deference*, 86–103.

Chapter 6

1. William Bartram, *Travels through North and South Carolina, Georgia, East and West Florida* (1792; Savannah, Ga., 1973), 34–35.

2. Braund, *Deerskins and Duffels*, 151–52.

3. Many students of the Yamasee War have concluded that it was caused by a combination of declining numbers of slaves and deerskins to trade, rising Indian indebtedness to abusive traders who threatened to enslave indebted trade partners, and English encroachment on Yamasee land. Only very recently have they also begun to consider the changing character of Anglo-Indian exchange relationships that made longtime friends appear so dangerous, and only William Ramsey and Steven Oatis have examined how Indians used the war to create new relationships in addition to destroying others. This chapter draws on many of their insights. Richard L. Haan, "The 'Trade Do's Not Flourish as Formerly': The Ecological Origins of the Yamasee War of 1715," *Ethnohistory* 28 (1982): 341–58; Crane, *The Southern Frontier*, 162, 166; Hahn, *Invention*, 79–80; Gallay, *The Indian Slave Trade*, 330–33. For examples of the newer approach, see Ramsey, "'Something Cloudy in Their Looks,'" 74–75; Oatis, *A Colonial Complex*.

4. For a discussion of "culture as argument," see David Warren Sabean, *Power in the Blood: Popular Culture and Village Discourse in Early Modern Germany* (Cambridge, U.K., 1984). See also, David Waldstreicher, *In the Midst of Perpetual Fetes: The Making of American Nationalism, 1776–1820* (Chapel Hill, N.C., 1997), 9.

5. Le Jau, *The Carolina Chronicle*, 39.

6. *JCHA (1702)*, 21; October 11, 1710, *TJCHA* 3: 475; January 24, 1702, *JCHA (1702)*, 21; October 11, 1710, *TJCHA* 3: 475; September 13, 1711, *JCIT*, 18.

7. Crane, *The Southern Frontier*, 124–25; Ramsey, "'Something Cloudy in Their Looks,'" 52–57; Oatis, *A Colonial Complex*, 96–99.

8. Ian Steele points out that 1705 was a pivotal turning point for Charles Town's commerce, but he does not connect this date with the raids against Apalachee in 1704. Converse D. Clowse, *Economic Beginnings in Colonial South Carolina, 1670–1730* (Columbia, S.C., 1971), 125–32; Steele, *The English Atlantic*, 32–33; Nairne, *Muskhogean Journals*, 57–58. For an excellent discussion of the mixed success of the Commissioners of the Indian Trade, see Ramsey, "'Something Cloudy in Their Looks.'"

9. For background on the war, see Gallay, *The Indian Slave Trade*, 259–87;

Oatis, *A Colonial Complex*, 84–91; Joseph W. Barnwell, ed., "The Tuscarora Expedition: Letters of Colonel John Barnwell," *South Carolina Historical and Geneological Magazine* 9.1 (1908): 28–54, quote from 32–33. For the possible presence of Tallapoosas, it is worth noting that the expeditions included at least one "Chatahooche" Indian, someone from an outlying village established by the Abeca town of Okfuskee in the valley that the Apalachicolas abandoned in 1690. The "Coosata King," who was probably from the Abeca town of "Coosate" (but perhaps the Alabama town of Koasati) on the upper reaches of the eponymous river, complained of the misappropriation of some of his captive Tuscaroras. May 4, 1714, May 20, 1714, *JCIT*, 53, 57; Nairne, Map of South Carolina, MS 152679, Huntington Library; Piker, *Okfuskee*, 19–20. On the lessons that southeastern Indians learned about their British allies, see also Merrell, *The Indians' New World*, 69–72.

10. *JCHA (1702)*, 48 (quote); Bienville to Pontchartrain, Fort Louis, March 2, 1712, *MPAFD* 3: 171–73; La Harpe, *Journal*, 84; Diron D'Artaguette to Pontchartrain, Bayonne, France, May 12, 1712, *MPAFD* 2: 60. Between 1703 and 1712, only three supply ships departed France for Louisiana. Banks, *Chasing Empire across the Sea*, 47.

11. Cadillac to Pontchartrain, Fort Louis, October 26, 1713, *MPAFD* 2: 172–73. As Cadillac notes in a marginal postscript, he sometimes had difficulty offering gifts because the colony's director of accounts (the *ordonnateur*), Jean-Baptiste du Bois du Clos, hated him intensely and frequently withheld funds. *MPAFD* 2: 172, fn.1.

12. Bienville to Pontchartrain, Fort Louis, June 15, 1715, *MPAFD* 3: 183.

13. Marcel Giraud, *A History of French Louisiana*, vol. 1, *The Reign of Louis XIV, 1698–1715*, trans. Joseph C. Lambert (Baton Rouge, La., 1974), 252–53, 323–28. Salaries come from Enclosure of Duclos to Pontchartrain, Fort Louis, October 25, 1713, *MPAFD* 2: 144, 146.

14. Almon Wheeler Lauber, *Indian Slavery in Colonial Times within the Present Limits of the United States*, ed. Faculty of Political Science, Studies in History, Economics, and Public Law (New York: Columbia University, 1913), 54: 233–40, 291; Kelton, *Epidemics and Enslavement*, 160–201; Gallay, *The Indian Slave Trade*, 301–2 (quote 302). Regarding the end of the slave trade and the causes of the Yamasee War, see Journal of Board of Trade, Whitehall, July 16–July 28, 1715, *TRBPROSC* 6: 137.

15. June 14, 1711, *TJCHA* 3: 557; Crane, *The Southern Frontier*, 167.

16. Autos y demas diligencias hechas sobre la benida de cuatro caciques principales, May 28, 1715, enclosed in Governor Francisco Córcoles y Martínez to King, January 25, 1716, AGI SD 843.

17. Ibid.

18. June 22, 1711, *TJCHA* 3: 570.

19. Langdon Cheves, ed., "A Letter from Carolina in 1715 and Journal of the March of the Carolinians into the Cherokee Mountains in the Yemasee Indian War, 1715–1716," in *Yearbook of the City of Charleston, 1894* (Charleston, S.C., 1894), 334–35.

20. Similar rumors regarding the enslavement of Indian children reached New York. Colonel Caleb Heathcote to Lord Townshend, Manor of Scarsdale, July 16, 1715, in *Documents Relative to the Colonial History of the State of New York*, ed. E. B. O'Callaghan, vol. 5 (Albany, N.Y., 1854), 433.

21. Ramsey, "Something Cloudy in Their Looks,'" 65–67; August 31, 1714-April 12, 1715, *JCIT*, 59–65. Regarding this detail, see Declaration of Francisco

Dominguez, October 18, 1717, enclosed in Governor Antonio Benavides to King, September 28, 1718; Fr. Joseph Ramos de Escudero to King, London, November 19, 1734, AGI SD 2591. Traders and agents among the various nations enumerated nearby peoples in early 1715, but the figures were not sent to the Board of Trade until 1720. Governor Robert Johnson to Board of Trade, Charles Town, January 12, 1720, *TRBPROSC* 7: 238–39.

22. Córcoles y Martínez to King, July 5, 1715, AGI SD 843.

23. Most students of the war rightly contend that the Ocheses, Tallapoosas, Abecas, and Alabamas fought in the Yamasee War to end the threat of enslavement. I believe that this was not merely a destructive effort but a creative one as well. Crane, *The Southern Frontier*, 254–55; Gallay, *The Indian Slave Trade*, 329–40; Oatis, *A Colonial Complex*, 104–5; Ramsey, "Something Cloudy in Their Looks,'" 74–75; Hahn, *Invention*, 81–120.

24. Autos y demas diligencias, May 28, 1715, enclosed in Córcoles y Martínez to King, January 25, 1716, AGI SD 843.

25. April 12, 1715, *JCIT*, 65; William R. Ramsey, "A Coat for 'Indian Cuffy': Mapping the Boundary between Freedom and Slavery in Colonial South Carolina," *South Carolina Historical Magazine* 103.1 (2002): 48–66.

26. Governor Francisco Córcoles y Martínez to King, July 5, 1715, AGI SD 843.

27. George Rodd to Unknown, Charles Town, May 8, 1715, *TRBPROSC* 6: 75; Ramsey, "'Something Cloudy in Their Looks,'" 69 ("were like women"). For a more detailed explanation that provides a deeper sense of confusion and anxiety, if a slightly different sequence of events, see Autos y demas diligencias, May 28, 1715, enclosed in Córcoles y Martínez to King, January 25, 1716, AGI SD 843.

28. Fitch, "Journal," 189–90.

29. Cheves, "Journal of the March," 333, 334.

30. *Boston News-Letter*, June 6–13, 1715.

31. George Rodd to Unknown, Charles Town, May 8, 1715, *TRBPROSC* 6: 77–78.

32. La Harpe, *Journal*, 90. It is worth noting that other scholars of the war believe that the Chickasaws did not join the conflict. Although this seems largely to be the case, the deaths of these few traders still makes clear that some Chickasaws, like their eastern neighbors, harbored grave doubts about their relationship with Carolina. Crane, *The Southern Frontier*, 169; Ramsey, "'Something Cloudy in Their Looks,'" 73.

33. Bartram, *Travels*, 247. This story raises a potential discrepancy in my description of the locations of towns in Apalachicola province. In chapter 4, I point to the relocation of Apalachicola town near the mouth of the Savannah River as evidence of increasing cooperation with the Yamasees. Bartram's story, however, suggests that the town of Apalachicola remained on the banks of the Chattahoochee River at the outbreak of the war. There are two possible explanations that allow for both locations to exist. One is that only some of the inhabitants migrated to the Savannah River. The other is that Bartram's teller was not so concerned with location when he described the fate of the traders. Both are problematic. Spanish documents strongly suggest that no towns remained in the valley by 1691. The oral history suggests otherwise, however, because a trader at Apalachicola actually took Bartram to see the presumed remains of the burned house. As I mention in chapter 4, I am inclined to accept the Spanish documentation as the more contemporary source, but the answer is far from clear. Auto, September 18, 1691, enclosed in Quiroga y Losada to King, April 10, 1692, AGI SD 227B, N. 89; Bartram, *Travels*, 246; Worth, "The Lower Creeks," 279.

34. Le Jau, *The Carolina Chronicle*, 152–54.

35. By August, epidemics ravaged the colonial capital. Le Jau, *The Carolina Chronicle*, 164.

36. George Rodd to Unknown, Charles Town, May 8, 1715, *TRBPROSC* 6: 85.

37. George Rodd to Joseph Boone and Richard Berresford, Charles Town, July 19, 1715, *TRBPROSC* 6: 103–7; Le Jau, *The Carolina Chronicle*, 169 ("reconciliation"); Cheves, "Journal of the March," 333 ("their friendship").

38. On traders' demotion from executors of policy to sources of information, see Fitch to Council, November 1, 1725, *TJGC* 3: 150. On the shift in administration of Indian policy, see Crane, *The Southern Frontier*, 187–205; Oatis, *A Colonial Complex*, 148–54.

39. July 24, 1716, *JCIT*, 89 ("to be sold"); Joseph Boone to Board of Trade, London, April 25, 1717, *TRBPROSC* 7: 15 ("Insulted"); July 24, 1716, *JCIT*, 84; December 5, 1717, *JCIT*, 238. On the endurance of gift giving after 1716, see Joel Martin, *Sacred Revolt: The Muskogees' Struggle for a New World* (Boston, 1991), 62–63. For purchasing power, see Edward Murphy, "The Eighteenth-Century Southeastern American Indian Economy: Subsistence Versus Trade and Growth," in *The Other Side of the Frontier: Economic Explorations into Native American History*, ed. Linda Barrington (Boulder, Colo., 1999), 155.

40. Hann, "St. Augustine's Fallout," 182, 184.

41. Governor Antonio de Benavides to King, August 12, 1718, AGI SD 842; Diego de Peña to Governor Antonio de Benavides, San Marcos, August 6, 1723, enclosed in Benavides to King, August 18, 1723, AGI SD 842; Boyd, "Peña's Expedition to Apalachee and Apalachicolo in 1716," 26; Mark F. Boyd, ed. and trans., "Documents Describing the Second and Third Expeditions of Lieutenant Diego Peña to Apalachee and Apalachicolo in 1717 and 1718," *Florida Historical Quarterly* 31.2 (1952): 116.

42. Autos y demas diligencias, May 28, 1715, enclosed in Córcoles to King, January 25, 1716, AGI SD 843 ("shelter and assistance"); Governor Francisco Córcoles y Martínez to King, January 25, 1716, AGI SD 843 ("voice and name").

43. Don Gregorio Salinas Varona, Governor of Pensacola, to Don Juan de Ayala y Escobar, Governor of Florida, Santa Maria de Galve, July 24, 1717, in Boyd, "Peña in 1717 and 1718," 127 ("good union"); La Harpe, *Journal*, 92; Bienville to Pontchartrain, Fort Louis, September 1, 1715, *MPAFD* 3: 188 ("produce"); Arrete of the Council of the Marine, Paris, June 10, 1718, AC C13A 5: 151 ("Emperor of the Caoüitas," "other nations").

44. Cheves, "Journal of the March," 330–45 (quotes 342, 344).

45. Carolina Assembly to Board of Trade, Charles Town, April 28, 1716, *TRBPROSC* 6: 185.

46. Fe de Juan Solana, scribe, April 4, 1717 (quote), and Razonamiento q se hizo alos casiques Principales Venidos de Apalachicolo adar la obediencia al Rey de España, April 6, 1717, both enclosed in Ayala to King, April 18, 1717, AGI SD 843 ("cell or dungeon," "ancient tradition," "stable and permanent"); Testimony of Diego de Peña, October 18, 1717, enclosed in Benavides to King, September 28, 1718, AGI SD 842 ("regaled them"). For Ayala's military, maritime, and commercial activities, see Juan de Ayala y Escobar, service relation, Madrid, December 7, 1702, AGI Indiferente 136, N. 55; John Jay TePaske, *The Governorship of Spanish Florida, 1700–1763* (Durham, N.C., 1964), 83–85.

47. Lords Proprietor to Board of Trade, London, June 14, 1717, *TRBPROSC* 7: 55–56 ("fall upon"); Boyd, "Peña's Expedition in 1716," 24–26; Hahn, *Invention*, 94.

48. May 24, 1717, *TJCHA* 5: 275 ("they are resolved"); May 29, 1717, *TJCHA* 5: 287; June 14, 1717, *TJCHA* 5: 319.

49. Lords Proprietor to Board of Trade, London, June 14, 1717, *TRBPROSC* 7: 54.

50. For an excellent overview of Brims and the Ocheses, including a discussion of his relatives, see Hahn, *Invention*, 86–113, 192–93.

51. Barcia, *Chronological History*, 359–60; Daniel H. Thomas, *Fort Toulouse: The French Outpost at the Alabamas on the Coosa*, ed. Gregory A. Waselkov (1960; Tuscaloosa, Ala., 1989), 6–14.

52. La Tour to Hubert, Fort Toulouse, March 18, 1718, AC C13A 5: 117 (quote); Bienville to Hubert, Fort Louis, September 19, 1717, *MPAFD* 3: 222–23; Boyd, "Peña in 1717 and 1718," 118. For more details regarding some of these events, see Hahn, *Invention*, 103–6.

53. November 15, 1717, *TJCHA* 5: 368; Testimony of Francisco Dominguez, October 18, 1717, enclosed in Benavides to the King, September 28, 1718, AGI SD 842; Testimony of Sunicha, principal of Cussita, December 22, 1717, enclosed in Ayala to King, December 22, 1717, AGI SD 843; Ayala to King, December 22, 1717, AGI SD 843.

54. La Tour to Hubert, Fort Toulouse, March 18, 1718, AC C13A 5: 117–18. The entire passage is worth reproducing: "Je ne seai sil pourout veunir car L'Empereur est un grand politique et fort traistre il a ce coeur Entiereur d'Espagnol, il aime ou craint les anglois, car il veut absolument les avoir, Il Ny a que quatre ou cinq jours qu'il fit menacer Mougoulacha grand chef de ce pais ei, de prendre garde a la fureur des Anglois, que tort ou tard ne manquerroient pas de luis couper la tete, sil ne se rangeroit pas de leur party vous devés juger de cette menace que le Empereur est dans les Interests des Anglois, il est encorplus dans celuy des Espagnols, dont il en a cinq chez luis qui sont de la garrison de pensacolee arrivée dans ce pais."

55. Barcia, *Chronological History*, 365; January 16, 1718, *JCIT*, 248; La Tour to Hubert, Fort Toulouse, March 18, 1718, AC C13A 5: 117; Joseph Primo de Rivera to Governor Juan de Ayala y Escobar, San Marcos, April 28, 1718, AGI SD 843.

56. Joseph Primo de Rivera to Ayala y Escobar, San Marcos, April 28, 1718, AGI SD 843. For more information on this agreement, see Primo de Rivera to Juan Joseph de Torre, Sabacola, May 29, 1718, AGI SD 2533; Barcia, *Chronological History*, 360–66.

57. Hahn, *Invention*, 116–18.

58. "A Governor Answers a Questionnaire, 1719/1720," in *The South Carolina Scene: Contemporary Views, 1697–1774*, ed. H. Roy Merrens (Columbia, S.C., 1977), 64 (quote); Usner, *Indians, Settlers, and Slaves*, 31–34, 48–49; Oatis, *A Colonial Complex*, 213–14. Regarding the colony's western interests, see Paul W. Mapp, "Atlantic History from Imperial, Continental, and Pacific Perspectives," *William and Mary Quarterly*, 3rd ser., 63.4 (2006): 21.

59. Antonio Pérez de Ecampaño to King, October 23, 1722, AGI SD 849.

60. Sirmans, *Colonial South Carolina*, 111–28; Walter B. Edgar, *South Carolina: A History* (Columbia, S.C., 1998), 73–74, 110–11; Weir, *Colonial South Carolina*, 101–2; L. H. Roper, *Conceiving Carolina: Proprietors, Planters, Plots, 1662–1729* (New York, 2004), 151–53.

61. Converse D. Clowse, *Measuring Charleston's Overseas Commerce, 1717–1767: Statistics from the Port's Naval Lists* (Washington, D.C., 1981), 54–69; Weir, *Colonial South Carolina*, 108–13, 141–45; Crane, *The Southern Frontier*, 184–85; Clowse, *Economic Beginnings*, 194–27 (quote 227). Regarding public debts, see June 7, 1712, *TJCHA* 4: 84; Sirmans, *Colonial South Carolina*, 130.

62. Jane Landers, *Black Society in Spanish Florida* (Urbana, Ill., 1999), 26–27.

63. Nairne, Map of South Carolina, MS 152679, Huntington Library.

64. January 16, 1718, *JCIT*, 248–49; August 16, 1720, *Journal of the Commissioners for Trade and Plantations from November 1718 to December 1722 Preserved in the Public Record Office* (London: His Majesty's Stationery Office, 1925), 198; Crane, *The Southern Frontier*, 201, 234, 239–46; Oatis, *A Colonial Complex*, 267–68.

65. December 12, 1717, *JCIT*, 246.

66. December 12, 1717, June 3, 1718, *JCIT*, 246, 281.

67. Verner W. Crane, "The Origin of the Name of the Creek Indians," *Mississippi Valley Historical Review* 5 (1918): 339–42. For the earliest uses of "Ochese Creeks," see *JCHA (1703)*, 95–97. For an instance where contextual evidence makes clear that "Creeks" referred to the peoples of central Georgia, see *JCHA (1707–8)*, 48–50. For examples of non-traders' use of the word, see, Le Jau, *The Carolina Chronicle*, 158. The latest references that I have found in which "Creeks" is synonymous only with "Ocheses" are Governor Robert Johnson to Board of Trade, January 12, 1720, *TRBPROSC* 7: 233–50, where he describes "desperate Creek Indians" (as distinct from the Tallapoosas, Abecas, and Alabamas) living near Apalachee, and also June 30, 1721, *TJGC* 1: 130, which mentions "Emperor Breem of the Creek Indians." The earliest definitive example of the broader English definition of Creek is July 7, 1718, *JCIT*, 303–4, where a store owner has orders to deliver goods to "the Oakfuskey Head Warrior (a Creek Indian)." Okfuskee was (and remains) a prominent Abeca town. As the Commissioners of the Indian Trade broadened their definition of "Creek," they distinguished among the "Upper Towns called Abekahs; . . . the Middle Settlements; and . . . the Cussitoes [Cussitas], being the lower Settlements." The meaning of "Middle Settlements" remains unclear, but it probably was the Tallapoosas. July 16, 1718, *JCIT*, 304.

68. July 19, 1718, *JCIT*, 309–11.

69. Creeks' talk to Governor Francis Nicholson, Charles Town, October 25, 1723, *TRBPROSC* 10: 175–92.

70. Braund, *Deerskins and Duffels*, 6.

71. Auto, February 18, 1726, enclosed in Testimonio de los autos, enclosed in Governor Antonio de Benavides to King, May 27, 1726, AGI SD 842.

72. Crane, *The Southern Frontier*, 237, 245–46.

73. John Barnwell to Governor Robert Johnson, April 1720, *TRBPROSC* 8: 1–10 (quote 1).

74. Oatis, *A Colonial Complex*, 268; Hahn, *Invention*, 124.

75. Theophilus Hastings to Assembly, Cussita, April 14, 1723, enclosed in Council Journal, May 15, 1723, CO 5/427: 13–14, PRO 24/1, Microforms Reading Room, LOC; Lieutenant Diego de Peña to Governor Antonio de Benavides, San Marcos, August 6, 1723, enclosed in Benavides to King, August 18, 1723, AGI SD 842.

76. John Woort to John Bee, Ocheese River, July 30, 1723, *TRBPROSC* 10: 131–32; The Governor's Talk to Oulatta and the Creek Indians, Charles Town, November 16, 1723, *TRBPROSC* 10: 181; Peña to Benavides, San Marcos, August 6, 1723, enclosed in Benavides to King, August 18, 1723, AGI SD 842 ("Casista"); Gerrard Monger to Governor Francis Nicholson, Fort Moore, September 24, 1723, *TRBPROSC* 10: 155–58 ("revenge," "dipt," 157).

77. Governor's Talk to Oulatta and the Creek Indians, Charles Town, November 16, 1723, *TRBPROSC* 10: 179–80 (quotes 179).

78. Oulatta's Talk to Governor, Charles Town, October 25, 1723, *TRBPROSC* 10: 177.

79. Governor's Talk to Oulatta and the Creek Indians, Charles Town, November 16, 1723, *TRBPROSC* 10: 180. The Tukabatchee Captain and Oulatchee (or Oulatchee Ifamico) were likely the same person because Oulatchee was identified at one point as from Tukabatchee and Oulatchee is a war title that combines the words *holata* (leader) and the suffix *hadjo* ("crazy," as in fearless in war). Governor's Talk to Oulatta and the Creek Indians, Charles Town, November 16, 1723, *TRBPROSC* 10: 179; Hann, *Apalachee*, 99; Swanton, "Social Organization," 101, 103.

80. June 5, 1724, *CRSC (1724)*, 12–13 (quote); June 11, 1724, *CRSC (1724)*, 26.

81. June 5, 1724, *CRSC (1724)*, 12–13; Council's instructions to Tobias Fitch, August 25, 1725, *TJGC* 3: 72.

82. Oulatta's Talk to Governor, Charles Town, October 25, 1723, *TRBPROSC* 10: 176.

83. Fitch, "Journal," 183 (quote); Tobias Fitch, Journal, August 4, 1725, *TJGC* 3: 56. Europeans recognized the utility of lying as well as anyone, and they used it as best they could to their own ends, often lying about the ambitions of their rivals in conversations with Indians. See Fitch, "Journal," 193, 200; Bienville to Maurepas, New Orleans, July 15, 1738, *MPAFD* 3: 719–20.

84. Oulatta's Talk to Governor, Charles Town, October 25, 1723, *TRBPROSC* 10: 176–77. On the Dog King's residence, see Gerrard Monger to Governor Francis Nicholson, Fort Moore, September 24, 1723, *TRBPROSC* 10: 158.

85. Oulatta's answer to the governor's talk, Charles Town, November 19, 1723, *TRBPROSC* 10: 184.

86. Swanton, *Early History*, 131.

87. Gerrard Monger to Governor Francis Nicholson, Fort Moore, September 24, 1723, *TRBPROSC* 10: 156 ("false report"); Theophilus Hastings to Governor Francis Nicholson, Cussitaws, October 9, 1723, *TRBPROSC* 10: 185–86.

88. Unknown to Joseph Boone, South Carolina, June 24, 1720, *TRBPROSC* 8: 25 ("good news"); Joseph Boone to Board of Trade, London, April 25, 1717, *TRBPROSC* 7: 15 ("hold both").

89. Richter, *The Ordeal of the Longhouse*, 205–9; Havard, *The Great Peace of Montreal*; Daniel K. Richter, *Facing East from Indian Country: A Native History of Early America* (Cambridge, Mass., 2001), 164–71 (quote 164).

90. Swanton, "Social Organization," 61. For another version, see James R. Gregory to Emmett Starr, August 29, 1898, Inola, Creek Nation, Indian Territory, James R. Gregory Papers, OHS. It is worth noting that Swanton attributed his version to Ispahihta (also known as Isparhetcher), who was also the source of many of Gregory's stories.

91. On the malleability and reliability of oral traditions, see Nabokov, *A Forest of Time*, 47–48; Richard White, *Remembering Ahanagran: Storytelling in a Family's Past* (New York, 1998). For examples of South Carolinians' self-serving revisionism, see Alexander Hewatt, *An Historical Account of the Rise and Progress of the Colonies of South Carolina and Georgia*, 2 vols. (1779; Spartanburg, S.C., 1962), 1: 212, passim.

Chapter 7

1. William Hatton to Francis Nicholson, "In the Charokees," November 14, 1724, *TRBPROSC* 11: 271–72.

2. John Sharp to Francis Nicholson, Noo yah wee, November 12, 1724, *TRB-*

PROSC 11: 266–69; Hatton to Nicholson, November 14, 1724, *TRBPROSC* 11: 271–72, 277. Hatton's letter is cited extensively in Gerald M. Sider, *Lumbee Indian Histories: Race, Ethnicity, and Indian Identity in the Southern United States* (New York, 1993), 193–96.

3. Fitch to Council, September 15, 1725, *TJCHA* 3: 154 ("warr"); Fitch, "Journal," 181 ("Expected"); Hatton to Nicholson, November 14, 1724, *TRBPROSC* 11: 273–74 ("for my Part").

4. In fact, Sharp heard another version of Steyamasiechie's talk in which he urged that "if they mett with white men there goods should be Taken from them." Fitch, "Journal," 192.

5. For other discussions of this event, see Sider, *Lumbee Indian Histories*, 196–97; Tom Hatley, *The Dividing Paths: Cherokees and South Carolinians through the Age of Revolution* (New York, 1993), 45; Hahn, *Invention*, 131; Oatis, *A Colonial Complex*, 223–24. The ignominy of near nakedness carried a clear message of protest. See Claudio Saunt, "'Domestick . . . Quiet Being Broke': Gender Conflict among Creek Indians in the Eighteenth Century," in *Contact Points: American Frontiers from the Mohawk Valley to the Mississippi, 1750–1830*, ed. Andrew R. L. Cayton and Fredrika Teute (Chapel Hill, N.C., 1998), 151.

6. Kenneth J. Banks, *Chasing Empire across the Sea: Communications and the State in the French Atlantic, 1713–1763* (Montreal, 2002), 27–37, 153–83; J. H. Elliott, *Empires of the Atlantic World: Britain and Spain in America, 1492–1830* (New Haven, Conn., 2006), 231–32.

7. Much of the information is summarized in An Exact Account of the Number and Strength of all the Indian Nations that were Subject to the Government of South Carolina . . . 1715, Governor Nathaniel Johnson to Board of Trade, Charles Town, January 12, 1720, *TRBPROSC* 7: 238–39; Swanton, *Early History*, 184–87, 254–58, 286–312, 432–35; Jason Baird Jackson, "Yuchi," in *Handbook of North American Indians*, ed. Sturtevant, vol. 14, *Southeast*, ed. Fogelson, 426–27. My discussion of the Yuchis and Shawnees also benefited from Stephen Warren, personal communication with author, April 25, 2006.

8. Recommendations of Committee on Indian Affairs, March 17, 1724, reprinted in December 22, 1736, *CRSC (1736)*, 112–13 ("proper Person"); George Chicken, "Colonel Chicken's Journal to the Cherokees, 1725," 101; Fitch, "Journal," 176.

9. Fitch, "Journal," 178 ("Sorry"), 179–80.

10. Ibid., 180.

11. Ibid., 181 ("nothing But Skins"), 192.

12. Ibid., 182–84; Fitch to Council, August 4, 1725, *TJGC* 3: 57.

13. Fitch, "Journal," 188 ("Kind"), 195 ("War"), 204–5; Fitch to Council, November 1, 1725, *TJGC* 3: 155–56; Governor Antonio de Benavides to King, November 20, 1725, AGI SD 842; Benavides to King, May 27, 1726, AGI SD 842. Fitch never says explicitly that Steyamasiechie and Seepeycoffee attacked together, but both headed to Fort San Marcos at the same time and Steyamasiechie's war party returned home via the Chattahoochee Valley, from which Seepeycoffee's would have departed.

14. Fitch to Council, August 4, 1725, *TJGC* 3: 59; Fitch to Council, Coweta, August 1, 1726, enclosed in Council Journals, October 8, 1726, CO 5/429: 14, LOC; Fitch, "Journal," 194, 197.

15. Charlesworth Glover, Journal, December 23, 1727–April 15, 1728, *TRBPROSC* 13: 130.

16. Fitch, "Journal," 200.

17. George Chicken, Journal, July 27, 1726, read in Council on September 1, 1726, CO 5/429: 7, LOC.

18. Sleigh Journal, *TJGC* 3: 279 ("stripped"); Chicken, Journal, July 27, 1726, read in Council on September 1, 1726, CO 5/429: 2, LOC ("Villain"). The Council called Sharp to Charles Town to answer the charges, but there is no record in the following year that he actually came. Council Journal, September 1, 1726, CO 5/429: 12, LOC.

19. A Journal from Samuel Sleigh, March 23, 1726–April 7, 1726, copied in *TJGC*, April 20, 1726, 3: 276.

20. April 26, 1726, *JCHA (1725–1726)*, 91.

21. April 26, 1726, April 28, 1726, April 29, 1726, *JCHA (1725–1726)*, 91, 97–99.

22. Sleigh Journal, *TJGC* 3: 277; Fe de Juan Solana, public scribe, May 11, 1726, enclosed in Testimonio de los autos . . . sobre la venida de los casiques y principales de la Provincia de Apalachecolo, enclosed in Benavides to King, May 27, 1726, AGI SD 842.

23. Fitch to Council, Coweta, August 1, 1726, enclosed in Council Journals, October 8, 1726, CO 5/429: 13, LOC. Fitch also qualified the good news, claiming, "Indeed, I never knew that the Cussetaws was at Warr with them."

24. Martin and Mauldin, *Dictionary of Creek/Muscogee*, q.v. cekehle.

25. General meeting of the Creek headmen at Tukabatchee, September 23, 1726, enclosed in Council Journals, October 8, 1726, CO 5/429: 39–40. For a related discussion of British understandings of gift giving, see Gregory Evans Dowd, "'Insidious Friends': Gift Giving and the Cherokee-British Alliance in the Seven Years' War," in *Contact Points*, ed. Cayton and Teute, 138–39.

26. January 11, 1727, *JCHA (1727)*, 59–61; January 25, 26, 1727, Council Journals, CO 5/387: 238–48, LOC, esp. 244 ("Different Nations"), 247 ("Spoilt").

27. Governor Arthur Middleton to Secretary of State Newcastle, June 13, 1728, *TRBPROSC* 13: 61–68; John Herbert, *Journal of John Herbert, Commissioner of Indian Affairs for the Province of South Carolina, October 17, 1727 to March 19, 1727/8*, ed. A. S. Salley (Columbia, S.C., 1936), 13; Charlesworth Glover, Journal, *TRBPROSC* 13: 101–2.

28. Oatis, *A Colonial Complex*, 277–79; Crane, *The Southern Frontier*, 246–49; Piker, *Okfuskee*, 14–28; Herbert, *Journal*, 6–7 (quote); Middleton to Newcastle, June 13, 1728, *TRBPROSC* 13: 69.

29. Charlesworth Glover, Journal, October 1727-April 1728, *TRBPROSC* 13: 87 ("great affront"), 93 ("no harm").

30. Ibid., 13: 108, 117, 163.

31. Ibid., 13: 136 ("Peace"), 155–56; Hahn, *Invention*, 142–43.

32. Glover, Journal, *TRBPROSC* 13: 142 ("all the Power"), 143 ("win"), 144 ("trade governs").

33. Ibid., 13: 128–29.

34. Governor Antonio de Benavides to King, September 10, 1727, AGI SD 844; Benavides to King, September 10, 1727, AGI SD 866; Governor Dionisio Manuel de la Vega to King, Havana, August 27, 1728, AGI SD 866; Alexander Parris to Wargent Nicholson, Charles Town, March 27, 1728, *TRBPROSC* 13: 187–88.

35. Glover, Journal, *TRBPROSC* 13: 163, 168 ("earnest").

36. Perier to Abbé Ragué, New Orleans, August 14, 1728, *MPAFD* 2: 585.

37. Officials had settled new colonists—especially Scots-Irish—in outlying settlements as early as 1718 in Massachusetts, Pennsylvania, and South Carolina,

but Johnson's township plan was the first to treat this idea as policy. Crane, *The Southern Frontier*, 293–94; Maldwyn A. Jones, "The Scotch-Irish in British America," in *Strangers within the Realm: Cultural Margins of the First British Empire*, ed. Bernard Bailyn and Philip D. Morgan (Chapel Hill, N.C., 1991), 295–96; Warren R. Hofstra, "'The Extention of His Majesties Dominions': The Virginia Backcountry and the Reconfiguration of Imperial Frontiers," *Journal of American History* 84.4 (1998): 1281–1312.

38. Usner, *Indians, Settlers, and Slaves*, 65–76; Gwendolyn Midlo Hall, *Africans in Colonial Louisiana: The Development of Afro-Creole Culture in the Eighteenth Century* (Baton Rouge, La., 1992), 107–10; Crane, *The Southern Frontier*, 274–80; Oatis, *A Colonial Complex*, 258–62.

39. Hahn, *Invention*, 152–54; King Louis XV to Bienville, Marly, February 2, 1732, *MPAFD* 3: 554.

40. Benoît to [Périer?], Fort Toulouse, March 29, 1732, *MPAFD* 4: 120–21; December 15, 1736, *CRSC (1736)*, 108–11; Piker, *Okfuskee*, 21, n. 10.

41. Phinizy Spalding, *Oglethorpe in America* (Chicago, 1977); Julie Anne Sweet, *Negotiating for Georgia: British-Creek Relations in the Trustee Era, 1733–1752* (Athens, Ga., 2005); Oglethorpe to the Trustees, Charles Town, June 9, 1733, in *Early American Indian Documents*, ed. Vaughan, vol. 11, *Georgia Treaties*, ed. John T. Juricek (Frederick, Md., 1989), 17 ("concluded a peace").

42. B. R. Carroll, *Historical Collections of South Carolina, Embracing Many Rare and Valuable Pamphlets and Other Documents Relating to the History of that State*, 2 vols. (New York, 1836), 1: 276; David Ramsay, *Ramsay's History of South Carolina from Its First Settlement in 1670, to the Year 1808* (1808; Newberry, S.C., 1858), 69; Trevor Richard Reese, *Colonial Georgia: A Study in British Imperial Policy in the Eighteenth Century* (Athens, Ga., 1963), 30, notes that during 1733–52, when the colony was run by the Trustees, Georgia received £136,000 from Parliament and only £16,000 from private donations.

43. David Armitage, *The Ideological Origins of the British Empire* (New York, 2000), 174–81.

44. From Bienville to King, summarized by Ministry of Colonies, August 25, 1733, *MPAFD* 1: 193.

45. Oglethorpe's Instructions to Patrick Mackay, April 27, 1734, in Juricek, *Georgia Treaties*, 34–35.

46. December 15, 1736, *CRSC (1736)*, 114 ("whip"), 120–21 (for a slightly different story), 140 (Hitchitis' council of war). For additional discussion of the Edwards event, see Piker, *Okfuskee*, 31–32.

47. December 15, 1736, *JCHA*, 115 ("Lives"); Mackay to Causton, Coweta, March 27, 1735, Juricek, *Georgia Treaties*, 48; Governor Francisco Moral Sánchez Villegas to King, May 23, 1735, AGI SD 2591.

48. December 15, 1736, *JCHA*, 114; Piker, *Okfuskee*, 31–33.

49. Governor Francisco Moral Sánchez Villegas to King, May 23, 1735, AGI SD 2591 ("leathers").

50. June 3, 1718, *JCIT*, 281; *Pennsylvania Gazette*, July 24, 1732; Peter C. Mancall, Joshua L. Rosenbloom, and Thomas Weiss, "Indians and the Economy of Eighteenth-Century Carolina," in *The Atlantic Economy during the Seventeenth and Eighteenth Centuries: Organization, Operation, Practice, and Personnel*, ed. Peter Coclanis (Columbia, S.C., 2005), 304. On this point, see also Ramsey, "'Something Cloudy in Their Looks.'"

51. Governor Francisco Moral Sánchez Villegas to King, May 23, 1735, AGI SD 2591; Mackay to the Trustees, Coweta, March 29, 1735, in *General Oglethorpe's*

Georgia: Colonial Letters, 1733–1743, ed. Mills Lane, 2 vols. (Savannah, Ga., 1990) 1: 148 (quote).

52. Waselkov and Smith, "Upper Creek Archaeology," 249; Hahn, "The Mother of Necessity," 109–13.

53. Benoît to [Périer?], Fort Toulouse, March 29, 1732, *MPAFD* 4: 121. Benoît refers to the leader simply as "our king," but it is clear from other letters that the French at Fort Toulouse considered Alabamas to be "their" Indians, because, as Bienville put it, they were "very brave and very devoted to the French" and because they welcomed (if not always listened to) a missionary among their towns. Bienville, Memoir on Louisiana, 1725 [probably 1726], *MPAFD* 3: 536; Marcel Giraud, *A History of Louisiana,* vol. 5, *The Company of the Indies, 1723–1731* (Baton Rouge, La., 1991), 367–68.

54. T. Dale Nicklas, "Linguistic Provinces of the Southeast at the Time of Columbus," in *Perspectives on the Southeast,* ed. Kwachka, 9–11, notes that the Alabama and Creek languages can both be considered part of a common group of Eastern Muskogean languages but that the former exhibits qualities that suggest a certain exclusivity from neighboring Muskogean speakers, including the Creeks. See also Swanton, *Early History,* 191–92; Swanton, "Social Organization," 42–45.

55. Bienville and Salmon to Maurepas, New Orleans, April 5, 1734, *MPAFD* 3: 652. Such connections were likely among the reasons that many Creeks considered the Alabamas, if not powerful, at least "men of intelligence and of good counsel." Bienville to Maurepas, New Orleans, July 15, 1738, *MPAFD* 3: 720.

56. Steven C. Hahn, "The Cussita Migration Legend: History, Ideology, and the Politics of Mythmaking," in *Light on the Path,* ed. Pluckhahn and Ethridge; Pennington, "Georgia Indian Lore," 197.

57. Thomas Causton to Trustees, June 20, 1735, in *Colonial Records for the State of Georgia,* ed. Milton and Ready, 20: 401.

58. Diron D'Artaguette to Maurepas, Mobile, October 24, 1737, *MPAFD* 4: 146.

59. Patrick Mackay to James Oglethorpe, Coweta, March 29, 1735, in Lane, *Oglethorpe's Georgia,* 1: 152–53.

60. Steven Hahn, personal communication with author, August 1, 2006.

61. Armitage, *Ideological Origins,* 175–78.

62. Crane, *The Southern Frontier,* 206–34; Stephen H. Cutcliffe, "Colonial Indian Policy as a Measure of Rising Imperialism: New York and Pennsylvania, 1700–1755," *Western Pennsylvania Historical Magazine* 64 (1981): 237–68; Timothy J. Shannon, *Indians and Colonists at the Crossroads of Empire: The Albany Congress of 1754* (Ithaca, N.Y., 2000). J. Russell Snapp, *John Stuart and the Struggle for Empire on the Southern Frontier* (Baton Rouge, La., 1996), argues that Carolinians and Georgians resented the intrusion of imperial authority into their relations with Indians, but he does not notice how this conflict was the unintended consequence of colonists' efforts to better regulate their relations with Indians.

63. Bienville to Maurepas, New Orleans, October 4, 1734, *MPAFD* 3: 673. The phrase "and carries to his nation an English flag" is found only in the French original, AC C13A 18: 206v.

Conclusion

1. Quoted in Armitage, *Ideological Origins,* 194–95.

Glossary of Native Place Names

Note: Because some prominent towns were also the namesakes for the provinces, or collections of towns, that they influenced, I have distinguished between towns and provinces in my definitions, when appropriate. Readers who are curious about the sources for my definitions should consult my references to these places in the text and endnotes.

Abeca (province): A province of about thirteen towns, including Abi-kudji, Coosa, and Okfuskee, located along the upper Coosa and Talla-poosa Rivers.

Abeca (town): A town along the upper Coosa River that was probably a tributary to the Coosa chiefdom before 1600. By 1670, its residents shared Woods Island with those of Coosa. Abecas were probably among those who established the town of Abikudji.

Abikudji: A white or peace town whose name means "Little Abika." It was located on Tallahatchee Creek, a tributary of the Coosa River, and its residents probably founded the town after splitting off from the amal-gamated settlement at Woods Island sometime after 1715.

Alabama: A province of towns in central Mississippi. Alabamas fled Choctaw attacks and relocated to the upper Alabama River before 1686. By 1720, they were associated with the Creeks.

Altamaha: Also known as Tama and La Tama, this town was a chiefdom along the upper Ocmulgee River during the sixteenth century. Between about 1540 and 1597, its chief probably owed tribute to the chief of Ocute. Westo raids in the 1660s forced Altamahas to scatter to the safety of the Apalachicolas, Apalachees, and Guales. During 1685 to 1715, the town was located near today's Port Royal, South Carolina, among the Yamasees.

Apalachee: A province of about eleven towns, including Ivitachuco and San Luís. Apalachee warriors drove off Spanish explorers in the 1500s but welcomed missionaries after 1633. Slave raids from the Ocheses and their English allies destroyed and dispersed the inhabitants in 1704. Apalachees numbered about nine thousand in 1700.

Apalachicola (province): A province of thirteen or fourteen towns, including Apalachicola, Coweta, Cussita, Osuche, and Savacola, located along the Chattahoochee River until most of it residents moved to the Oconee Valley in 1691.

Apalachicola (town): The principal town of Apalachicola province, located on the Chattahoochee River until 1691. The town was located along the lower Savannah River before 1708, but Apalachicolas moved back to the Chattahoochee in late 1715 or early 1716.

Atasi: A town located along the lower Tallapoosa River that had close ties to Tukabatchee and Coweta. Some Atasis relocated to the Oconee Valley when Cowetas and other Ocheses lived there from 1690 through 1715.

Cahokia: The largest Mississippian archaeological site, located across the Mississippi River from today's St. Louis, but also part of a series of mound sites spread throughout the region known as the American Bottom. Residents probably began construction of the earthen mounds after 1000 C.E. and the population probably peaked at ten thousand people before the city collapsed sometime before 1300.

Cemochechobee: A small archaeological site along the Chattahoochee River occupied between 1200 and 1300 C.E.

Chacato: People who lived northwest of the towns of Apalachee and east of the Apalachicola River. Spaniards reported them to be very warlike before 1639. They welcomed missionaries in 1675 before a brief revolt the following year. When slave raiders destroyed the missions after 1704, most of those who eluded capture fled west to the sanctuary of the French at Mobile.

Cherokee: A province of two or three dozen towns whose residents lived in the eastern foothills of the southern Appalachian Mountains and west into the upper Tennessee Valley. Cherokees probably numbered between sixteen thousand and twenty thousand in 1708.

Cherokeeleechee's Town: An unnamed Lower Creek town that was located at the confluence of the Flint and Chattahoochee Rivers after

1715 and was home to Cherokeeleechee, a strong supporter of ties to St. Augustine.

Chickasaw: A province located in today's northern Mississippi. Most Chickasaw allied with Carolina and participated heavily in the slave trade before 1715 and directed many attacks against the Choctaws. Their population in 1700 was about three thousand to six thousand.

Chisca: A group of people originally living in the Appalachian Mountains in 1540 who moved to the outskirts of a number of Spanish missions shortly before 1624. After encouraging Apalachees' unsuccessful revolt against the Spanish, Chiscas moved west to the Apalachicola Valley.

Choctaw: A province of several dozen towns located in today's central Mississippi. During the early 1700s, most Choctaws allied with the French to seek protection from slave raids. During the 1720s, their population may have reached thirty thousand.

Coosa: A chiefdom located along the upper Coosawattee River in northwestern Georgia from about 1400 to 1600. Coosas relocated over the following century to sites further down the Coosa River. By about 1670, they had joined with the people of Abeca to establish a town at Wood's Island before 1725, when they had settled a smaller town where Talledega Creek joins the Coosa River.

Coweta: A red or war town founded when its residents separated from the town of Cussita sometime between 1662 and 1675. Cowetas initially lived across the Chattahoochee River from Cussita before 1690, when they moved to the Oconee Valley. Some moved to the Tallapoosa River about this time as well. After 1715, Cowetas returned to the Chattahoochee Valley.

Creek: A collection of towns that initially included the towns along Ochese Creek but that after 1715 also included Creek allies in the Alabama, Tallapoosa, and Coosa Valleys. (*See also* Lower Creek; Ochese; Upper Creek.)

Cussita: A white or peace town that migrated to the northern end of the Apalachicola province in the Chattahoochee Valley sometime before 1662. After 1690 its residents relocated to the Oconee Valley in central Georgia before returning to the Chattahoochee Valley in 1716.

Etowah: A chiefdom located on the Etowah River in northwestern Georgia that achieved its greatest influence between 1200 and 1375 C.E.

Guale: A province of about five towns that was located along the sea islands of Georgia. Most Guales joined the missions in the 1590s. Spanish officials relocated Guale towns south of the Altamaha River after a series of slave raids and pirate raids after 1680. Those who were not killed or dispersed by the slave raids of the early 1700s lived on the outskirts of St. Augustine.

Lower Creek: A province of towns located on the Apalachicola River after 1715 and consisting primarily of Ochese towns that abandoned central Georgia after the outbreak of the Yamasee War.

Mobila: A chiefdom probably located on the upper Alabama River where the chief Tascaluza ambushed de Soto's invasion force in 1540. Mobilas and their allies moved to the mouth of the river sometime before 1686, when Marcos Delgado brokered a peace between them and the Tawasas at the headwaters of the river.

Mocama: A Timucuan province of towns located along the Atlantic coast north of St. Augustine and south of Guale.

Moundville: A very large town and mound center on the Black Warrior River in western Alabama that was home to perhaps two thousand people between 1200 and 1400 C.E.

Ochese: A province of about a dozen towns, including most of the Apalachicola province but also some Westos, Yuchis, and others who inhabited the Oconee Valley and traded with the English between 1690 and 1715. (*See also* Creek; Lower Creek.)

Ocute: A chiefdom on the upper Oconee River that probably had influence over Altamaha and other towns in the valley during the 1500s. By 1600, it seems to have lost this influence. Like Altamaha, Ocute fragmented following Westo attacks in the 1660s. Another town of the same name was among the Yamasees between 1685 and 1715.

Osuche: A town in Apalachicola province located upriver from Apalachicola town before 1690 and after 1715. Osuches relocated to the Oconee Valley in the intermediate period.

Rood's Landing: An archaeological site on the east bank of the Chatta-hoochee River that was occupied at different times between 1300 and 1600 C.E.

Sabacola: An Apalachicola town located at the confluence of the Flint and Chattahoochee Rivers that briefly hosted a Spanish mission from 1675 to 1679 and 1681 to 1692.

San Pedro: A Mocama mission founded on Amelia Island in 1595, whose chief, Juan, received gifts from the Spanish governor Gonzalo Méndez de Canzo to promote the conversion of interior peoples.

Singer-Moye: An archaeological site several kilometers east of the Chat-tahoochee River and about twenty-eight kilometers southeast of Rood's Landing that was occupied sometime between 1100 and 1450 C.E.

Tallapoosa: A province of towns, including Atasi and Tuckabatchee, located along the lower Tallapoosa and Coosa Rivers.

Tawasa: A province of towns located at the headwaters of the Alabama River as early as 1675. Tawasas' unwillingness to participate in English slave raids convinced many to relocate closer to the French on Mobile Bay in the early 1700s.

Timucua: A province located between the Atlantic and Gulf coasts of the Florida peninsula. At the time of the first Spanish invasions and into the middle seventeenth century, most of these towns formed part of one of several chiefdoms.

Tocoy: A Spanish mission on the St. Johns River, along the path that con-nected St. Augustine to the missions of central Timucua. In 1628 one of its missionaries was accused of selling food illegally to private citizens of the colony.

Tuani: A town located in the Tennessee Valley before its residents fled English and Westo slave raids and relocated on the upper Alabama River before 1686.

Tukabatchee: A white or peace town located along the lower Tallapoosa River as early as 1620. Tukabatchees had close ties with Coweta and some relocated to the Oconee Valley when Cowetas and other Apalachi-colas lived there from 1690 through 1715.

Upper Creek: The collective name for the Abeca, Alabama, and Talla-poosa provinces after Ocheses joined them in a larger and more cohesive Creek alliance after 1715. (*See also* Creek; Lower Creek.)

Westo: Iroquoian people from the shores of Lake Erie who moved to the Savannah River Valley about 1659 and began taking neighbors captive for sale to English traders. Some of Carolina's Native allies destroyed and dispersed the Westos in 1680. They were also known as Eries or Rechahecrians.

Yamasee: The collective name for various migrants who fled to the Apalachees, Apalachicolas, and Guales after Westo attacks in the 1660s. Many of these migrants came from the Oconee Valley. After 1685, many of these same refugees reconstituted a new confederacy of about ten towns near today's Port Royal, South Carolina. By 1700, Yamasees numbered over four thousand.

Yuchi: A collection of towns located in the Tennessee Valley at the time of de Soto's invasion in 1540. Most Yuchis fled to the Savannah, Ochese, and perhaps Tallapoosa and Coosa Valleys following attacks from Cherokees and English and Westo slave raiders in the 1670s and afterward.

Index

Acknowledgments

This book is the fruit of many gifts. I began the research with support from an Andrew Mellon Fellowship in the Humanities from the Woodrow Wilson Foundation and a University fellowship from the University of Wisconsin-Madison. A Fulbright/IEE fellowship sponsored my research in Spain, and an Andrew Mellon Postdoctoral Fellowship provided me with an invaluable year of research and writing at the Huntington Library. Pre-tenure leave from Bates College allowed me to spend the year at the Huntington. A grant from the National Society of the Colonial Dames of America in the State of Wisconsin, alumni fellowships from Amherst College, and faculty development grants from Bates College covered additional expenses.

All of this generosity would have been meaningless without the assistance of so many librarians and archivists. For all of the help they offered and for all they do to make their collections such wonderful places to work, I thank the staffs of the Wisconsin State Historical Society, the South Carolina Department of Archives and History, the Oklahoma Historical Society, the Archivo General de Indias, the Howard-Tilton Library Special Collections at Tulane University, the Library of Congress, the Huntington Library, and the George and Helen Ladd Library at Bates College.

A number of Muscogees (Creeks) were generous teachers. Buddy Cox informed and inspired me with his broad knowledge of Creek history. Joyce Bear and Tim Thompson of the Muscogee (Creek) Nation's Cultural Preservation Department answered incessant questions during my brief visit to the Muscogee Nation and continued to assist via email. Wilbur Gouge, Keeper Johnson, and Valeria Littlecreek imparted lessons that the notes can only suggest.

In a speech to Bates College graduates several years ago, the children's book author Eric Carle advised, "Follow your dreams, but get a good editor." Many eyes have kept this book from becoming too surreal. With a tight scrawl that was well worth the trouble to decipher, Chuck Cohen at Wisconsin taught me about clear writing and coherent argument. Steve Stern, Jeanne Boydston, and Paul Nadasdy provided additional guidance while I was in Madison. Bob Lockhart and Dan Richter at the University of Pennsylvania Press helped turn dense early drafts into a more readable book; I could not have asked for a more diligent and more considerate pair of editors. Melissa Sundell conducted her own crusades against opaque prose, and she and Bob enjoy the distinction of independently recognizing what this book was about before I did. Lucky for me they did not keep it a secret.

For their attention to various chapters of this evolving manuscript, I am grateful to many, including Charles Beatty, Amy Turner Bushnell, David Chang, Robbie Ethridge, Sarah Fatherly, Leo Garofalo, Alan Gallay, Lillian Guerra, Steven Hahn, Peter Mancall, Paul Mapp, Karen Melvin, James Merrell, Monica Najar, Joshua Piker, Louise Pubols, Ileana Rodríguez-Silva, Claudio Saunt, Sissel Schroeder, Marvin Smith, and Mark Williams. Claudio commented on an early and late version of the manuscript as an anonymous reader for the press, and Robbie was also kind enough to read an entire draft. Candid comments from students in my History 390S seminar at Bates College proved crucial for Chapter 7. Editors and outside readers have also assisted with portions of Chapter 2, which has appeared already in "Between Old World and New: Oconee Valley Residents and the Spanish Southeast, 1540–1621," in *The Atlantic World and Virginia, 1550–1624*, ed. Peter Mancall (Chapel Hill, N.C., 2007), and others helped me lay the foundation for Chapter 5 in the forthcoming essay "Anxious Alliances: Apalachicola Efforts to Survive the Slave Trade, 1660–1704," in *Indian Slavery in Colonial America*, ed. Alan Gallay (Lincoln, Neb.). Seminar discussions sponsored by the McNeill Center for Early Modern Studies at the University of Pennsylvania, the Center for Early Modern History at the University of Minnesota, and the Early Modern Studies Institute at the University of Southern California and the Huntington Library provided me with feedback and encouragement. For her retyping of these countless drafts I am indebted to Sylvia Hawks. The history departments at SUNY-Fredonia and Bates College supported me with their collegiality and daily lessons about sharing the people of the past with those of the present.

But the gifts of love have been the richest. My parents, Jane and Joseph Hall, and siblings, Michaela Gouveia, Alana Hall, and Jonathan Hall, have offered a lifetime of support. My sons, Oliver and Simon, have enriched the last eight years with questions and interests of their own. And Melissa, besides being an editor and supporter par excellence, has shared her life with me. Thank you.